THE CHINESE OF SEMARANG:

A Changing Minority Community in Indonesia

The Chinese of Semarang:

A Changing Minority Community in Indonesia

By DONALD EARL WILLMOTT

*Published under the auspices of
the Modern Indonesia Project
Southeast Asia Program
Cornell University*

Cornell University Press

Ithaca and London

CORNELL UNIVERSITY PRESS

This work has been brought to
publication with the assistance of
a grant from the Ford Foundation.

First published 1960
Second printing 1970

International Standard Book Number 0-8014-0453-3
Printed in the United States of America
by Valley Offset, Inc.

TO LIEM THIAN JOE

the Semarang historian, journalist, and friend
who has given this study its foundations in the past

Preface

This book attempts to present a comprehensive picture of a minority community in a rapidly changing, non-Western, urban setting. Because of the nature of the community and the interests of the writer, description has been supplemented with analysis and interpretation of social and cultural change throughout the book, ending in the Epilogue with an attempt to formulate a theory of change. Chapters I and II provide the geographic, demographic, and historical background necessary to an understanding of the changes taking place. The remaining chapters describe various aspects of community life, such as economic activities, religion and magic, ethnic group relations, and community leadership.

For the purposes of this research, the writer and his wife spent twelve months in Semarang, after three months of preliminary work in Djakarta, the capital of Indonesia. They had learned to speak and read simple Indonesian before they arrived, and eventually acquired facility in reading and adequacy in conversation and interviewing. Because the writer lived in China for some years, he was also able to speak Chinese with many who had studied Mandarin in school. Indonesian or English was used, however, with numerous informants who might have preferred Dutch or one of the "dialects" of South China.

During the period of field research, the writer regularly read and clipped three local newspapers and one weekly magazine. In addition, many Indonesian and Chinese-language periodicals, books, and other publications were collected and studied. A research assistant translated considerable material from Dutch-language sources. Much of the information here presented is based upon these various printed materials. Rather than give repeated warnings throughout the text, the writer prefers to emphasize, at this point, the fact that many of the publications used are not thoroughly reliable. No better information was available, however. The sources of information based upon printed materials alone are given in footnotes. The writer intends these references to indicate tentativeness, not authority.

In addition to formal and informal interviewing and the study of printed materials, the writer spent a good deal of his time visiting homes, observing family celebrations, attending meetings and programs of various kinds, visiting such institutions as temples, churches, schools, and business enterprises, and observing public ceremonies and festivals. Three other research techniques—a questionnaire survey, an analysis of municipal government documents, and an interview survey—are described and evaluated in Appendixes I, II, and III.

All the field research was carried out in late 1954 and 1955. Wherever the present tense is used, it refers to that period and not to the date of publication. Since 1955, a number of important changes have taken place. For instance, the Indonesian government has considerably increased its regulation and control of Chinese schools and business enterprises. Such developments may have halted or even reversed the trend toward assimilation which the writer observed during his stay in Semarang. In any case, the reader should keep in mind that words such as "now," "today," and "the present" in this study refer, at the latest, to 1955.

The reader must also be cautioned that the situation in Semarang cannot be taken as typical of all large Indonesian cities. In the major cities of Java alone, the Chinese communities seem to have taken quite different courses of development.

Several other limitations of this study should be kept in mind. In the course of his work in Semarang, the writer's most frequent and intimate associations in the Chinese community were primarily among Indonesia-born businessmen and professionals. Although many contacts were made with other groups, these may not have been sufficient to eliminate a bias toward the upper socio-economic level of the Peranakan group (that is, Chinese born in Indonesia who do not speak Chinese). Furthermore, the writer is keenly aware that many errors and omissions must exist in his work. The pressure of time was such that some of the information obtained was not adequately checked, and important areas of information were left unexplored.

For illustrative purposes, many anecdotes, accounts of particular individuals or families, and personal opinions have been included in the text. In most cases fictitious names have been used and, where necessary, slight changes of fact have been made in order to conceal identities.

It is frequently contended that the word "Indonesian" should not be used in any way which excludes Indonesian citizens of Chinese or other origin. The writer agrees with the logic of this contention and sympathizes with the humanitarian or equalitarian motives of those who advance it. It would, however, be cumbersome and confusing, if not grammatically impossible, to substitute the words "Chinese and Indonesians of Chinese descent" for the word "Chinese" in a book which uses the term several times in each paragraph. Again, there is no convenient and suitable term, other than "Indonesian," to designate the indigenous (if not original) population of these islands. Therefore the writer has decided to use the terms "Chinese" and "Indonesian" as mutually exclusive. This practice may be at least partially justified by the fact that we are speaking in this book of ethnic groups, not of nationalities.

In the presentation of Chinese terms and names, the spelling current in Semarang has been used. This is based upon the Dutch romanization of South China "dialects." [1] In order to avoid excessive use of italics, foreign words which are proper nouns are not italicized. The writer has taken the liberty of using the English plural form with some of these, for instance, "Peranakans" and "Hakkas."

I should like to thank the Appleton-Century-Crofts Company for permission to quote from *Acculturation in Seven American Indian Tribes*, edited by Ralph Linton. I am also indebted to the authors and publishers of the following books, from which much material was drawn: Liem Thian Joe, *Riwajat Semarang* (Boekhandel Ho Kim Yoe, Semarang); Nio Joe Lan, *Riwajat 40 Taon dari Tiong Hoa Hwe Koan—Batavia (1900–1939)* (Tiong Hoa Hwe Koan, Djakarta); Kam Seng Kioe, *Sam Po* (Toko Buku "Liong," Semarang).

The present study would have been impossible without substantial grants from the Social Science Research Council, the Canadian Social Science Research Council, and the Cornell Modern Indonesia Project. I am deeply grateful to these institutions not only for the substantial financial assistance granted, but also for the complete freedom which they allowed me in the planning and execution of the research in accordance with my own abilities and interests.

I am also indebted to Professors Gordon F. Streib, George McT. Kahin, William W. Lambert, and Lauriston Sharp for their suggestions and criticism during both the field research and the preparation of the manuscript. The letters of Professors Streib and Kahin were especially appreciated for their guidance and encour-

[1] For most of the Chinese terms and names used in the text, the Chinese characters and Wade-Giles romanizations may be found in the glossary of the following source: Donald E. Willmott, "Sociocultural Change among the Chinese of Semarang, Indonesia" (doctoral dissertation, Cornell University, 1958), pp. 486–493.

agement. I should like also to acknowledge my very great indebtedness to Dr. G. William Skinner, who took much time from his own research in Thailand and Indonesia to give suggestions, advice, and constructive criticism at every stage of my research and writing.

Among the many people who helped me to make adequate arrangements for our stay in Semarang and who introduced me to others in a position to give assistance or information, I should like to mention especially Professor George McT. Kahin, Dr. Edward Ryan, Mr. Sumarno of the Indonesian Ministry of Information, Mr. R. Roosdiono and Mr. R. Kosim Adisapoetra of the Ministry of Home Affairs, and Dr. and Mrs. J. H. Feenstra. I am also greatly indebted to Mr. Liem Tjiauw Khing, of the firm Liem Kiem Ling in Semarang, for providing office space without charge.

I should like to acknowledge my indebtedness to the government officials of many departments who gave assistance, to the high school principals who co-operated in the questionnaire survey, and to the many friends and informants who spent long hours answering questions and giving information. Their names are too numerous to mention, but special acknowledgment is certainly due Liem Thian Joe, the journalist and local historian, and Liem Ek Hian, for whom I have special regard as a teacher and friend.

After I began to analyze the data and prepare the manuscript, I found it necessary to correspond with persons in Semarang to get further information and to check what I had written. In addition, one or more well-informed citizens of Semarang were asked to read each chapter and to point out errors, misinterpretations, or omissions. For their letters containing indispensable information, suggestions, and criticisms, I should like to acknowledge my indebtedness to Jauw Bing Lang, Tan You Kiong, Liem Thian Joe, Liem Ek Hian, Mrs. Liem Tjiauw Khing, Kao Tseng-tun, Tan Tjien Lien, Liem Siauw Tjong, Oei Tiong Djioe, Ko Tjay Sing, LL.M., Tan Tjong Yan, LL.M., and Tan Siang Swie, LL.M.

I am grateful also to Dr. Olga Lang, whose suggestions and materials contributed substantially to the preparation of the questionnaire.

Among the people who have been associated most closely with the present study, I should like to mention Miss Tjan Hei Kiauw, who served with patience and competence as research assistant; Miss Liem Tjiep Nio, who undertook the interviewing with courage and understanding; my parents, who did much painstaking work on the manuscript; and my wife, whose numerous and varied contributions were indispensable.

In spite of the generous and competent assistance of so many people, mistakes and misinterpretations have undoubtedly crept into this study. For these, I alone must take full responsibility, especially since I have not always followed the advice or accepted the corrections suggested to me.

I should like to end these acknowledgments by mentioning, with gratitude, the words of the principal of a pro-Peking Chinese school. In introducing me and my questionnaire to one of his classes, he said:

"Social science knows no boundaries of nation or ideology."

I should like this to be the motto of my study.

                                                    D. E. W.

Saskatoon, Saskatchewan
March 1960

Contents

THE CHINESE OF SEMARANG:

A Changing Minority Community in Indonesia

CHAPTER I

The City and Its People

Five hundred and fifty years ago, on the coastal flatlands where the city of Semarang now lies, there was nothing but open fields, wasteland, and water. Today Semarang is an important commercial metropolis, capital city of the province of Central Java, and home of 360,000 people. The Indonesian inhabitants ascribe the founding of the city to the revered Moslem leader Ki Pandan Arang, whose father forsook a princely throne to devote himself to religious teaching. But the local Chinese have learned a different story from their grandfathers.

About five hundred and fifty years ago, it is said, the illustrious Ming Dynasty Emperor Bing Sing Tjouw sent a great armada to the South Seas in search of a miraculous jade Seal of State, which had been carried away by a gigantic white elephant. Commanded by the Grand Eunuch, Sam Po, the fleet visited many lands, from the islands of the Pacific to Arabia, and brought many kingdoms under the benevolent rule of the Chinese Emperor.

While they were sailing along the north coast of Java, Sam Po's Second in Command, Ong King Hong, became seriously ill. Sam Po ordered his fleet to anchor in the bay which is now the harbor of Semarang, and then explored the small Garong River in his own ship.

A small cave was found in a hillside not far from the coast, and this served as temporary quarters for Sam Po while some of his followers built a small house for his sick lieutenant. Sam Po concocted some medicine, and Ong King Hong's condition gradually improved. After about ten days, however, Sam Po decided to continue with the voyage, and Ong King Hong was left behind with a ship, ten men, and plenty of provisions.

During a long convalescence, Ong King Hong directed his followers in the clearing of land, planting of crops, and building of houses. Even when completely recovered, he did not return to China, but used his ship for trading up and down the north coast of Java. His followers took Indonesian wives, and the little colony became so prosperous that many other Indonesians established farms nearby and became part of the community.

Like Sam Po, Ong King Hong was a devout Moslem, and he spent much of his time teaching his Indonesian and Chinese followers the moral precepts, the spiritual truths, and the religious practices of Islam. In addition, he taught them to revere the high achievements and the exalted character of Sam Po. He had a small statue of Sam Po placed in the cave, and he took his followers to worship there at regular times. When Ong King Hong died at the age of eighty-seven, he was given a Moslem burial. He became known as Kiai Djuru Mudi Dampo Awang, or the Venerable Navigator of Sam Po, and was worshiped by both Chinese and Indonesians on days fixed according to the Javanese calendar. In the same manner, Sam Po received the honorary title of Sam Po Tay Djien, or the Great Sam Po, and the local people came to worship before his statue on the first and fifteenth day of every month of the Chinese lunar calendar. The settlement grew and prospered, and the people never flagged in their devotion to Sam Po and his chief officer. Thus did the city of Semarang come into being, and thus was Sam Po deified as its patron god.[1]

[1] This version of the legend is an arbitrary compilation of various parts of the accounts given in the following sources: Liem Thian Joe, *Riwajat Semarang* (Semarang, c. 1933), pp. 1–2; Tju Kie Hak Siep, *Riwajat Sam Poo Tay Djien* (Semarang, c. 1954), pp. 1–19; *Buku Petundjuk Alamat Pedagang dan Perusahaan Djawa Tengah* (Semarang, 1955), pp. 22–27; Kam Seng Kioe, *Sam Po* (Semarang, c. 1955), pp. 17–51.

Historical records indicate that Sam Po was none other than the great Ming Dynasty voyager, Cheng Ho, who actually did visit many parts of the "Southern Ocean," including Java, between 1405 and 1433.[2] His exploits are recounted in the legends, and his idol is worshiped in the temples of many Chinese communities in different countries of Southeast Asia. However, the stories of his coming to Semarang vary so greatly in detail that it is impossible to separate historic fact from legend. Kiai Djuru Mudi Dampo Awang, for instance, appears variously as one of Sam Po's officers, as his Indonesian navigator, and as a local Indonesian Moslem teacher. The cave where Sam Po Tay Djien is now venerated was dug only in 1704; it is said that the original one, which was close by, caved in during a storm, entombing a newly married couple who were worshiping there.[3]

Nevertheless, the Chinese of Semarang have never doubted that Sam Po did come there, and that he landed near the site of the present cave and temple built in his honor. Whether or not this was so, it seems probable that the first settlement of Chinese traders in the Semarang area grew up in that locality.

In the seventeenth century, when the Dutch East India Company extended its commercial activities and military power into central Java, every important town had a colony of Chinese merchants and traders. These enterprising businessmen brought household pottery and porcelain, cotton goods, silk, and paper from China and exchanged them for pepper, nutmeg, and cinnamon, which they sent back to China in their junks. They established sugar-cane mills to refine sugar for local markets and for export. Part of the sugar was also used in the production of wine. Almost every Chinese residence was a small candle factory, and many manufactured peanut oil as well. Moreover, local Indonesian rulers had established a system of farming out monopoly tax rights, including import and export duties, the head tax, market fees,

[2] Victor Purcell, *The Chinese in Southeast Asia* (London, 1951), pp. 22–23.
[3] Tju, *op. cit.*, pp. 14, 20.

gambling concessions, and taxes on wine manufacture and the trade in salt, rice, and wood. These monopolies were an additional source of income for the wealthy Chinese merchants who held most of them.[4]

Over the centuries, it has been the hope of almost every immigrant to return to his home village after making his fortune overseas, and many have done just that. Others returned with almost as little as they had had when they set out, but those who did not prosper usually settled down in Indonesia. Still others, although making their homes in Indonesia, visited their native land as often as they could afford it. At certain times during the Ch'ing Dynasty, the return to China of emigrants was forbidden or hampered by imperial and provincial authorities. In any case, almost every immigrant regularly sent a part of his earnings back to his family in China.

The Chinese community of Semarang prospered and grew rapidly. There was a steady flow of new arrivals from China, especially in the turbulent years around 1644, when the Manchus overthrew the Ming Dynasty. In addition, there was a growing population of Indonesia-born Chinese.

In 1678, Semarang and the surrounding lands and villages were made over to the Dutch East India Company by the Sultan of Mataram.[5] Hitherto the company had maintained a number of fortified trading posts in the main coastal towns such as Semarang, Djepara, Djuana, and Pekalongan. From this time on, however, the company extended its political and military power over an ever-widening area in central Java.

A system of "indirect rule," in which the company backed the authority of local Indonesian "regents" with its military forces, was found to be the most expedient form of government. The system was applied also to the Chinese, by appointing leading Chinese merchants as "captains," "lieutenants," and, later on, "majors." So long as these various functionaries maintained peace

---

[4] Liem, *op. cit.,* pp. 11–19.   [5] *Ibid.,* p. 13.

and order in their communities and assured a flow of raw materials and taxes out of them, the company was content to let them handle all other affairs in their own way. The first Chinese officer of Semarang was appointed in 1672—Captain Kwee Kiauw.[6]

After the wanton massacre of several thousand Chinese by the Dutch in Batavia in 1740, the Chinese of Semarang took part in a country-wide revolt against the company. Although they gained the support of strong Indonesian forces, the Chinese were finally defeated in 1742. With this one exception, the relations between the company and the Chinese in Java were generally good. The Chinese merchants and traders were indispensable to the company, because it was they who brought the products of the land to the Dutch trading posts and sold to the native population the goods which the company imported. On the other hand, the Chinese benefited greatly from the peace and security which company military power maintained throughout wide areas. In addition, the company extended the system of farming out monopoly tax rights and concessions, and this constituted a lucrative source of income for leading Chinese merchants.

A Chinese traveler, who visited Semarang in about 1783, included the following description of the city in an account which was translated into English over one hundred years ago:

Semarang is a district subject to Batavia, but superior to it in appearance. Its territory is more extensive, and its productions more abundant. Merchant vessels are there collected, and its commerce is superior to all the places in these south-western regions. Pacalongan, and Lassam form its right and left wings; Ulujami is its granary, and Tese and Japara constitute its door-ways. The country which is under its government extends to hundreds of miles; the fields are fertile and well-watered, and the people rich and affluent; whence it may be considered the crown of all those lands. With respect to climate, the air is clear and cool, and thus superior to Batavia; the inhabitants are seldom troubled with sickness, provisions are reasonable and easily obtained,

[6] *Ibid.,* p. 9.

while throughout the whole region for ages past they have not known the calamity of famine; the manners of the people are so inoffensive, that they do not pick up things dropped in the roads; and the laws are so strictly enforced, that men have no occasion to shut their doors at night.[7]

The bankruptcy of the company and the substitution of Dutch government authority for company rule in 1800 did not materially affect the livelihood of the Chinese in Semarang. Neither did the brief period of British rule, from 1811 to 1816, although the reforms of Sir Stamford Raffles, if carried out there, would have curtailed their monopoly rights on the one hand and extended their opportunities for usury on the other.[8]

The position of the Chinese suffered severe setbacks during the period between 1820 and 1850, when a system of restricted residence and travel passes was progressively put into effect. Chinese were required to obtain special passes from the authorities for every trip outside of Semarang, whether they were traveling to another city or merely trading in nearby markets. A small part of the city was designated as the Chinese quarter, and Chinese living elsewhere were required to move their residences into this "ghetto." Violations of the travel and residence regulations, and other minor criminal offenses, were dealt with by police courts known as the *politie rol*. These courts had wide arbitrary powers and were regarded by the Chinese as extremely unjust.[9]

These and other grievances, combined with modernist influences from China, gave impetus to a strong Chinese nationalist movement among the Indies Chinese from about 1900 on. Fearing the alienation of the Chinese, the Dutch government progressively re-

[7] Ong Tai Hae, *The Chinaman Abroad; or, A Desultory Account of the Malayan Archipelago, Particularly of Java* (English trans., Shanghai, 1849), pp. 7–8.

[8] John Bastin, *The Native Policies of Sir Stamford Raffles in Java and Sumatra* (Oxford, 1957), pp. 56–57 and *passim*.

[9] Liem, *op. cit.*, pp. 87–90.

moved the grievances and, through political and educational measures, succeeded in orienting a small part of the Chinese population
toward the Netherlands before the Japanese occupation of the
archipelago in 1942.

Further details about the historical development of the Chinese
community in Semarang will appear in succeeding chapters, where
their relation to various aspects of contemporary Chinese society
will be examined.

The People of Semarang

The great majority of the people of Semarang have always been
of native Indonesian stock. According to 1920 census figures, Indonesians comprised 80 per cent of the population of 158,036. This
percentage has changed but little in recent decades, in spite of
very rapid population growth. Of the 1955 population of about
360,000, approximately 81 per cent were Indonesians.

According to one source, about 180 Dutch traders, soldiers,
sailors, and artisans were living in the fortress of Semarang in
1678. It was not until much later that Dutch women came to the
colony. Therefore, not only was there a good deal of prostitution,
but many Dutch men took Indonesian mistresses or wives. The
result was a growing population of Eurasians. As early as 1746, an
institution was established to care for Eurasian children.[10] From
those times onward, the Eurasian population has lived as a community apart. But they have always had the same legal status as
the Dutch and were included with "Europeans" in census enumerations.

In 1930 there were 12,587 Dutch and Eurasian people living in
Semarang. In 1950, after the turbulent period of Japanese occupation and revolutionary war, only about 5,000 remained. Many had
lost their lives, but the majority had left the country. In 1950 and
1951 Dutch nationals residing in Indonesia were allowed to choose
between Dutch and Indonesian citizenship. According to munic-

[10] *Buku Petundjuk Alamat,* p. 21.

ipal government statistics based on the reports of the *lurah*, or headmen, of 114 wards,[11] there were about 3,000 Dutch nationals living in Semarang in 1954 and about 2,300 Indonesian citizens of Dutch descent. Presumably, almost all of the latter group were Eurasians, but there were also many Eurasians among the Dutch nationals.

As for other minorities, the same municipal statistics for 1954 show about 1,500 Arab and 120 Indian residents. In each case less than a third were Indonesian citizens. In addition, there were several dozen residents of other nationalities: British, American, German, Swiss, and other.

The Chinese have always been the largest minority. According to census figures, there were 19,727 Chinese living in Semarang in 1920, more than double the number in 1900. The annual flow of immigrants from China finally reached a peak in the mid-1920's. The last complete census, taken in 1930, enumerated 27,423 Chinese residents of the city. During the Japanese occupation from 1942 to 1945 and the revolutionary war which followed it, a large number of Chinese from surrounding areas sought refuge in Semarang, and many of them remained. Immigration had continued at a slower rate during the 1930's, but a large number of pro-Kuomintang refugees came to Semarang between 1946 and 1950. By 1950 the Chinese population was more than double that of 1930.

Like the Dutch, Chinese born in Indonesia were given a chance to choose between Indonesian and Chinese citizenship between December 27, 1949, and December 27, 1951. Those who preferred Chinese citizenship had to make a court declaration rejecting Indonesian citizenship. Those who made no such declaration became Indonesian. The status of wives and children followed that of the family head, except that foreign-born fathers had to make a declaration on behalf of their Indonesia-born children if they

[11] For an evaluation of the reliability of Semarang municipal statistics, see Appendix II.

wanted them to be Chinese citizens. Out of approximately 46,000 Indonesia-born Chinese residents of Semarang, about 5,000 became Chinese citizens through rejection of Indonesian citizenship. The remainder, about 89 per cent, became Indonesian citizens.

In January, 1955, the municipal statistical records indicated a total of about 60,000 Chinese in Semarang's population of 360,000. Of these, about 17,000 were Chinese subjects and 43,000 were citizens of Indonesia.

Geography and Physical Features of the City

Semarang is situated on the north coast of Central Java. The main part of the city lies on flat ground between a mile-wide strip of coastal swampland and the hills about three and a half miles inland. It is a city of contrasts. There are wide boulevards skirted by modern buildings and residences landscaped with lawns, trees, and gardens. Close by may be found narrow muddy alleys with the tiny wooden houses of the common people crowded along them. Cars, buses, trucks, and motorcycles share the road with bicycles, trishaws (bicycle taxis; *betjak*), oxcarts, and horse carriages. Dutch businessmen holding high positions in the big banks and trading companies, wealthy Chinese, and a few Indonesian government officials live in mansions worthy of Hollywood. On the other hand, thousands of homeless people live on the public squares and under the eaves of public buildings. The majority of the people, Indonesian, Chinese, and Eurasian, live in small, overcrowded houses of wood or brick, with very inadequate plumbing and simple furnishings.

Semarang has an artificial inland harbor of some size, but large steamships must anchor in the outer bay, where they are tended by tugs and barges. The harbor area, which stretches about a mile inland from the coast, contains many docks, warehouses, and industrial establishments, including a rice-milling factory and a large spinning mill. There is practically no resident population, however, since most of the area is under military surveillance and can be entered only after obtaining a special permit from the police.

Just south of the harbor area is the main commercial district, an area about three-eighths of a mile square. This is the old Dutch city. Along its streets are to be found the major banks, insurance companies, newspaper and printing establishments, office buildings, and trading companies, as well as a number of government buildings and small factories. The main railway station is in the northeast corner of this section. Tightly fitted between business buildings are many very old residences. These were once occupied by the wealthy Dutch, but are now the homes of middle-class and poor Chinese and Indonesian families. In this section, as in others, many Chinese families live in parts of their shops, factories, or warehouses.

Semarang's main street, Bodjong, stretches for about a mile and a quarter to the southwest from the commercial district. At its northern end are situated the provincial government building, the city's largest market and public square, a theater, the central mosque, the major hotel, the post office, and several other government buildings. Next is the main shopping center of the city—three or four blocks of the best stores of all kinds. Most of these are owned by Chinese, but a few are Dutch, and there are half a dozen Indian-owned textile stores. Along the second half of Bodjong Street are located the most important garages and automobile dealers, the imposing headquarters of the Dutch Shell Oil Company, the city hall and other government buildings, several theaters, and many once-fine residences (some of them now converted into schools and pensions). The street ends at a monument to the Heroes of the Revolution, which is surrounded by several large military and police buildings.

In striking contrast to Bodjong is Mataram Street, which runs due south for over two miles from the eastern side of the old commercial district. Along it are located several clubs, theaters, schools, and churches. But for the most part it is closely bordered by what

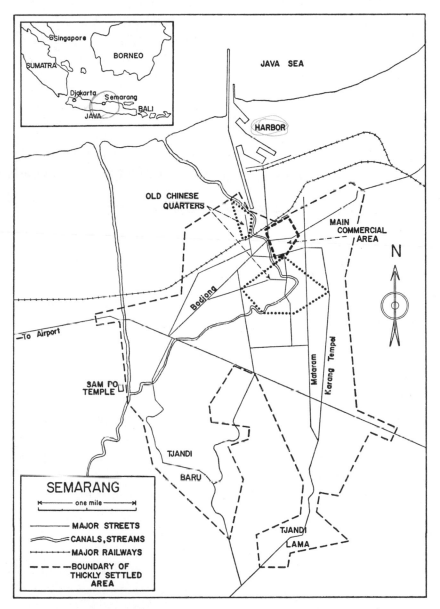

Main features of the city of Semarang

seems an endless number of Chinese shop-homes. These are built side by side in long rows, each one having a series of three or four small rooms along one side of a hallway reaching back from the street. The front room, the shop, is usually completely open to the street, though it is boarded up at night. The walls separating one house from another are usually a single thickness of woven bamboo plastered on both sides, but are sometimes made of wood or brick.

Karang Tempel Street, which runs parallel to Mataram, is typical of the best old residential streets. It is lined with spacious homes and gardens, many of them over a hundred years old and looking it. The Dutch have long since moved to newer, more comfortable homes, leaving these for Eurasians, Chinese, and a few Indonesians.

Just south of the major commercial district, and between the main streets of Bodjong and Mataram, is located the old Chinese quarter, an area little more than half a mile square. During the "ghetto period" from about 1830 to 1916, the Chinese were confined to this quarter, plus a very small section near the harbor. It is still one of the most crowded areas of the city. The streets are very narrow, and the houses are narrow too, with no space between them. There is hardly space for a tree or a patch of grass in the whole district. It is impossible to calculate the exact population of this area today, but there must be well over 20,000 Chinese residents, in addition to at least 5,000 Indonesians.

The Chinese quarter has all the appearances of an old Chinese city in the homeland. The houses and buildings are usually very old and are built in Chinese architectural style. The signs over shops and doorways are almost all in Chinese. And there are ten traditional temples in the area.

Just south of the old Chinese quarter, and in several other parts of the city, there are areas of modern homes. These are built on a more modest scale than the grand old residences of Karang Tempel Street, but they are much more attractive and comfortable. Their occupants are mostly Chinese, but again, especially in several pre-war municipal housing areas, there are also a fair number of Eurasians and Indonesians.

Running east and west between the main part of the city and the hills is a less thickly populated residential area. A municipal stadium and swimming pool, the major secondary schools of the city, a large school of navigation, the zoo, several churches, the local radio station, and the military, municipal, and Chinese hospitals are also located in this district.

On top of a low range of hills in the south are Tjandi Lama and Tjandi Baru, the best residential areas of the city. In Tjandi Lama, or "Old Tjandi," the houses are much older and their grandeur has faded considerably. Therefore few Dutch people have remained there, and the houses are occupied mostly by Eurasians, Chinese, and Indonesian government or military officials. Nevertheless, the Dutch social club, the Dutch sports club, and the residence of the Dutch Commissioner are all to be found in this area.

"New Tjandi," to the west, was not begun until 1905. It is now a beautiful residential area of luxurious homes and gardens. Almost the entire Dutch population of the city now lives in this area, in addition to a small number of wealthy Chinese and high Indonesian government officials. The fine Dutch Catholic hospital is also located there.

There are twenty-three markets and a large number of mosques and schools scattered throughout the city. Shops and industrial establishments are distributed almost as widely. The large modern cigarette factory of the British American Tobacco Company is an imposing landmark in the extreme northeast corner of the city. A few traces of the traditional Chinese block specialization are still to be found. For instance, three-quarters of the forty Chinese gold shops in Semarang are located on one relatively short street. Hardware and household-supplies stores and shoe stores are disproportionately numerous on three streets. Batik textile shops and furniture stores are similarly clustered, and the big garages and car dealers are also close together.

The majority of the people of Semarang live in the *kampung* areas back of the buildings along the main streets and in the outskirts of the city. In these areas one finds a network of narrow streets and alleys which are only wide enough for bicycles and pedestrians. The houses, which consist of two or three tiny rooms, usually have wooden walls and tile roofs. They are even smaller than the typical Chinese shop-homes or the old houses in the Chinese quarter, but they frequently have a tiny yard and a tree or two, and quite often are built as separate houses with narrow spaces between.

A large number of Chinese live in Indonesian-style houses in *kampung* areas. They are therefore referred to as *"kampung* Chinese." As in the higher-class areas, they may occupy almost a whole street, or their homes may be scattered here and there among Indonesian homes. In either case, the *"kampung* Chinese" have closer contact with their Indonesian neighbors than do more well-to-do Chinese. This is due not only to their physical proximity, but also to more frequent interlocking activities and a similar way of life.

Of the city of Semarang's 114 wards, about 40 have no Chinese residents, and the Chinese constitute the majority of the population in about 20 of them. Chinese homes are often clustered together even when there are only a few of them in a neighborhood. But many Chinese families have Indonesian neighbors on all sides. Thus it is evident that residential segregation has decreased rapidly since the end of the "ghetto system" in 1916.

Boundaries of the Chinese Community

From the foregoing description, it will be clear that the "Chinese community" in Semarang does not have as well-defined boundaries as does a preliterate tribe or an American town.

Spacially, Chinese residences and places of work are widely scattered among those of the Indonesians and the Dutch. There is a great deal of social interaction between the different ethnic groups. Culturally, boundaries are very indistinct, since acculturation toward the European way of life on the one hand and the Indonesian on the other have proceeded very far among certain groups of Chinese. Furthermore, as will be shown in Chapter IV, the Chinese population is socially divided into two major groups, Totoks and Peranakans, each of which might be called a separate community.

The justification for speaking of the "Chinese community" and for treating it as a single social system lies in the fact that in spite of internal differences, and with few exceptions, the Chinese interact much more frequently and intimately with one another than with Indonesians or Europeans. The Peranakan and Totok groups are viewed by this writer as subsocieties within the social system of a single Chinese community.

There is virtually no ambiguity about who is to be considered Chinese. Although a great many Chinese men have taken Indonesian wives, especially before World War I, the children of these marriages have almost always been raised as Chinese. Even the most assimilated and acculturated Chinese families have usually retained their Chinese names. Therefore the Chinese community of Semarang which is described in this book comprises all people bearing Chinese names who reside in the municipality.

CHAPTER II

Sources of New Currents in the Chinese Community

Chinese society and culture in Semarang today are very different from the traditional society and culture of the homeland communities along the South China coast. For hundreds of years immigrants arrived in Semarang familiar only with the traditional Chinese way of life. Yet they developed quite a different way of life—a society and culture which were distinct from Chinese, Indonesian, or Western civilization, but which included elements of all three. In this chapter the main sources of Indonesian, Western, and modernist-Chinese influences will be examined. The effects of these influences on the Chinese community will be left to subsequent chapters.

Indonesian Influences

Of the various outside influences on immigrant Chinese society and culture, the earliest were those arising out of the concrete circumstances of life in Indonesia. Primary among these were the new economic position of the immigrants and their intermarriage with Indonesian women.

For most Chinese immigrants, coming to Indonesia involved an immediate change in occupation and economic status. The majority of them had been laborers, farmers, peddlers, and petty traders. They left China because they could not make a satisfactory living there. Of those who went to other parts of Southeast Asia, many took jobs as laborers in mines, factories, or plantations. But there has never been a significant demand for Chinese labor in Java. The typical immigrant there, after working as a peddler or shop assistant for a time, set himself up as a shopkeeper, trader, or merchant. Most immigrants were able to take good advantage of the economic opportunities Indonesia offered them and to increase their income and property fairly rapidly. This socioeconomic mobility was in striking contrast to the relative rigidity of traditional Chinese society. Moreover, the conditions of business were different in Indonesia, where Chinese traders were dealing for the most part with people outside their own community—the Indonesian people and, in some cases, the Dutch merchants. These differences in their economic position were bound to have effects on their society and culture.

A second stream of Indonesian cultural influences flowed into the Chinese community through the Indonesian wives and concubines which the immigrants acquired. Chinese women did not emigrate to Indonesia in significant numbers until after World War I. According to a Chinese writer in Indonesia, this was partly because the voyage to Indonesia by junk was a hard one for women to endure, and the passage fares were high; but even more important was the fact that traveling overseas would have involved a degree of outside contact which was forbidden to decent Chinese women, and it would have violated the traditional family duties of women, especially of married women to their parents-in-law.[1] Similarly, another authority states that prior to 1893 unmarried women never emigrated unless they were bought and taken overseas as prostitutes or concubines; married women were forbidden to emigrate by family lineage councils, which were afraid of losing

[1] Liem Thian Joe, *Riwajat Semarang* (Semarang, c. 1933), pp. 12, 90.

the family entirely.[2] In any case, all emigration was officially illegal
until 1894, and the law was applied more strictly to women than
to men. Therefore, although most immigrants had wives and children in China, they did not transport them overseas. But whether
they had families in China or not, many of them took Indonesian
women as second wives or concubines.

Thus there came into existence an increasing population of
locally born Chinese who had Indonesian mothers, grandmothers,
or great-grandmothers. They were called "Peranakan," as distinct
from the China-born "Totok" Chinese. And even though Peranakans were always considered Chinese, they never escaped the cultural influences of their Indonesian mothers.

In the first decade of the twentieth century a Japanese steamship
line, the Nippon Sho Sen Kaisha, opened a passenger service con-
necting emigrant cities in China with Indonesian ports, including
Semarang. This made travel to Indonesia safe for the first time and
much more inexpensive and comfortable. At about the same time
the modernist movement was gathering momentum in China, and
traditional restrictions on women began to break down. Thus
the physical, financial, and social barriers against the emigration
of Chinese women were largely removed, and by 1920 large numbers were coming to Semarang and other Indonesian cities.

By this time also, the Peranakan population, in which there was
the usual slight excess of women over men, had outgrown the
Totok population, which had fewer women than men. Therefore
the sex ratio in the Chinese community as a whole was rapidly ap-
proaching normal. By 1954 there were well over 90 women for
every 100 men among the Semarang Chinese.[3] With a Chinese
wife available for almost every Chinese man, intermarriage with

---

[2] G. William Skinner, *Chinese Society in Thailand: An Analytical History*
(Ithaca, N.Y., 1957), p. 161.

[3] Exact calculation of the sex ratio of the Semarang Chinese is impossible
because Indonesian wives of Chinese are enumerated as Chinese in population
reports—a practice carried over from Dutch census-enumeration methods.

Indonesians is very uncommon in Semarang today. Thus one of the major sources of direct Indonesian influences on the Chinese community has virtually ceased. But many of the cultural patterns which it initiated pass from generation to generation.

Dutch Influences

Elements of Dutch and Western culture have reached the Chinese community in Indonesia through four main channels of influence: government regulation, education, the mass media, and the living example of the local Dutch community.

With the exception of the period from 1824 to 1855, European law in commercial affairs was applied to the Chinese, and in these matters they were tried in the *Raden van Justitie*, the courts for Europeans, rather than in the *Landraden*, the courts for the Indonesian population. In criminal matters, the Chinese were tried in the *Landraden* and the arbitrary *politie rol* courts, and it was not until 1918 that Chinese began to come under what was substantially European law. Under Dutch rule, however, the Chinese never attained full equality with the Dutch in criminal matters. From 1919 on, Dutch family and inheritance laws (with only a few exceptions, such as in the case of adoption) were applied to the Chinese in Java who were Dutch subjects—that is, to the Peranakans. Totoks were tried according to the laws prevailing in China.[4]

On January 8, 1931, the institution of Chinese community officers officially came to an end in Semarang, and from then on the Chinese were governed directly by the Dutch administration.[5]

But of even greater influence was Dutch education. Throughout the period of Dutch rule, Chinese were rarely admitted either to the schools for Dutch children or to the government schools established after 1854 for the Indonesian population. This was greatly resented by the Chinese, who considered that they were

[4] Victor Purcell, *The Chinese in Southeast Asia* (London, 1951), pp. 506–511.

[5] Liem, *op. cit.*, p. 286.

paying more than their fair share of taxes and that the government should therefore provide schools for their children. After 1900, Chinese communities all over Indonesia began establishing their own schools. The curricula and language of instruction in these schools were Chinese, and the government became alarmed at the spread of Chinese nationalist feelings engendered by them. The government therefore undertook to establish rival schools, known as Dutch-Chinese Schools, beginning in 1908. The language of instruction was Dutch, and the curriculum was the same as in the elementary schools for Dutch children. By 1914 there were 27 of these schools in Java, with an enrollment of 5,203 pupils.[6] By 1937 there were 106 Dutch-Chinese Schools, both government and private, with over 30,000 pupils.[7] And by this time too, a significant number of well-to-do Chinese were receiving higher education in the Dutch colleges of medicine, law, and engineering in Java and in universities in Holland. The first Dutch-Chinese School in Semarang was established in 1909.[8] By the time of the Japanese occupation in 1942, there were several schools in which Chinese pupils were taught in the Dutch language, including mission schools.

In 1916 the Chinese English School was established in Semarang, in order to give a secondary schooling to Chinese wishing to enter colleges and universities in China and English-speaking countries. The headmaster was an Englishman.[9] These various schools brought Chinese into close contact with Europeans and with European culture and thought.

As early as 1829 a Dutch newspaper was being published in Semarang, and in the second half of the nineteenth century there was a continual increase in the number of Dutch papers, magazines, and books available. Semarang's first newspaper in the Malay

---

[6] *Ibid.*, p. 222.

[7] M. Hutasoit, *Compulsory Education in Indonesia* (UNESCO; The Netherlands, 1954), p. 80.

[8] Liem, *op. cit.*, p. 194.   [9] *Ibid.*, p. 232.

language, beginning publication in 1860, was published by a
Dutch firm and edited by a Chinese.[10] Since World War II, American as well as Dutch magazines and books have flooded into the
bookshops and newsstands of Semarang, and Western moving pictures, especially those from Hollywood, have become extremely
popular among the Chinese.

In addition, there has always been the example of the local
Dutch community. It was, of course, the public features of Dutch
life in Semarang which were most apparent to Chinese eyes: their
business practices, their technology, their clothing, their architecture, and their greeting and parting customs, for instance.

There is no doubt that the superior economic and political position of the Dutch gave them great prestige in the eyes of the
Chinese and Indonesian populations. The Dutch had a monopoly
of political authority and the military and police power to maintain it. They also had decisive economic power, as was demonstrated in 1927, when Dutch commercial interests succeeded in
bringing about the bankruptcy and collapse of the one large Chinese bank in Semarang, the Be Biauw Tjoan Bank. Furthermore,
there were many regulations designed to inculcate respect for the
Dutch and acceptance of their superiority. For example, Chinese
and Indonesians were not allowed to pass through the central area
of Dutch government buildings except on foot. If they were on
horseback or riding in a carriage or any other kind of vehicle, they
were required to descend and to walk until they had reached the
opposite boundary of the restricted area.[11]

In addition, there was an elaborate series of regulations to prevent Chinese or Indonesians from acquiring Dutch characteristics.
They were not allowed to wear European-style clothing until 1905,
and many a young Chinese was heavily fined for cutting off his
queue. Before 1905 a few prominent Chinese had been able to
obtain, from the Dutch Resident, special permits to wear Western
clothes. But even this right was won only in about 1889, when

[10] *Ibid.*, p. 144.   [11] *Ibid.*, p. 88.

Major Oei Tiong Ham, of Semarang, had his Dutch lawyer take the matter to the Governor General.[12] In 1887 a wealthy Chinese merchant, Be Soe Ie, was fined a large sum for putting up a building that resembled the main Dutch government building in Semarang. Moreover, he was required to remodel his building and to add a pointed roof, even though he maintained that he needed a flat roof for a sun-drying process involved in his business.[13]

Originally Chinese and Indonesians were not allowed to use the Dutch language. Even in 1906, when the Semarang municipal council was established, it was necessary for the chairman to translate the gist of every speech into Malay for the benefit of the few Chinese and Indonesian members.[14] Segregation was a policy of the Dutch. With only a very few exceptions, Chinese and Indonesians were excluded from Dutch residential areas, Dutch social and sports clubs, Dutch hotels, Dutch resorts, and Dutch schools.

All these policies caused considerable resentment among the non-Dutch population. But at the same time they heightened Dutch prestige. Respect for everything associated with the Dutch became a part of the psychological make-up of the great majority of the Semarang Chinese and Indonesian population, even including many of those who were most opposed to Dutch political policy. Developments since World War II, however, have generally resulted in the broadening of this respect to include Western culture as a whole, especially American culture.

Thus, although exclusivist Dutch policies originally prevented the spread of Western culture, they enhanced the tendency of Chinese and Indonesians to value and accept elements of that culture once the restrictions were removed.

Modernist Chinese Influences

As late as 1880, a competent observer might well have predicted that within a few generations the Chinese in Indonesia would become almost completely acculturated to the Indonesian way of life. At that time the amount of immigration from China was rela-

---

[12] *Ibid.*, p. 154.   [13] *Ibid.*, p. 150.   [14] *Ibid.*, p. 185.

tively small, intermarriage was still common, the influence of
Indonesian mothers or grandmothers was very apparent, Dutch
culture was not accessible, and the Indonesian Chinese took no
interest in China as a nation. There was certainly no loyalty to the
Manchu government. Many of the overseas Chinese were exiled
rebels, and all of them had violated the Manchu ban on emigration. Those who tried to return to China (mostly Totoks) were
harassed by the authorities, as well as by swindlers, and were often
severely punished if they could not pay large bribes. In 1784 the
family of the deceased Captain Tan Lik Sing had his remains
shipped home to China for burial. Claiming that he had been an
outlaw, Chinese officials put every kind of obstacle in the way of
the burial—until the family paid out large bribes in all directions.
The Semarang community was outraged by the news of the skul-
duggery and corruption of Chinese officials in this case, as in
others.[15] The situation did not improve during the nineteenth
century.

In the first decade of the twentieth century, however, a nationalist movement among the Indonesian Chinese reached such
proportions as to alarm the Dutch government—even before the
fall of the Manchu regime in 1911. This nationalism resulted
from the concurrence of two major factors: the widespread dissatisfaction of the Indonesian Chinese with the restrictions placed
upon them by the Dutch government, and a sudden influx of
modernist and nationalist influences from China itself.

Various grievances of the Chinese have already been mentioned
in previous sections. Chief among these were the "ghetto" and
travel-pass systems, the unequal and sometimes unjust administration of justice, the lack of government schools for Chinese, and
discriminatory tax assessment.[16] There was also an important eco-

[15] *Ibid.,* p. 55.

[16] Fuller accounts of these and other grievances of the Chinese may be
found in the following sources: P. H. Fromberg, *Verspreide Geschriften*
(Leiden, 1926), pp. 405–446; Purcell, *op. cit.,* pp. 507–508, 522–524; W. de
Veer, *Chineezen onder Hollandsche Vlag* (Amsterdam, 1908), pp. 1–66.

nomic stimulus to group solidarity. In 1900 it was decided to extend the government monopoly of pawnshops throughout the Indies and to establish agricultural credit banks to provide loans to farmers at more reasonable rates than the private moneylenders, chiefly Chinese, had claimed. Thus the important pawnshop revenues were lost to the leading Chinese merchants, and government loans threatened to constitute serious competition for the moneylending activities of the Chinese population from the wealthy businessmen down to the small shopkeepers. Soon after, the government took over the opium monopoly, which had been farmed out to Chinese merchants, and also restricted opium sales. In the previous thirteen years, Major Oei Tiong Ham, as the opium monopoly holder for Semarang and three other residencies, had made a profit of 18,000,000 guilders.[17] These various legal and economic restrictions stimulated unity in the Chinese community vis-à-vis the Dutch government and encouraged them to turn their loyalties more and more toward China.

It was about this time, too, that the Imperial Chinese government was waking up to the potentialities of the overseas Chinese as a source of political and financial support. The 1860 treaties with the Great Powers had provided that emigration from China should be allowed, and this had reduced the obstacles to travel abroad. But it was not until 1894 that the ban was officially lifted and that corrupt officials could no longer accuse emigrants of breaking the law. The humiliation of defeats and encroachments by the European powers, and by Japan in the Sino-Japanese War of 1895, had inspired modernist and reformist movements among the intelligentsia of China, and had contributed to antiforeign movements among the peasantry. Reform measures begun in 1898 were only briefly halted by a *coup d'état* of the Empress Dowager, and the movement to strengthen and modernize the military, administrative, and educational systems continued. Both Manchu reformers and anti-Manchu revolutionaries realized the political

[17] Liem, *op. cit.*, p. 181.

and commercial importance of the overseas Chinese, and a vigorous competition for their loyalty ensued. For the first time, the Indonesian Chinese began to see China as a nation and to identify themselves with it.

For the purposes of the present study, it is not necessary to trace the historical development of nationalism among the Chinese of Indonesia.[18] The significance of the movement for a study of culture change lies in the specific cultural models and values which it presented to the Chinese community and in the emotions it aroused which served to motivate acceptance of these new traits. In the remainder of this chapter, therefore, the various sources of the new cultural patterns and attachments which appeared in the nationalist and modernist movement will be considered.

At this point, however, it should be emphasized that the early modernists were modern in that they wanted Chinese to acquire the military, administrative, commercial, and technical "know-how" of the West; but most of them had no intention of disrupting the basic features of traditional Chinese society. On the contrary, they attempted to use Confucian and classical philosophy and morality as a basis for public-spiritedness, national unity, and reconstruction.

Chinese Schools

The modernist Chinese school system which grew up in Indonesia was a major source of cultural influences. It began with the founding of the Tiong Hoa Hwe Koan in Batavia in 1900. Within a very few years, Chinese communities all over Java had established similar or identical organizations. Their purpose was to promote Chinese nationalism on the basis of Confucianism, and to

---

[18] For fuller information on the development of the Chinese nationalist movement in Indonesia, see Lea E. Williams, "The Rise of Overseas Chinese Nationalism in Netherlands India, 1900–1916" (doctoral dissertation, Harvard University, 1956); Donald E. Willmott, *The National Status of the Chinese in Indonesia* (Cornell Modern Indonesia Project, Ithaca, N.Y., 1956).

break down the barriers which existed between Peranakans and Totoks and between the various speech groups—the Hokkians, the Cantonese, the Hakkas, and others. Their main function was to operate Chinese schools. From the first, these schools used Mandarin, or the national dialect, as the language of instruction, and imported most of their textbooks and almost all their teachers directly from China. The Tiong Hoa Hwe Koan associations also served as wedding and funeral societies, and generally endeavored to promote adherence to Chinese customs, culture, and religion. After 1911, their orientation gradually shifted from cultural to political nationalism, and by 1925 they were ready to eliminate the promotion of Confucianism from their statement of purpose.[19]

The Tiong Hoa Hwe Koan School of Semarang was established in 1904. It had 80 pupils the first year. By 1930 the enrollment had grown to about 1,000. In 1911, there were already 93 Tiong Hoa Hwe Koan schools in Java, and by 1920 this number had grown to 442, with a total enrollment of almost 20,000 pupils.[20] Throughout the period of Dutch rule, the number of pupils in Chinese schools far outnumbered those in Dutch-Chinese Schools. Postwar figures are highly speculative, but a UNESCO source reported that there were 1,000 Chinese schools in Indonesia in 1950, with an enrollment of 250,000, whereas only about 50,000 Chinese children were attending government schools.[21]

From 1906 on, the Chinese schools maintained close ties with China. Between 1906 and 1911, an inspector of education from Peking made regular inspection tours of the Chinese schools in Java and endeavored to standardize their curricula, textbooks, and teaching methods.[22] At the same time, these schools were invited to send their graduates to the Chi Nan Hsüeh T'ang, a government school in Nanking, for secondary schooling. Up to the time

---

[19] Nio Joe Lan, *Riwajat 40 Taon dari Tiong Hoa Hwe Koan-Batavia (1900–1939)* (Batavia, 1940), *passim.*

[20] Liem, *op. cit.,* pp. 174, 177, 198.   [21] Hutasoit, *op. cit.,* p. 81.

[22] Nio, *op. cit.,* pp. 80–82.

of the 1911 revolution, about two hundred Chinese from Indonesia studied there, with all expenses paid by the Imperial government.[23] After the 1911 revolution, the Ministry of Education in China continued to supply the Indonesian Chinese schools with curriculum plans, textbooks, and teachers,[24] and a great many Chinese, both Totok and Peranakan, studied in high schools and universities in China or Hong Kong.

Chinese Chambers of Commerce

Between 1902 and 1911, with the encouragement of the Imperial government, prominent Chinese merchants established Chambers of Commerce in major cities throughout Indonesia. The Chinese name of these organizations, Tiong Hwa Siang Hwee, literally means "Chinese commercial association," but they were by no means confined to commercial affairs only. In addition to local social and welfare work and the championing of Chinese business and community interests before Dutch government authorities, they formed the major link between the Chinese communities in the Indies and the governments of China, both Manchu and Republican.

The Sianghwee of Semarang was founded in 1907. How it served to increase contacts with China and heighten Chinese patriotism may be seen from some of its many activities. In the ten-year period from 1907 to 1917, it collected substantial contributions from its members ten times for flood relief in China and six times for direct support of the Chinese national treasury. It helped to sell either Chinese government bonds or shares for private enterprises in China fifteen times in the same period. In 1913 it delegated its director to attend a conference held in Peking for the purpose of choosing a number of overseas Chinese representatives to sit in the new parliament. On several occasions it requested the Chinese government to intercede with the Dutch government on behalf of the Indies Chinese. It held frequent receptions and meetings

[23] *Ibid.*, pp. 101–107. [24] Hutasoit, *op. cit.*, p. 80.

for visiting dignitaries from China. Except from 1926 to 1931, when there was an official Chinese consulate in Semarang, the Sianghwee carried out all the functions of a consulate, including the issuing of passports. And in its headquarters the latest newspapers and periodicals from China were always available.[25]

Chinese Nationalist Organizations

From 1908 on, Sun Yat-sen's revolutionary movement was reflected in Indonesia by the founding of Soe Po Sia organizations in various cities, including Semarang. Beginning as study clubs with evening courses on national (Chinese) and international affairs, these groups became the center of Nationalist organization and influence among Indonesian Chinese after the 1911 revolution. They were later reorganized as branches of the Kuomintang Party and, except during the Japanese occupation, have been active up to the present day.

A number of radical and secret nationalist organizations also became active in the decade following 1911—for instance, the Ten Men League, the Kong Tong labor federation, the Blood and Iron Union, and the National Salvation Brigade. These organizations were considered dangerous by the Dutch government, and in 1920 they were suppressed or outlawed, and some of their leaders were deported.[26]

In addition, associations organized for the purpose of collecting funds for the support of the Chinese government were active from time to time. For instance, at the time of Japan's notorious Twenty-one Demands in 1915, the Fonds Tjinta Negri, or Ay Kok Koan (the Love China Fund), was established in order to give financial aid for strengthening China against Japan.[27] The Hoa Kiauw Kioe Kok Houw Wan Hwee was founded in 1934 for the same purpose.[28]

[25] *Boekoe Peringetan, 1907–1937, Tiong Hwa Siang Hwee, Semarang* (Semarang, 1937), *passim.*

[26] Liem, *op. cit.*, pp. 247–249.   [27] *Ibid.*, p. 231.

[28] *Boekoe Peringetan*, p. 13.

Visitors and Emissaries from China

Chinese nationalism in Indonesia was greatly stimulated by a series of visitors and emissaries from China. The first of these was K'ang Yu-wei, the leading reformist who escaped the Empress Dowager's purge in 1898. He thenceforth traveled among the overseas Chinese communities preaching nationalism and reform. His visit to Java in 1903 gave great impetus to Chinese community solidarity and a nationalist outlook in trade, education, and culture. In particular, he encouraged the establishment of schools and set in motion a movement to eliminate the wearing of Javanese dress, the chewing of betel nut, the filing of teeth, and other Indonesian customs then current among Peranakan women. The founding of the Tiong Hoa Hwe Koan in Semarang is attributed to his influence.

The inspector of education, Ong Hong Siang, who arrived in Semarang in 1907, was the first official of the Manchu government to be received there. A Peranakan newspaperman and local historian described the reaction of the Chinese community in these words:

The arrival of this inspector fired the enthusiasm of Chinese Peranakans for closer relations with their fatherland, even though all power there was still in the hands of the Manchus. In small towns which had not set up Tiong Hoa Hwe Koan schools, the inspector stimulated their establishment. In Semarang, Mr. Ong Hong Siang received an extraordinarily warm welcome.[29]

More dramatic, however, were the visits of two Chinese naval vessels to Semarang in the years 1907, 1909, and 1911. While Peranakans and Totoks came from far and wide to see the proud sight of modern warships manned entirely by smartly uniformed Chinese, the visiting emissaries were busy creating closer political and commercial ties with local Chinese leaders.[30]

[29] Liem, op. cit., p. 191. All translations from Chinese and Indonesian sources are by the present author unless otherwise indicated.

[30] Ibid., pp. 191–192.

From that time until the Japanese occupation, hardly a year passed in which the Semarang Chinese did not entertain one or more visiting dignitaries from China—for instance, a representative of the Bank of China (1912); the Chinese Minister to the Netherlands (1913); a personal representative of Vice-President Li Yuan Hung (1913); China's all-star soccer team, Loh Hua (1929); the Minister of Communications, Chen Kung Po (1934); a troup of Boy Scouts from Amoy (1934); the ex-Minister of Foreign Affairs, Wang Ching Ting (1935); and a Chinese trade mission, including a representative of the Shanghai Commercial Press (1936).[31]

Chinese Consuls

In 1912 the first Chinese Consul General arrived in Batavia. In the 1911 Consular Agreement with the Netherlands, China had been forced to concede that its consuls would have no jurisdiction over Chinese who were Dutch subjects according to Dutch law—that is, the Peranakans. But in practice, the Chinese consuls were active among all groups of Chinese, both Totok and Peranakan. Their purpose was to win the loyalties and open the pocketbooks of as many Chinese as possible.

When the Consul General first visited Semarang in 1915, it was for the purpose of selling Chinese government bonds. Two years later he wrote to the Semarang Sianghwee asking for contributions for flood relief in China. The reply was 13,800 guilders.[32] Not long after, he returned to Semarang, this time selling shares in a Chinese steamship company.[33] He also tried to encourage the buying of more products from China. On the invitation of Semarang Chinese, a consulate was opened in Semarang in 1926. It ran into financial difficulties, however, and in spite of contributions from the Sianghwee and other organizations, it was finally closed in 1931.

[31] *Boekoe Peringetan, passim.*   [32] *Ibid.*, pp. 12–13.
[33] Liem, *op. cit.*, p. 258.

Chinese consuls not only sought financial support from the Indonesian Chinese, but attempted to gain political allegiance as well. Several times the consulates tried to register all Indonesian Chinese, including Peranakans, and once an effort was made to organize a country-wide election of representatives to the Chinese National Congress.[34]

The Chinese Press

By the turn of the century, newspapers, periodicals, and books were already being published by Chinese in the Indies, mostly in the Malay language. This activity increased rapidly in the first two decades of the twentieth century. A large proportion of the Chinese press was dedicated to reviving the interest of Peranakans in Chinese customs, Chinese history and culture, and a Chinese point of view. As China itself developed toward a modern national state, the Chinese press in the Indies, like the Tiong Hoa Hwe Koan organizations, added more and more political nationalism to its cultural nationalism.

In 1909 the first Chinese newspaper in Semarang, the *Djawa Tengah*, began publication. At first it had both a Malay and a Chinese language edition, but the latter had to close down in the following year. The Malay edition, still in publication in 1938, outlived several other Malay Chinese newspapers which were established later, such as the *Warna-Warta* and the *Sinar Djawa*. The Batavia newspaper *Sin Po* has had readers in Semarang since its inception in 1910. It has always been an ardent advocate of Chinese political and cultural nationalism. Its Chinese edition quickly became the most influential Chinese-language newspaper in Indonesia, and the Malay edition has only recently been eclipsed by the more moderate *Keng Po*.

Two Chinese daily newspapers are published in Semarang to-

[34] Purcell, *op. cit.*, p. 545; George McT. Kahin, "The Political Position of the Chinese in Indonesia" (master's thesis, Stanford University, 1946), pp. 79–87.

day, both in the Indonesian language, the *Kuangpo* and the *Sin Min*. In 1955, both were supporting Indonesian nationalism and the Ali Sastroamidjojo cabinet. But they criticized government policy toward the Indonesian Chinese; and cultural nationalism appeared in many of their articles and news items. With regard to Chinese politics, the *Sin Min* favors the Peking government, and the *Kuangpo* is pro-Kuomintang.

Many of the Indonesian-language books which have been printed locally are translations from the Chinese, and Chinese bookstores in Semarang have imported a great many Chinese-language publications from China. Classical novels, such as *The Three Kingdoms,* have been published again and again, not only in Chinese and Malay, but also in Javanese. They are even appearing in comic-book form today. The writings of the modern Chinese author Lu Hsün have been equally popular, among both Totoks and Peranakans.

As in the case of Western culture, in recent years Chinese culture has reached the Semarang Chinese community through the moving pictures. And here again, both classical dramas and stories of modern life in China are popular.

Influences from Communist China

Since the end of World War II, and especially since the founding of the People's Republic of China in October, 1949, a new stream of cultural influences has flowed into the Chinese community. The Semarang Chinese on the whole have paid very little attention to the political and ideological content of Chinese communism, and they are not prone to anti-individualist, anticapitalist ways of thinking. But their identification with China as a nation and their pride in the economic, diplomatic, and even military successes of the new regime lead many of them—including, perhaps, the majority of young people—to value many of the new social and cultural patterns now developing in China.

In Semarang there are several bookstores which specialize in publications from Communist China. There are also several which deal almost exclusively with publications from Hong Kong and Taiwan. In both cases a great many books and attractive magazines are available, but the pro-Peking literature tends to be cheaper and to include more material in the Indonesian language.

There is much going and coming between China and Indonesia. The exchanging of cultural missions and of delegations to labor, youth, and professional conferences receives considerable attention in the Indonesian press. Official delegations to China are usually composed almost entirely of Indonesians, but every year at least several dozen Indonesian Chinese are invited to attend the October 1 celebrations in Peking and to visit various parts of China. In 1954, two Peranakan Chinese went from Semarang. Most of the members of these various missions and delegations are non-Communist, and some even anti-Communist. Their reports, often given at length in public speeches and in newspaper columns and serials, give details about the new social and cultural patterns in China.

A Chinese cultural mission which gave performances of Chinese music, dancing, and classical opera in the major cities of Indonesia during the summer of 1955 received a good deal of attention and press publicity from all sides. Many Semarang Chinese were disappointed that it did not make a public appearance in their city, but rather in the neighboring Indonesian cultural centers of Jogja and Solo. Hundreds of them made an overnight trip to one or the other of these two cities in order to see the Chinese presentation.

When two teachers from China came as fraternal delegates to a conference of the Persatuan Guru Republik Indonesia (Federation of Indonesian Teachers), which met in Semarang in November, 1954, pro-Peking Chinese associations organized welcoming festivities hardly less grand than those given the imperial emissaries who visited Semarang almost fifty years earlier.

There is no Chinese consulate in Semarang today, but several local organizations act as representatives of the Djakarta consulate general. Their work includes the arranging of passports and travel papers for people returning to China. Among those who "return," the majority are high school students who have never been in their "homeland" before. In 1955, about fifty Semarang students went to China to continue their studies, even though they were warned by Indonesian authorities that they would not be allowed to re-enter Indonesia. In addition, a number of individuals and families go back to China every year. The following announcement, which appeared in an Indonesian-language Chinese newspaper, is an example:

LEAVE TAKING

On August 2, 1954, as passengers aboard the "Tjiluwah," leaving from the port of Semarang, we:

Hoe Joe Pien and wife and Hoe Fang Soeng

departed for our ancestral land. From all our relatives, brothers and sisters, and friends, we hereby take leave. If in our relations we have unintentionally given offense, we wish to take this opportunity to express our sincerest regrets.

We wish you well in parting! Until we meet again, farewell!

Optician with diploma from Leiden
ex-Hing Sing Optical—Semarang

The Semarang Chinese receive many letters from China, both from relatives who live there and from recent returnees. This means that most members of the Semarang community hear about developments in China, at least occasionally, through letters written to them or to their acquaintances. From time to time the pro-Peking Semarang newspaper *Sin Min* prints letters or news from former Semarang residents who are now in China. It may well be that these informal letters are a more influential source of new ideas from China than are imported books and magazines, since the latter tend to reach only those who are already oriented toward "New China."

Among the Chinese schools of Semarang, three are Peking-oriented. These schools foster sympathy and loyalty toward the China of Mao Tze-tung, and they provide, in classroom and assembly hall, considerable information about new social, economic, and cultural developments in China. Actually, they cannot be correctly described as "Communist" schools. The majority of the people associated with them—the students, the teachers, the staff, and the boards of directors—are non-Communist. Many dislike or disapprove of world communism, and others take no interest in politics whatever. But most are Chinese nationalists, with varying degrees of sympathy or enthusiasm for the Peking regime.

Summary

In this chapter the major conditions, situations, and events which have modified the traditional society and culture of the Chinese community in Semarang have been discussed. These may be briefly listed as follows: (1) a new physical environment, (2) the Indonesian economy, (3) Javanese culture, especially as presented by the native wives of the Chinese, (4) the government, the schools, the publications, and the living example provided by the Dutch, and (5) communication with a changing China, through visitors and emissaries, consuls, political and charitable organizations, the press, and modern schools with teachers and textbooks from China.

CHAPTER III

Occupations and
Economic Activities

Occupations

Figures on the occupational distribution of the population of Semarang do not exist. The Dutch and Eurasian population, however, is known to be almost entirely engaged in business and commercial enterprise, with the Eurasians filling lower positions or owning the smaller businesses. Indonesians are predominantly occupied in government service and skilled and unskilled labor. The Indonesian business group is very small, but is growing rapidly. The Chinese are, of course, mostly occupied in trade. There is only a very small number of professional people in Semarang, but Indonesians, Chinese, and Dutch are all well represented in it.

Table 1 gives a more detailed picture of the occupational distribution of Chinese men in Semarang. The percentage figures in the first column, derived from questionnaire replies,[1] indicate the occupations of the parents of Chinese high school students. It must be assumed that a disproportionately large number of men in the higher socioeconomic groups is included in this column, both because they can afford to have their children attend high school

[1] See Appendix I for a description and evaluation of the questionnaire survey made by the writer.

and because they are older men who have had time to improve their position over men between twenty and forty years of age. The second column shows the percentage distribution of occupations among Chinese men who registered their marriages in 1954.[2] Again, these cannot be taken as representative of the whole community, because men in the lower socioeconomic groups are more

Table 1. Occupational distribution of gainfully employed Chinese men, Semarang, 1954–1955

Occupational group	Fathers of high school students *	Men registering marriages in 1954 †	All employed men (estimated)
Professionals	4.2%	.6%	2%
Owners and managers of big businesses	3.6	2.7	2
Business and trade, small and middle	77.0	50.5	50
White-collar clerks and employees	10.1	33.0	27
Government employees	1.7	3.8	2
Technicians and craftsmen	1.3	8.8	12
Unskilled labor	2.1	.6	5
	100.0%	100.0%	100%

* Based on questionnaire replies from 473 Chinese high school students in Semarang, 1955.

† Based on the occupations stated in the records of the Civil Registration Office, Semarang, for 182 Chinese men who married in 1954.

delinquent in registering their marriages, and because more newly married men hold lower positions than would be found among all gainfully employed men. The third column of percentages shows the occupational distribution of all gainfully employed Chinese men in Semarang, as estimated by the writer. Allowances have been made for the above-mentioned sources of error in the other two columns, and the percentages reflect also the absolute numbers in

[2] See Appendix II for details about the civil registration records and for an evaluation of the validity of basing conclusions on them.

various occupational groups as estimated in succeeding paragraphs.

According to statistics based upon the reports of the *lurah* (ward headmen), there were about 17,000 adult male Chinese in Semarang at the beginning of 1955. Of these, it will be assumed that about 15,000 were gainfully employed. The occupations in which these men were engaged will now be considered in greater detail.

There is a distinct group of professionals whose work requires an advanced academic degree—that is, the doctors, dentists, lawyers, and engineers. There are about 55 Chinese in this group, as compared to about 30 Dutchmen and 35 Indonesians. Among professionals may also be included all other occupations which require a comparatively advanced education, but which do not come under the heading of business, trade, or commerce: nurses, opticians, newspapermen, writers, teachers, preachers, and the administrators of nonbusiness organizations. It is estimated that about 250 Chinese men are employed in such occupations. This brings the Chinese professional group to a total of a little more than 300 persons, or about 2 per cent of those gainfully employed.

When asked to state their occupations, most Semarang Chinese automatically respond: "Trade." This term, however, includes both commerce and industry, and covers everything from peddlers to big businessmen. The latter, to avoid any misapprehension, usually specify that they are owners or managers of certain well-known business establishments. Such specific responses were given in 3.6 per cent of the questionnaire replies and in 2.7 per cent of the marriage registrations. However, not more than three or four hundred Chinese firms have telephones, as listed in the 1955 telephone book, so the number of Chinese "big businessmen" has been arbitrarily estimated at 300, about 2.0 per cent of the gainfully employed. Only a handful of these would rate as big businessmen in the West, however. A telephone in one's office, a car in one's garage, an imported refrigerator, a large and comfortable home, and large charitable donations are enough to ensure acceptance within the top business circles in Semarang.

As can be seen from Table 1, about half of the gainfully employed Chinese men in Semarang are businessmen and traders.
This means that they are owners or part-owners of business enterprises, however small, or at least that they make a living in trading
activities.

In the white-collar group clerks, typists, bookkeepers, cashiers,
office assistants, and sales clerks have been included. It is very
difficult to draw a line between this group and the category of businessmen and traders, because many "white-collar" functions are performed by brothers, sons, or other close relatives who may be considered as part-owners in the smaller businesses. The estimate,
setting white-collar workers at 27 per cent of the gainfully employed, is intended to include only those who are employees in
the sense that they are wage earners.

Government service does not suit the interests and aspirations
of most Indonesian Chinese. In any case, under former Dutch
rule, Chinese were not allowed to take the civil service examinations, and only a very few were employed in any kind of government service. After the war there was a drastic shortage of personnel, so a much greater number of Chinese were employed by
the government, especially in Dutch-occupied areas. The number
has been declining in recent years, however. This is at least partly
due to the reluctance of government officials to employ Chinese.

In Semarang are found the headquarters of provincial, residency, regency, and municipal governments, with tens of thousands of employees. Yet not more than a few hundred Semarang
Chinese are in government service. The estimate shown in Table 1,
2 per cent of all gainfully employed Chinese, is set closer to the
questionnaire results than to the marriage registration figure because virtually all Chinese employed by the government find it
necessary to have registration papers, whereas a great many other
Chinese do not.

The questionnaire results indicate that about half the Chinese
working for the government are in white-collar jobs, such as book-

keepers and post-office clerks. Others are in positions requiring special training, such as auditors. A small number are in the police force and the army. A few are in positions of some authority—for instance, there are several Chinese administrators in the Department of Taxes and Excises. But there are no Chinese *lurah* (ward headmen) even in wards with almost exclusively Chinese populations. Chinese teachers in government schools, doctors who do part-time work for the Health Department, and employees of the government-owned railways are, strictly speaking, government employees, but they have been put in other categories.

Among technicians and craftsmen the following occupations have been included: cooks, bakers, barbers, tailors, shoemakers, carpenters, tinsmiths, goldsmiths, blacksmiths, radio repairmen, photographers, printers, electricians, mechanics, and taxi, bus, and truck drivers. Many of the men in these occupations own and manage their own businesses. The unskilled laborers are janitors, watchmen, untrained handy men, and manual workers. There are virtually no Chinese servants or factory laborers in Semarang. The estimates for the categories of "technicians and craftsmen" and "unskilled labor" in the third column of Table 1 have been increased over the figures in the other two columns because many of the less well-to-do members of these two groups do not send their children to high school or register their marriages.

Fields of Business Enterprise

Very few Chinese enterprises are devoted solely to finance. There are only four Chinese or part-Chinese banks in Semarang. One of these, the Oei Tiong Ham Bank, is not a public bank. It is engaged primarily in financing the various enterprises of the Oei Tiong Ham Concern. The Great Eastern Bank (Ta Tung Yin Hang) was established in Semarang by Totok Chinese in 1954. Two other banks, the Gadjah Mada and the Bank Timur, are owned jointly by Indonesians and Chinese of Indonesian citizenship. The Dutch banks and Indonesian government banks are larger, more important, and more numerous than the Chinese banks. These Chinese banks often act as intermediaries between individual Chinese borrowers and the Dutch banks.

The field of insurance is dominated by Dutch companies in Semarang, but there is one large Chinese concern, the Lloyd Indonesia. This company established two subsidiaries in 1953. Among about a dozen leading Chinese brokers and commission agents, most have a regular business of their own in addition to their activities as intermediaries.

There are about forty Chinese gold and silver shops in the city, and these perform an important financial function. It is customary for a large part of the Indonesian population and the poorer Chinese to invest their savings in gold and silver trinkets. When in need of cash, they pawn or sell back their jewelry.

No doubt the majority of Chinese businessmen in Semarang are engaged wholly or partly in retail trade. The little Chinese shops selling provisions, rice, dried foods, candy, soft drinks, cigarettes and tobacco, matches, candles, various kinds of oil, and cheap household articles are too numerous to estimate. Many of the shopkeepers are also engaged in buying up local agricultural produce for delivery to processors and exporters. Some of them still make a good profit from extending cash loans to trusted Indonesian customers, usually to be repaid in produce at a very high rate of interest.

There are a large number of Indonesian-owned small shops in Semarang, but in the field of middle sized and large stores the Chinese have little competition. In the retail business, as in other fields discussed below, the 1955 telephone book proved valuable in assessing the relative proportion of businesses owned by Chinese. The Chinese and Indonesian languages, even when both are written in Latin script, cannot be confused. Most Chinese enterprises have Chinese names, so there is no doubt about their ownership. In addition to the name of each enterprise, the telephone book often gives the name of the owner. Here again Chinese owners are easily distinguishable. On the other hand, Eurasian names are usually not different from Dutch names, and this writer is not able to distinguish many Arab and Indian names from Indonesian names. Therefore it was possible to divide businesses listed in the telephone directory into only four groups: (1) those which are unmistakably Chinese, (2) those which are Dutch or Eurasian, (3) those which are Indonesian, Indian, or Arab, and (4) those which have Dutch or Indonesian-sounding business names, but no owner's name given. The majority of the enterprises in the very last group can be assumed to be wholly or partly Chinese-owned, at least in most fields, since more and more Chinese businessmen are giving their enterprises Indonesian names (and sometimes taking on Indonesian business partners) in order to avoid various kinds of official and unofficial discrimination.

The writer attempted to analyze the distribution of ownership of the enterprises listed not only in the telephone book, but also in two current Semarang trade directories.[3] The latter included many businesses which have no telephones, and were therefore much more complete; but they did not give the names of the owners. Nevertheless, judging only by the names of enterprises, the writer found that the proportions which could be assigned to the different ethnic groups were very close to those found in the telephone directory.

Of 238 retail stores listed under various general headings in the telephone book, 70 per cent were unmistakably Chinese, 5 per cent were Dutch or Eurasian, 8 per cent were Indonesian, Arab, or Indian, and 17 per cent were undeterminable. Thus it can safely be assumed that from 75 to 80 per cent of all fair-sized retail stores in Semarang are owned by Chinese. This includes stores selling the following types of merchandise: furniture and wood products, textiles and household supplies, clothing, shoes and leather

---

[3] Bakoenoen, *Buku Penundjuk Alamat Dunia Dagang Kota Semarang* (Semarang, 1954); *Buku Petundjuk Alamat Pedagang dan Perusahaan Djawa Tengah* (Semarang, 1955).

goods, hardware, iron goods, bicycles, cars, radios, electrical supplies, photographic supplies, clocks and watches, toys, books, flowers, and food products.

In the service trades, the proportions are more varied. Dry-cleaning establishments, garages, and the main restaurants are almost all Chinese-owned. The larger tailoring establishments are almost all Chinese-owned, but they employ some Indonesians, and independent Indonesian tailors probably outnumber the Chinese. The majority of barbers are Indonesian, and almost all beauty shops are Chinese. Eight of the nine moving picture theaters are owned by Chinese; the other is run by a municipal foundation. The three classical Javanese dance-drama theaters are owned by Indonesians. There are seven Dutch- or Eurasian-owned hotels and pensions, about a dozen Chinese hotels, and over thirty Indonesian hotels—the size and comfort varying in accordance with the relative economic position of the three groups.

In the field of transportation the Chinese role is varied. The railway is state-owned, and none of the shipping lines is Chinese. There is a small coastal trade by Chinese junks, and some of these may come from as far as Singapore. But the volume of goods carried is insignificant. On the other hand, of about 80 bus lines, trucking and moving companies, and car rental services which are listed in the telephone directory, 82 per cent are Chinese, 6 per cent Dutch or Eurasian, 6 per cent Indonesian, and 6 per cent undeterminable. Among the many individual taxi owners, there may be a higher proportion of Indonesians. The thousands of three-wheeled bicycle taxis (betjak) in Semarang are operated almost entirely by Indonesians, but are usually owned by Chinese merchants or bicycle dealers.

In the field of manufacturing it is much more difficult to assess the role of the Chinese, because there is still so much small-scale and home industry. And regarding the larger concerns, the number of enterprises is not so significant as figures for the volume of production would be. The telephone directory once again provides

information. Of 134 "factories" making about 30 different kinds
of products, 71 per cent were Chinese, 7 per cent were Dutch or
Eurasian, 10 per cent were Indonesian, Arab, or Indian, and 12
per cent were undeterminable. The number of workers employed
in these establishments varies from about a dozen to several thousand, the average (technically, the mode) probably being about
one hundred. The largest factories in Semarang are not Chinese-
owned—a spinning mill, which is in the course of being national-
ized, and the cigarette factory of the British American Tobacco
Company. The most important Chinese factories manufacture or
process the following products: *kretek* (clove-scented) cigarettes,
rubber goods (especially sandals), soft and hard drinks, light machinery and tools, books and periodicals, coconut oil, weighing
scales, yarn, textiles, patent medicines, soap and cosmetics, glassware, floor tiles, batteries, umbrellas, incense, ice, tea, and coffee.
Smaller but more numerous are the establishments which produce
shoes and leather goods, furniture, batik sarongs, and numerous
food products. There is one large rice mill in the harbor area and
half a dozen others not far outside the city; all are owned by
Semarang Chinese.

Although the Chinese own at least three-quarters of the concerns
operating in the above-listed fields of production, it should be
remembered that the European-owned enterprises probably have
a higher average volume of production and that the significant
volume of Indonesian home industry is not accounted for in this
figure. A considerable proportion of the latter type of production
is organized under a "putting out" system in which Chinese merchants supply the raw materials and pay relatively low piece rates
to the home producers. Batik making, for instance, is often organized in this way. Then too, there is also a sizable volume of
small-scale Chinese industry, such as food processing, which is not
included in the figures derived from the telephone directory.
Thus it is safe to say that by far the greater part of Semarang's
total volume of production is turned out by Chinese enterprises.

Between the raw-material producer and the consumer, products are usually handled by a series of middlemen, such as buyers, processors, importers and exporters, wholesalers, distributors, and dealers. These various functions are often combined in one or two concerns. All such enterprises will be designated as "trading companies," and their owners as "middlemen" or "traders." These terms, however, should not be allowed to obscure their diverse functions.

By far the greater part of Semarang's import-export trade with Europe is handled by the big Dutch trading companies. In the twentieth century there has never been a significant amount of trade with China, since Chinese products have not been able to compete with those from Japan either in price or in suitability for the Central Java market. Efforts of patriotic Chinese merchants to increase the sale of Chinese products ended in repeated failure. Only umbrellas from Fukien and various food products (mostly for the Chinese community itself) were regularly imported from China. Today the umbrellas are made locally, and even the import of China-made provisions has slowed to a trickle.

Nevertheless, there are many dozens of Chinese "import-export" companies in Semarang. Usually using the big European companies as intermediaries, they import a fairly large volume of European and American manufactured goods, including textiles, radios. bicycles and motorcycles, machinery and tools, refrigerators, prepared foods, pens and pencils, watches and clocks, and other luxury goods. Without the help of European firms, they import cheaper-grade manufactured goods from Singapore, Hong Kong, China, and Japan: enamelware, kitchen utensils, flashlights, textiles, socks, underwear, prepared foods, bicycles, and so forth. Importing rice from Rangoon and Bangkok was once a lucrative business for Chinese merchants. Under government regulation, however, this trade is now in the hands of Indonesian importers.

Whether goods are imported by Chinese or European companies, they generally pass into Chinese hands as soon as they reach Semarang. European firms have never developed widespread distributing agencies, and Chinese wholesalers and distributors have always performed this function. Recently a large number of Indonesian or joint Indonesian-Chinese companies have entered this field, with government encouragement. If present government restrictions are continued, it is likely that strictly Chinese companies will gradually have to move into other lines of enterprise. If one visits the Chinese quarter today, one can see empty shelves and slowed-down activity in the headquarters of some of the biggest old Chinese trading companies.

Another traditional function of the Chinese middlemen has been to gather the produce of the land and deliver it to the large exporters for shipment to Europe and elsewhere, or to transport it to markets in other parts of Indonesia. Chinese trading companies in Semarang are still busy with this activity. The most important products handled are coffee, tea, sugar, rice, tobacco, kapok, lumber, cassava, tapioca, red peppers, copra, rubber, soybeans, peanuts, and oil seeds. In this field too, Chinese firms are meeting with increasing competition—this time mostly from co-operative marketing organizations. But their position is still dominant.

In summary, it can be said that in 1955 the Semarang Chinese owned and managed from three-quarters to four-fifths of Semarang's retail, transport, manufacturing, service, and wholesale enterprises. They were less important in banking and finance, and their position in the import-export field, always secondary to the European firms, was being challenged by Indonesian or part-Indonesian companies.

Some of the reasons for the dominant position of the Chinese in the economy should be mentioned at this point. From the early days of the Dutch East India Company, discriminatory Dutch policy strengthened the position of the Chinese as economic middlemen and practically eliminated the native merchant class. On the other hand, government regulations and the educational system discouraged the Chinese from entering government service, but channelized the aspirations of Indonesians, especially the native aristocracy, in this direction. The latter tendency was strengthened by certain feudalistic attitudes characteristic of native society. These are some of the historical reasons why, even today, most Indonesians prefer to seek careers in government service, whereas most Chinese are attracted to business enterprise. Other reasons, based upon culturally determined, individual predisposition, will be discussed in later sections of this chapter.

Finally, it should be noted that the dominant economic position of the Chinese is now being challenged. The influence of modern Western values on the outlook of many Indonesians and the government policy of encouraging Indonesian business enterprise have initiated a trend toward the increasing participation of Indonesians in the private sector of the economy. Co-operatives also have provided serious competition for the Chinese (though mostly in rural areas), and government enterprises may become increasingly important.

The Internal Structure of Chinese Business Enterprise

The most striking feature of Chinese business organization in Semarang is the familism which, in the great majority of cases, forms its core. Before this statement is discussed further, two examples of Chinese enterprise will be examined. The anonymity of the first will be maintained by using assumed names and altering a few unimportant details, but the second has been in the public eye for so long that anonymity is impossible.

About 1880, a young immigrant by the name of Tjan San Go arrived in Semarang by junk. He had used almost his whole savings to pay for the passage, and, unlike many immigrants, he had no relatives in Semarang to receive him. However, a wealthy Semarang merchant with the same surname, Tjan Tan Sing, gave the young man work until he had enough experience and savings to start trading on his own. This was in accordance with the traditional belief that all persons of the same surname are related and all relatives must be helped when in need.

Tjan San Go finally established a little store in the outskirts of town. In 1890 he married a local Chinese girl considerably younger than he. They had six children, three boys and three girls. As the boys grew up, they helped to extend their father's business by trading trips to other towns. The eldest brother, Sie Ming, proved the most capable. He established himself in the farm-produce trade in nearby Ambarawa and gradually became one of the town's leading merchants. He was the first Ambarawa trader to mechanize his enterprise: in 1925 he acquired a truck for transporting local produce to Semarang.

The second brother, Sie Ping, stayed with his father. For some reason, he refused to get married. When old San Go decided to retire, Sie Ping took over the store. By this time, the third brother, Sie King, had set up his own store in another part of town. He sold flour, tobacco, rice, paper, oil, beans, and other staples. His enterprise flourished, and he raised a family of five boys and two girls. While he was out on business, his wife took charge of the store, and even the children were often required to help.

Just before World War II, Sie King installed a refrigerating unit in his store and thus began a profitable side line in various kinds of meat. He sent his eldest son to commercial school. His second son got a clerical job in a business run by the son of his grandfather's benefactor, Tjan Tan Sing. The two families had always maintained business and friendly relations.

During the Japanese occupation, Sie King had to close his store because of the shortage of goods. He refused to ask his wealthy brother, Sie Ming, for help, even though his other brother had obtained a generous "loan." He considered Sie Ming "filthy rich" and would have nothing to do with him. But his worries got the best of him, and he died not long after. The store was rented, and his wife, Kie Nio, moved with the younger children into another house.

On Kie Nio's side of the family there were ten brothers and sisters. After the war, one of her sisters, who had married well, lent Kie Nio a good deal of money to get the store going again, and a brother, Tji

Ting, took over the management. The same sister helped another brother to get started in the tobacco trade, and a brother-in-law in the restaurant business. Not long ago, when it was discovered that Tji Ting had been misusing family funds, his nine brothers and sisters held a council and decided to oust and disown him. Tji Ting moved to another city, and the store is now managed by Kie Nio's fourth and sixth brothers jointly. Her own sons are employed elsewhere.

In many ways this story is typical of Chinese enterprise in Indonesia. In spite of various successes and failures, this family has managed to maintain a simple but fairly comfortable standard of living through several generations. Indonesia has seen spectacularly successful Chinese enterprises too. For example, here is the case of the Oei Tiong Ham Concern, which has been of great importance in the Semarang Chinese community in many ways.

About twenty years before Tjan San Go arrived in Semarang, another penniless immigrant had come there as a refugee from the devastations of the T'ai P'ing Rebellion. The newcomer, Oei Tjie Sien, established a produce business and did well. But his son, Oei Tiong Ham, did even better. He cornered the sugar market and by 1890 had enough money to lease the opium monopoly for the Semarang area. He expanded his business and his monopoly holdings until he was the wealthiest man in Semarang. He was appointed the Major of the Chinese community and was showered with other honors.

As was expected of wealthy Chinese in those days, Oei Tiong Ham gave huge contributions to charitable causes, and took five or six wives. He had twenty-six children. Mindful of the proverbial dangers of business failure in the third generation, he trained eight of his sons to carry on his empire. The rest inherited generous cash allotments, but no share in the business.

Today the Oei Tiong Ham Concern is the biggest and best-organized Chinese enterprise in Indonesia. It has offices in nine major Indonesian cities and fifteen overseas commercial centers, including London, Amsterdam, and New York. It owns at least ten factories and mills, producing sugar, kapok, rubber, and other products. It operates a bank and an insurance company and owns much real estate. Among its imports are textiles, drugs and chemicals, flour, machinery, newsprint, glassware, and piece goods. Its exports include rubber, sugar, kapok, tapioca, rice, leather, gums and resins, and tea. In Semarang, besides manufacturing, financial, and trading activities, the Oei Tiong Ham Concern owns and operates a pharmacy, a number of large warehouses, and the biggest Chinese building and construction company.

Long before his death in 1924, Oei Tiong Ham laid down the concern's strict personnel policy. It was considered revolutionary because it rated brains, ability, and training above family connections. Nevertheless, even though the concern is a limited-liability company today, its ownership and top management are kept within the Oei family. Several of Oei Tiong Ham's sons have died, but they are now being replaced by grandsons. It is still common for the concern to employ many members of one family, including several generations. If the company always looks for the best-qualified man for a job, at least it starts looking among relatives.

Several characteristics of Chinese business organization in Indonesia will now be considered. With regard to size, the Tjan family stores are more typical than the Oei Tiong Ham Concern. The great majority of Chinese enterprises are small enough for one family to handle without employing outsiders above the level of workers or clerks. Such an enterprise consists of an office or a shop and a warehouse; usually the family living quarters are in the same building. When the business expands, it is generally by opening a branch in another town—another office or shop, with its warehouse and living quarters, under the direction of a member of the family.

This leads to a second characteristic, diversity of lines of business. There are many Chinese businessmen who stick to one line —textiles, for instance. But the tendency is to stop the expansion of one line at a certain point, in order to enter into new fields. Chinese manufacturers, for instance, rarely employ more than a few hundred workers; rather than expand their factories further, they invest elsewhere. The Oei Tiong Ham Concern is a prime example of diversity, but some of Semarang's lesser large firms are more typical.

The Sien Bie Kongsie operates a photo-offset (printing) establishment for producing cigarette-paper booklets. It also imports cigarette paper, office machines and supplies, construction iron and steel, enamelware, and wheat flour; and it exports tea, tapioca, and other local products. It has branches in Japan and Amsterdam.

The Hiap Liong Company, a family enterprise, operates a rice mill, a kapok factory, and a diversified export-import business.

The Sidodadi Company imports General Electric refrigerators and electrical appliances, medical and dental equipment, X-ray machines, and automobiles and parts; it also has a secondhand department, a garage, and a wrecker (derrick-truck) for rent.

It may be that the diversity characteristic of middle- and large-size Chinese businesses is partly the result of a desire to keep administrative units small, with family management close to the work in each line. It is also a practical way to utilize the various members of a family in one business with the least amount of subservience of one to another. No doubt equally important is the fact that diversity offers a kind of insurance against the vicissitudes of the market.

This brings up a third characteristic of Chinese business enterprises in Indonesia, instability. The outside world tends to remark only the spectacular successes among Chinese businessmen, but the Chinese community itself is well aware of the constant failures, sellouts, and bankruptcies. The saying that Chinese enterprises never last more than three generations is common among the Indonesian Chinese, and the special measures Oei Tiong Ham took to avert this fate have already been noted. The typical instability of the small enterprises of the Tjan family has also been brought out. Successive crises in the sugar market during the 1920's bankrupted a dozen of the leading merchants of Semarang, including the near-millionaires Oei Tjoe, The Ing Tjhiang, Siek Djwee Kioe, and Kwik Djoen Eng. Other big enterprises, such as the Java Ien Boe

Kong Sie printing works, went bankrupt, but were bought out and continued under the same name by new owners. Among the Chinese firms which were prominent enough to be elected to membership on the governing board of the Sianghwee between 1907 and 1935, only one-quarter are still in existence. Of the major Chinese enterprises in Semarang today, only about a dozen were founded before 1910; and, so far as the writer was able to ascertain, only four are now in the hands of third-generation owners. Liem Kiem Ling and Company, founded in 1862, has the distinction of being the oldest Chinese firm in Semarang and the only one now managed by a fourth-generation descendant of the founder. The advertisements of a certain Semarang dry-cleaning and laundry establishment boast of continuous service since 1918 with the same pride that New York banks display their eighteenth-century founding dates.

Chinese business failures are often ascribed to the "speculative nature" of the Chinese. That speculation is characteristic of a good part of Chinese business in Indonesia cannot be denied. But it is doubtful whether Chinese entrepreneurs are any more speculative in business than their counterparts in other ethnic groups. At any rate, there are many objective reasons, in addition to unwise speculation, for the rather frequent failures among Chinese business enterprises. For one thing, a considerable amount of their business is dependent upon world market prices, the fluctuations of which are not only beyond their control, but usually beyond their ken. In addition, the comparatively small scale of their business organization as well as the constant dividing of fortunes among many inheritors means that Chinese business enterprise must operate with a minimum of ready capital. In many families the sons do not care to take on their father's business, and the enterprise dies with the father. Finally, it must be emphasized that Indonesia, during the period under discussion, has experienced world war, Japanese occupation, revolution, and internal revolt. In view of these various factors, the rather short life of the average Chinese business enterprise is not at all surprising. Relative to comparable small business in Western nations, the Chinese concerns would seem, if anything, more stable. Relative to their own business ideology, however, they are seen as characteristically unstable.

A fourth aspect of Chinese enterprise is its familistic personnel structure. In the Tjan family the whole family was expected to help in the store. In the Oei Tiong Ham Concern a situation which is typical of the larger Chinese businesses was found: where there are more than two or three outside employees, many of them are closely related to one another. Thus the personnel core of most Chinese businesses is either one family or a single family and one or more satellite families. However, the exceptions are many. Close friends and schoolmates are considered to make good business partners or assistants, and more and more nonrelatives are being employed on the recommendation of relatives or friends. In addition, a few individuals are beginning to offer or to seek employment through newspaper advertising. This represents a complete break with Chinese tradition. In one of the Chinese newspapers of Semarang, an average of three or four such "want ads" appear each day. Of these, probably less than half are put in by Chinese advertisers. Here are some examples:

WANTED: *1 (One) Nursemaid*—Chinese, between ages of 30 and 40. Good wages.

WANTED: *Employment or Business Partnership*—by two CHINESE WOMEN who are experienced in tailoring; no objections to location outside city.

WANTED IMMEDIATELY: *Administrative Assistant* who is a skilled typist and a graduate of elementary school at least.

POSITION WANTED: Chinese youth of Indonesian citizenship seeks position as chauffeur; has driving license A, diplomas in Indonesian-language stenography and typing, and experience as a bill collector. Willing to work anywhere.

Such advertising is unusual in Indonesia even for European companies, which tend to adopt familistic policies in the employment of Chinese and Indonesian personnel.

The fifth characteristic of Chinese enterprise is familistic ownership. In the cases described so far, ownership has been kept entirely within the circle of one family and its close relatives. This is very often true even in the more modern limited-liability companies (which are called *naamloze vennootschap* and given the initials "N.V."). Semarang needs no stock exchange. Almost the only way to acquire shares in a company is to marry into the family owning it. The Indies government's commercial code, which is still in effect today, allows as few as two shareholders in a registered corporation. Thus family businesses can easily be incorporated, if limited liability is desired.

There are a small but growing number of corporations owned by a number of individuals, and partnerships are very common. But even when corporations and partnerships are not family businesses, some or all of the owners may be distantly related or may possess a common surname. Recent figures on the ownership of Semarang corporations are not available, but it has been reported that, of 55 Chinese enterprises granted corporate charters in the Semarang area in 1922 and 1923, 35 (60 per cent) were organized by only two persons, 18 (about 30 per cent) were established by three or four persons, and only 4 (less than 10 per cent) were formed by more than four persons. In these corporations, an average of 68 per cent of the stock was held by the principal shareholder. In some cases a single shareholder owned from 90 to 99 per cent of the stock.[4]

The discussion of ownership leads to a sixth characteristic of

[4] J. L. Vleming, door den Belasting-Accountants dienst, *Het Chineesche Zakenleven in Nederlandsch-Indië* (Weltevreden, 1926), pp. 77 and 80, as quoted in Lea E. Williams, "Chinese Entrepreneurs in Indonesia," *Explorations in Entrepreneurial History*, vol. V, no. 1 (Oct. 15, 1952; Cambridge, Mass.).

the internal structure of Chinese business enterprise, informal organization. With occasional exceptions, Semarang Chinese have always preferred the informal, personal relations of the partnership or family enterprise, rather than the formalities and supposed risks of the public corporation. In a letter to the present writer, one Chinese businessman put it this way:

Most China-born Chinese do not like to organize their business under the "N.V.-law." The reason is this: by nature disliking "complications" and having a "creepy" feeling against visiting the court of justice, they always keep themselves as far as possible from the "N.V." business, the organization of which entails drawing up deeds with the Notary Public, registering with the Court, employing a Public Accountant, issuing shares, etc. etc. All these to them are "troublesome." . . . The Family N.V. is most popular among the wealthy Indonesian-born Chinese.

This quotation illustrates the suspicion and distaste with which many Chinese businessmen regard the formalities involved in corporate enterprise of any kind. Especially strong reluctance to participate in public corporations is evident in the following two examples:

In 1917, the sugar merchants of Semarang held a special meeting to discuss what could be done about the drastic fall in world sugar prices. At the suggestion of Dutch bankers, plans were laid for a joint-stock company in which all the sugar merchants would be members. With a capital of 10,000,000 guilders, the company would be in a better position to regulate and control the sugar trade for the benefit of its members. On the third day of the meeting, however, the whole plan broke down because of the unwillingness of many of the merchants to give up their independence to this extent.[5]

In 1935, the kapok division of the Sianghwee tried to organize a special corporation for the export of kapok, so that the Chinese kapok producers could export through a jointly owned company. The gov-

[5] *Boekoe Peringetan, 1907–1937, Tiong Hwa Siang Hwee, Semarang* (Semarang, 1937), pp. 3–4.

ernment favored the plan and promised export licenses. But repeated visits to the various kapok producers failed to induce them to invest even the 50,000 guilders necessary for a start. The whole project collapsed.[6]

The earliest successful large Chinese corporations were the insurance companies Indische Lloyd, founded in 1916, and Chineesche Lloyd, founded in 1920. Shareholders of the latter subscribed a total of some 5,000,000 guilders. However, the company was collapsed by the bankruptcy of the Be Biauw Tjoan Bank in 1927. The Indische Lloyd is still in business today.

There is a growing number of Chinese limited-liability companies, but they are still mostly partnerships and family enterprises, and they are far outnumbered by unincorporated businesses. From the 1955 telephone book and the two current trade directories mentioned earlier, some idea is obtained of the proportion of limited companies among all Semarang enterprises with unmistakably Chinese names—for example, one out of nine coffee producers, two out of five rubber-goods factories, and 36 out of 214 trading companies. Among a dozen rice mills, ten soft-drink producers, and seven soap factories, none are organized as limited companies.

Thus far strictly Chinese enterprise has been discussed—that is, businesses owned entirely by alien Chinese or by Indonesian citizens of Chinese descent. Since Indonesia declared its independence in 1945, however, a new type of organization has appeared, the joint Indonesian-Chinese enterprise. This development has been largely due to the economic policies of the Indonesian government. Under successive cabinets, policies have varied in detail and degree of effectiveness. But all have been based upon a desire to build up an Indonesian middle class which would come to have a position of economic welfare and power equal to or stronger than that of the Chinese.

[6] *Ibid.*, pp. 19–20.

These policies will not be examined in detail here.[7] The essential features of all of them have been certain kinds of restrictions on the activities of Chinese (mostly alien Chinese) businesses, and preferential treatment for enterprises wholly or partly owned by native Indonesians. Under Iskaq Tjokrohadisurjo, Minister of Economic Affairs during the time of the present study, the respective restrictions and privileges were considerably increased. Iskaq proposed that, in order to share in the privileges, Chinese entrepreneurs should find Indonesian business partners and make them codirectors and joint owners of their firms. The statutes of such firms should guarantee that at least 50 per cent of the company's shares are owned by native Indonesians. In most cases, Iskaq admitted, the Indonesian partner would not have sufficient initial capital, and therefore he should be given one-half of the company's shares at the outset, with the understanding that he would gradually pay for them out of his share of the profits. Furthermore, said Iskaq, existing Chinese firms should reorganize their management staff in such a way as to allow the participation of native Indonesians, and Chinese-owned factories should offer facilities for training Indonesian technicians.[8]

The reaction of many Chinese to these policies was to extend their business activities in fields not yet touched by government controls—for instance, small-scale manufacturing not requiring equipment or materials from abroad; building and construction; or the handling, processing, and trading of local products. Others adopted a wait-and-see attitude, while putting their capital into jewelry, gold, and other nonproductive savings. A certain number resorted to bribery of officials or illegal operations through Indonesian "front" enterprises.

On the other hand, many Chinese businessmen have reorganized their businesses in accordance with government instructions.

[7] See Donald E. Willmott, *The National Status of the Chinese in Indonesia* (Cornell Modern Indonesia Project, Ithaca, N.Y., 1956), chs. vi and vii.

[8] *Times of Indonesia,* June 28, 1954.

There are in Semarang a considerable number of new jointly owned trading companies. Two Semarang banks are based on Indonesian as well as Chinese capital. Some Chinese manufacturers have taken on Indonesian business partners. And a few new Chinese-Indonesian productive enterprises have been established. For instance, the "Insel" singlet factory, which began operations in 1954 with a capital of about a million rupiahs, is partly owned by Chinese and partly by native Indonesians.

In some cases these jointly owned companies are genuine partnerships. There are, however, only a very small number of Indonesians with business experience and some capital of their own who are interested in going into partnership with Chinese. Therefore, the usual relationship between partners or "codirectors" of "jointly owned" firms is far from equal. With less business experience and little or no capital of his own, the Indonesian naturally plays a secondary role, even if half of the company's shares are signed over to him. Usually a division of labor occurs in which the Chinese partner manages the business while the Indonesian handles public relations and especially relations with government authorities. In some cases the Indonesian partner is very inactive and may even have another full-time job. Thus it may be concluded that for the most part the "new" structure of jointly owned Chinese-Indonesian enterprises is as yet not very different from the old: management and control are still largely in the hands of the Chinese.

External Relations of Chinese Business Enterprise

In this examination of the regularized relations between individual Chinese enterprises or businessmen and various significant outside groups, relations with the Dutch will be considered first.

As already noted, the Dutch and European trading companies neither retail nor widely distribute the goods which they import for sale in Indonesia. They do not gather the products of native agriculture or transport them to the big commercial centers for export abroad. These functions have always been carried out by Chinese merchants.

With regard to imports from Europe, the strength of the Chinese is in their knowledge of local markets, whereas their weakness lies in their small accumulation of ready capital. In the usual arrangement, therefore, a Chinese merchant places an order with a Dutch importer for European products that he knows will sell well. The importer advances credit to cover the greater part of the cost of the goods, and demands repayment only after the Chinese merchant has had time to sell them. In this way, Chinese firms can handle a volume of goods valued at many times the amount of their own capital.

In general, the economic relations between Chinese and Dutch businesses have operated smoothly and with mutual benefit. Moreover, the Dutch Chamber of Commerce and the Sianghwee have maintained co-operative relations ever since the founding of the latter. For example, on Dutch initiative, they co-operated in forcing down the wages of stevedores in 1920 by announcing a joint project to import Chinese coolie labor from Singapore; and in 1922, the Sianghwee supported the Dutch Chamber of Commerce in petitioning the Dutch government to lighten taxes.[9] In addition, they have regularly exchanged a certain amount of commercial information.

The relations between Chinese businessmen and the Dutch government were not always so friendly. Again, a certain amount of commercial information was regularly exchanged between the two, and government regulation of commerce was sometimes of considerable benefit to Chinese merchants. But, as brought out earlier, one of the purposes for which the Sianghwee was established was to oppose certain legal, social, and commercial regulations which adversely affected the Chinese community. In the first few years of its life, it applied pressure on the government to improve the treatment of Chinese immigrants (1907) and to abolish

[9] *Boekoe Peringetan,* p. 5.

the *politie rol* courts (1909), the travel-pass system (1910), and the "ghetto" restrictions (1916). Scarcely had these grievances been removed when there arose new contentions over some of the government's commercial regulations and restrictions. These began with a World War I decree forbidding the import and the internal transport of rice. Other examples were the import quota and licensing system introduced in the early 1930's, and price controls and quality standards. In various petitions to the government the Sianghwee opposed or suggested alterations in such restrictions. It also took up such causes as the defense of Chinese graves against real-estate developments, and support of the system of Chinese community officers.[10]

With increasing government regulation of commerce, there was even more need for the Sianghwee and other organizations to represent the interests of Chinese merchants. Yet the history of commercial organizations among the Semarang Chinese reveals a great reluctance on the part of businessmen to take part in any organized activities. They have always had their guilds and trade associations, but these have been more or less moribund except in times of crisis. The history of the Sianghwee provides various examples.[11]

The Semarang Sianghwee was established in 1907, largely as a result of the legal and social grievances and the rising nationalism of the Chinese community. Three years later an effort was made to unite the Sianghwee organizations of various cities into a federation in order to take co-ordinated action in various fields. This effort failed; but the plan was revived from time to time, and a federation was finally established in 1934.

In 1919 there were crises in the coffee and sugar markets. The Sianghwee called several meetings of coffee merchants, and an

---

[10] *Ibid., passim.*

[11] The information in the paragraphs that follow is taken from a history of the Sianghwee written by Liem Thian Joe, who was given access to all its records, correspondence, and minutes of meetings. The history was published in a memorial booklet by the Sianghwee itself: *Boekoe Peringetan, 1907–1937, Tiong Hwa Siang Hwee, Semarang* (Semarang, 1937).

organization was finally set up to control prices and regulate trade in this field. The organization collapsed nine months later, however. With the sugar merchants, the Sianghwee was more successful. They succeeded in establishing a permanent organization, which later federated with the sugar merchants of Surabaja. A federation of rice merchants was not finally organized until 1933.

In 1927 and again at the end of 1929, there were periods of several months' duration when no one could be found to accept the position of chairman of the Sianghwee, and the organization had to operate without top officers.

In 1935 the federation of Sianghwee organizations, which had been organized according to statutes and regulations customary in China, was reorganized in accordance with Dutch regulations. The federation was forced to make this change in order to become a chartered corporation, but it did so only after gaining the assent of the Chinese government. The member Sianghwee organizations followed suit.

At the end of 1934, it was decided that the interests of different groups of merchants could best be served by establishing separate departments for different trades: kapok, rice, tobacco, coffee, and so on. A circular letter was sent out asking all of the Semarang Sianghwee's 112 members which departments interested them. Only five or six replies were received. Nevertheless, the officers of the Sianghwee went ahead with the organization of three departments, kapok, rice, and coffee. Less than half the kapok producers of the area took part in the kapok department, but officers were elected and considerable work was done. It was this organization, however, that could not raise enough capital to establish the much-needed export corporation mentioned in the previous section. The rice department had only seven members. They did not elect officers and showed very poor co-operation in the fixing of quality standards. The coffee department was even less active. With the gradual improvement in business conditions during 1936, seventeen members dropped out of the Sianghwee.

In 1955, however, the Sianghwee was much more active. It had about 230 members, and departments for the following trades: food-product imports, textiles, tobacco, sugar, coffee, tapioca, rice, red peppers and melon seeds, and Chinese herbs and medicines. Each of these departments reflected a specific need for co-operation. The Chinese medicine dealers, for instance, had received no foreign exchange credit from the government and had therefore been unable to replenish their supplies from China.

There are more commercial and trade organizations in Semarang today than ever before—for example, the Federation of Central Java Importers, the Association of Printers, the Federation of Bakeries, and Textile Bond, the Association of Soft-Drink Producers, the Semarang Union of Cigarette Manufacturers, the Association of Trishaw (*Betjak*) Owners, the Federation of Motorized Transport Companies, the Sugar Trade Association, and the Semarang Rice Mill Union.

A more difficult economic situation and the very great increase in government regulations and controls since the establishment of the Republic of Indonesia in 1945 have had the effect, not only of increasing the number of Chinese trade organizations, but, in many cases, of bringing about another significant change—the inclusion of Indonesian merchants in these organizations or the establishment of new joint Chinese-Indonesian trade associations. This is also partly the result of an assimilationist trend in Chinese thinking on the minority-group question. There is even a group in the Sianghwee who want to eliminate the words "Tiong Hoa," that is, "Chinese," from the official name of the Sianghwee and to open its membership to non-Chinese. In most cases, however, the association of Chinese and Indonesian businessmen has been encouraged by more practical considerations of mutual benefit. The Chinese bring to such organizations greater economic strength and more business experience, while the Indonesians assure favorable treatment from government agencies. This division of responsibility is symbolized in the almost universal custom of electing Indonesian chairmen and Chinese treasurers. An example is the Persatuan Pedagang Pasar Djohar Semarang (the Association of Traders of the Semarang "Djohar" Market):

The Djohar Market is a very large roofed-over area in which there are hundreds of little stalls and shops selling everything from textiles and imported flashlights to bananas and parrots. No matter what you are interested in buying, if you cannot find it elsewhere, you will be told by residents of Semarang: "Go to the Djohar Market!" The petty merchants of the market are partly Indonesian, partly Chinese, with the Indonesians, perhaps, predominating in numbers. In 1954 their trade association was headed by Suroto, an Indonesian, and the treasurer was Soen Tjhing Kie, a Chinese; the other officers were about equally divided between Chinese and Indonesians. One of the functions of the association is to serve as a co-operative buying agent for certain products, such as wheat flour, sugar, and kerosene, which are controlled by the government and sold only to large wholesalers.

Some joint Chinese-Indonesian trade organizations deliberately exclude Chinese businessmen who are not Indonesian citizens. For instance, the Federation of Trucking Associations of Indonesia has taken this course, partly to co-operate with the government's attempt to exclude foreign Chinese from this field and partly, perhaps mostly, in order to qualify as a buying agent for tires and automobile parts, which are sold on a preferential basis to organizations with 100 per cent "national" capital. On the other hand, some trade associations are still divided along ethnic lines.

In 1954, from over a hundred applicants, the government selected five wholesale organizations for the privilege of handling all the government-controlled textiles allotted to the Semarang area. One of these was the Gabungan Textiel Semarang (Textile Union of Semarang), an organization of fifty-four Chinese-owned textile stores. The day has come when Chinese businesses, because of their limited size and economic strength, must join together in organizations or perish.

Another aspect of the external relations of Chinese business enterprises is the settlement of disputes. The Chinese rarely take their business disputes before the courts. In the first place, they are very much averse to laying bare their business relations to public view. Secondly, there is a traditional dislike and distrust of government authorities, because of their impersonality, their arbitrary or unjust acts in the past, and their non-Chinese outlook and personnel. Finally, business deals among the Chinese are usually based upon word-of-mouth agreements and are rarely supported by contracts or legal documents such as could be made the basis of court action.

The usual way of settling disputes is by the arbitration of trusted individuals or organizations. In Semarang the Sianghwee and the Chung Hua Tsung Hui (Federation of Chinese Associations) often perform this function. The Sianghwee has a regular arbitration committee. It consists of a board of judges, three of whom hear and decide each case. It is called upon to arbitrate about half a dozen cases each year.

Occasionally the loser in an arbitration case is required to undergo the humiliation of public apology. The following announcement, taken from an Indonesian-language newspaper, is an example. In order not to magnify and prolong the penance, the names of all parties involved have been changed.

ANNOUNCEMENT

The undersigned, Sik Oh Sin, some time ago ordered pepper from Mr. Yauw Lan Yap of Semarang. Because of a misunderstanding on my part, which was not in accord with the regulations of commerce, a controversy arose. With the help of the Chung Hua Tsung Hui and Mr. Kwik Say Hoo, this controversy has been settled amicably. Mr. Yauw Lan Yap has now forgiven me and has delivered the pepper to me. Here I wish to express my regret for any words of mine which may have reflected on the good name of Mr. Yauw Lan Yap.

Semarang, 19 October 1945   Sik Oh Sin

When dealing with European firms, Chinese businessmen have generally been required to follow Western business practices, especially in the matter of contracts. The Chinese long ago learned that almost every transaction had to be covered by a signed contract, breach of which led to court action. It was at the insistence of Dutch merchants that Dutch commercial law was applied to the Chinese in 1855, in order that business disputes involving Chinese could be tried in the European court system.[12] Chinese taken to court in Semarang had to employ Dutch lawyers until 1926, when Chinese lawyers first established an office there. Since that time the number of Chinese lawyers has grown to over a dozen, and the number of court cases involving Chinese has steadily increased.

The final aspect of the external relations of Chinese enterprises to be discussed is their credit system. Loan and credit facilities are very important to enterprises having only a relatively small amount of available capital. As already noted, one source of credit for Chinese importers and wholesalers is the large European import firms, which offer liberal short-term credit arrangements for orders placed with them. Banks, especially the Chinese banks, are another source, though a less important one. In 1955, the interest on bank loans was 7 per cent per annum. But the average small businessman has neither the security nor the connections necessary for obtaining a loan from a bank. Furthermore, there are certain government restrictions on bank loans at present. A number of private individuals make a business of moneylending, but their interest rates are exorbitant. It is common for several small firms to pool their resources temporarily in order to co-operate in a particular business venture which requires considerable capital.

It is also common, especially among Totoks, to obtain direct loans from friends and relatives. It was mentioned earlier that members of the Tjan family made fairly large loans to less successful brothers, in order to get them started in business or to pull

12 Victor Purcell, *The Chinese in Southeast Asia* (London, 1951), p. 507.

them out of difficulties. No interest is paid on such loans, and in some cases they are never repaid. One of the prominent Chinese productive enterprises of Semarang was established many years ago with capital borrowed from a close relative. The original borrower died, and his family have never mentioned repayment. The sum involved was large, and the lending family, though they would never think of asking for repayment, have not forgotten it.

Among Totok Chinese a traditional Chinese method of raising loans is still sometimes used—the co-operative loan group. Perhaps Lee King Gin needs about 50,000 rupiahs for a business deal. He finds nine friends who are willing to join a loan group and who trust one another. As the organizer of the group, he invites them to a feast, and each one brings 5,000 rupiahs. The money is pooled and the pool goes to Lee King Gin. At two-month intervals thereafter, the group holds similar meetings, with the members bringing the same amount of cash every time. At each meeting those who have not yet won the pool draw lots or throw dice for the privilege. After ten meetings each man has had the use of a large amount of money at one time, for which he has paid out an equal amount in ten installments. The group is then dissolved.

The variations in loan-group practices are endless. The regular interval between meetings varies from one month to one year. The number of members and the amount of money involved differ greatly from group to group. Sometimes a complicated interest system is introduced. But in all cases the organizer gets the first "loan," each member wins it once, no one loses, and the members enjoy many evenings of social intercourse. Although once popular, loan groups are less frequently organized today.

In the external relations of Chinese business enterprises—that is, in relations with Dutch businesses and the government, in trade associations, in the settlement of disputes, and in the credit system—there is a strong tendency to maintain traditional Chinese practices based upon family ties, personal contacts, and maximum independence. Nevertheless, extensive change has taken place as a result of dealings with European business firms and adjustment to government regulations, and the extent of change in outlook and attitudes behind the traditional structure should now be ascertained.

Business Orientations

In connection with the business orientations of Chinese entrepreneurs, what is the view that they take of themselves? The following statement is from an article written in 1936 by Tan Tek Peng, an executive high in the Oei Tiong Ham Concern. Published in a special edition of a Semarang Dutch newspaper, the article appeared under the headline "Chinese Initiative Restrained."

Chinese entrepreneurs of light industry and the wholesale business are free traders par excellence. They find their strength in individual action in circumstances as free as possible. That is why limited companies are almost unknown in Chinese commercial circles. Each entrepreneur works for himself, his family, and his relatives. Individual driving power, great devotion to the family business, and austerity in life have brought prosperity, and sometimes great wealth, to many a Chinese family.

The Chinese individualist in trade was well adapted to times of freedom, when high personal qualities in the commercial field tipped the scale in striving after business success. But times have changed and present other exigencies. The days of freedom are gone and will not return in the near future. In their place have been substituted government regulations regarding price, quality and quantity, country of origin, and so on, such that a quick adaptation of the commercial mentality is required, in order to keep one's place in this new system.

Up till now the Chinese businessman has lacked this adaptation. Combined action to attain joint success does not fit into his nature; he has not been able to see the consequences of certain government regulations, and when he has finally taken action, either individually or together with others, it has often been too late. . . .

One of the most adverse consequences of strong Chinese individualism is mutual rivalry, particularly among the stores selling dry goods, and food and drinks. They try to co-operate, but fail again and again because people will not stand by group decisions. In the field of co-operation, Chinese still have much to learn.[13]

Here Mr. Tan has touched upon many of the significant personal characteristics of the Chinese businessman: extreme individualism, family loyalty, "driving power," hard work, austerity, independence, and poor ability to co-operate. In addition to these, even the Chinese themselves usually mention materialism and "money-mindedness." Instead of categorizing such characteristics as "virtues" or "vices" in order to praise or blame—the usual way of viewing them—Mr. Tan has considered them in the context of potentiality for adjustment to new conditions. With the same analytic purpose, the origins, development, and change potential in Chinese business orientations will now be discussed.

The Indonesian Chinese are only a few generations away from their homeland society, in which the highest traditional values were familistic. The members of that society acquired a keen sense of the historical continuity of their families. They felt a deep responsibility not only to their living family and relatives, but also to their ancestors and their descendants. Their duty to their ancestors was shown in honor and respect, in ceremonial attention, and in maintaining the good name of the family. Their obligation to their descendants was to enhance the family fortune, both in wealth and in position. This deep sense of responsibility to the wider family, past, present, and future, no doubt contributed much toward the characteristics of frugality, striving, willingness to work very hard, and individualistic competitiveness vis-à-vis nonrelatives.

A second factor which supported these same characteristics was the poverty and population pressure characteristic of the areas in China from which the immigrants had come. Competition in the

[13] Tan Tek Beng, "Chinese Initiative Restrained," in "Semarang Vooruit," a special number of *De Locomotief,* June 30, 1936.

struggle for existence had been keen and relentless, and the immigrants carried with them habits appropriate to that struggle. Once they arrived in Indonesia, they were cut off from the moral controls of their home communities and had little reason to fear that their behavior would reflect upon their family name and reputation. They had to make their livelihood from dealings with a people whom they did not respect and whose codes and standards they little knew or understood. These conditions set the stage for business practices of the most unrestrained, individualistic, and competitive kind. The Chinese immigrants felt a minimum of obligation to the Indonesian people and to each other. Their sole purpose was to advance the economic prosperity of their own families.

As settled communities of Peranakans grew up in Indonesia, relations among themselves and with others were tempered by considerations of personal reputation, family honor, community status, and maintenance of smooth and peaceful intercourse with both the Indonesian people and the Dutch. Even to this day Peranakans are said to be less aggressive, less "sharp" in their business practices, less willing to take advantage of others, and less prone to extralegal practices than are Totoks. Since immigration has now virtually ceased, a growing proportion of the Chinese in Indonesia are Indonesia-born and have their roots in local communities. This may be expected to have a continuing effect of tempering unrestrained individualism in business practices. Two other equally important factors in this direction are the increased vulnerability of the Chinese as a minority group and the rising amount of government regulation of commerce.

Nevertheless, even the settled Chinese community has inherited an extremely individualistic business orientation. A Peranakan businessman told the writer that in his group even the best of friends rarely give each other information about their business dealings. It has already been brought out how reluctant they are to co-operate in organized action, how highly they value independence, and how seldom they have undertaken corporate business organization.

These orientations tend to slow down the trend toward large-scale corporate business organization which might be expected under present circumstances. But another factor supports the trend—that is, the increasing acceptance of contractual relations, as opposed to the traditional system of trusting relations only. In the emigrant villages of China there were few strangers. Village populations were small, and everyone knew everyone else. This was not true, of course, in the towns and cities; yet there, too, it was customary to have none but the most superficial relations with strangers. Virtually all relations were based upon mutual trust arising out of family relationship or long personal acquaintance. The institution of go-betweens was essential to this system. For any kind of dealings with strangers, from marriage arrangements to trade agreements, go-betweens who knew and were trusted by both parties were sought out. There were professional go-betweens, but even more important was the widespread use of friends and relatives as informal go-betweens. This is the hallmark of a society based upon personal trust relationships rather than impersonal contractual relationships.

Chinese immigrants coming to Indonesia brought with them the habits and institutions of trust relationships. This is evidenced in the custom of depending on word-of-mouth agreements instead of contracts in business deals, in the preference for arbitration rather than litigation, in the inability to co-operate with strangers, in the loan clubs and the borrowing of money from friends and relatives rather than from banks, and in employment policies. It appears also in the inability of many Chinese to function impersonally, according to codes and regulations only—in their desire always to add the personal touch, such as the intercession of a friend or the invitation to a feast. Even in retail and trade relations with the Indonesian people, Chinese businessmen established trust relations as soon as possible, through the *langganan* system. A *langganan* is a regular client or customer or his opposite, the regular dealer or supplier. The *langganan* businessman and his client enter into an explicit or implicit agreement to trade exclusively with each other in a certain field, and thus they develop a prolonged acquaintance, mutual obligations, considerable trust, and even friendship. In some cases the relationship goes so far as to involve visiting and even eating in one another's homes.

Chinese merchants have often been praised for their high sense of business honor. On the other hand, they have been widely condemned as cheaters and swindlers. Even this writer has referred to the unrestrained individualism and "sharp" business practices of many Chinese immigrants. There is an apparent, not a real, contradiction here. In customary Chinese morality there was an implicit distinction between relatives and friends on the one hand and strangers on the other. Moral obligations were strongly felt toward the former group, but to a much lesser extent toward the latter. If Western merchants found stones in bales of cotton bought from Chinese traders, it was because they had not taken the trouble to build friendship with their Chinese opposites—to establish trust relations. Where such relations existed, payments were prompt, and the quality of goods exchanged was up to standard. In a trust-relationship system the businessman who violates the trust will soon fail. To keep customers and clients it is necessary to live up to promises and to fulfill expectations. Moreover, the family name must be maintained in good repute.

Thus the Chinese have a high sense of business honor, and for some this is not incompatible with cutthroat competition or sharp practices with strangers. It should be added that the impact of nationalism and the modern Chinese morality of the reformists and revolutionaries, in addition to the necessity of co-operation in ever-widening fields, have considerably extended the moral obligations felt by Chinese businessmen. Today, in their dealings with strangers and the public in general, they appear neither more nor less honest than businessmen of other groups.

In spite of deeply ingrained habits of dealing only through trust relationships, Chinese businessmen, as was brought out in previous sections, have begun to enter into more and more impersonal, contractual relations. By "contractual relations" is meant not only dealings guaranteed by signed contracts, but all dealings between relative strangers which are based only on economic or legal sanctions and not on mutual trust. By this definition, when a businessman obtains a permit from a government official or when he becomes a member of a trade association, he is involved in a contractual relationship. In each case he has certain obligations and rights, but they are the result of regulations or group standards and not primarily of a personal, trusting relationship.

From the first, the majority of dealings of Chinese merchants with European firms and with the government have necessarily been of this kind. But even among themselves, contractual relations are increasing. Corporations, Western-type banks, trade associations, price-fixing agreements, and the occasional employment of strangers are evidence of this. Even where contractual relations are forced by circumstances, such as government regulations, they help to form new habits of thought and action. The basis for complete dependence upon trust relationships—that is, the small, stable, and exclusive community—no longer exists in the urban Chinese communities of Indonesia. Urbanization and industrialization, though they tend to aggravate individualism, also increase impersonal, contractual relationships. One of the effects of this changing orientation is an increasing willingness to join with others in large-scale corporate enterprise. Already there is a significant group of Chinese businessmen whose "commercial mentality" is the same in these respects as that of the European businessmen with whom they deal.

A final aspect of the business orientations of the Chinese which should be discussed here is their characteristic frugality, perseverance, and willingness to work hard. As already mentioned, these traits were originally fostered by severe economic hardship in China and the traditional deep sense of responsibility toward the extended family, including ancestors and descendants. Many of the Chinese who came to Southeast Asia accepted extremely arduous jobs as miners or plantation laborers, working long hours for little pay. Yet they usually managed to save enough to get started in trading activities or to send considerable sums home to their families. The Chinese of Semarang, and of Java generally, rarely did such physically exhausting manual labor. But they demonstrated the same qualities in their long hours of work and in their willingness to forgo personal leisure and comfort in a constant struggle to build up the family business. The typical businessman, even when he had the means to do so, did not employ outside help merely to provide leisure time for himself and his family. Even among the wealthy there was little idleness. There were luxury and "conspicuous consumption," but very few lived beyond their means.

These various characteristics are still very much in evidence today. Yet there are signs of change. An editorial writer in an Indonesian-language Chinese newspaper put it this way:

People of Chinese descent in the old days—yes, and the older generation living today—have always considered perseverance in work as the primary form of capital necessary to business. Beside this, capital in the form of money or property was only secondary. They worked hard, not only in their own enterprises, but also when employed by others. . . .

But great changes are evident in the young generation of today. In life, they are impatient for luxury; even if they are only workers, they want to outdo their employers in outward splendor. In work, they want as little as possible, and as easy. They lack responsibility. They make almost no effort to examine the work methods of their colleagues, or to understand what makes a business "live" and "progress," in order to widen their experience and increase their ability in the field in which they are working. Perseverance in work is declining greatly.[14]

No doubt the author of this piece is one of the older generation himself. Certainly his view of the degeneracy of the younger generation is exaggerated. But there is some truth in it.

[14] *Kuangpo,* Dec. 16, 1954.

For one thing, the Western business practice of fixing regular hours of work is more and more widely accepted. So is the progressive Western and modernist Chinese idea that employees should work no more than eight hours a day. New leisure-time activities have become popular, such as moving pictures, picnics and outings, and all kinds of sports. Books, magazines, films, and the example of local Westerners have aroused a new range of economic wants. The same factors, combined with the high prestige of imported articles, have encouraged "conspicuous consumption."

In addition, family ties are becoming less important. Young people are not so duty-bound to obey and serve their parents and older relatives. Those who have jobs are under less obligation than formerly to give financial assistance to relatives and are less concerned about the "family fortune." A growing number are attending secondary schools and thereby considerably postpone the time when they are required to assume economic responsibilities.

Without doubt there has also been considerable influence from the more easygoing Javanese culture. The more leisurely, less anxiety-laden way of life of the people around them may have appealed to a certain number of Chinese. In addition, the writer believes that an important effect of Javanese culture may well have been introduced through the different child-rearing practices of Indonesian mothers and nursemaids.

From unsystematic observation and reading, the writer gained the impression that the Javanese are much more lenient and permissive with their children than are traditional Chinese parents, and that the latter place higher requirements upon their children for the achievement of success in various fields, such as academic standing. These observations led to the hypothesis that Javanese child-rearing practices tend to produce a personality characterized by less striving, less anxiety for achievement, and lower aspiration levels than in the personality usually produced by traditional Chinese methods.

Unfortunately, this hypothesis was not conceived until after the questionnaire project was well under way. Therefore no direct tests of the hypothesis were included among the questions asked. Nevertheless, the results provide a certain amount of support for the observation that Indonesian child-rearing practices are more lenient. In a series of questionnaire items concerning the respondent's childhood, the following question was asked: "Were you ever spanked or beaten by your parents?" Table 2 shows the distribution of replies given by boy students.

Table 2. Frequency of childhood corporal punishment as reported by male students of different parentage

Frequency of corporal punishment	Chinese, both parents China-born	Chinese, one parent China-born *	Chinese, neither parent China-born	Indonesian, both parents Indonesia-born
Often	15%	6%	7%	8%
Occasionally	43	24	28	19 †
Rarely	43	64	44	48
Never	0	6	21 †	25 †
	101% ‡	100%	100%	100%
Number of cases	47	33	100	194

* The China-born parent was the father in all but three cases.

† These percentages are significantly different at the .01 level from the corresponding figures in the first column. On the basis of the chi-square test of significance, the third and fourth columns, taken separately, differ significantly from the first, at the .05 and .01 levels respectively.

‡ Because of rounding off figures, the total comes to more than 100%.

These results indicate that China-born Chinese parents administer corporal punishment more frequently than do either Indonesian parents or Indonesia-born Chinese parents. The writer does not contend that less frequent corporal punishment in itself produces a more easygoing personality structure. Corporal punishment is here taken only as an index of a whole range of parental attitudes and practices. It is assumed that less frequent corporal punishment is an indication of a generally more permissive and lenient way of raising children, and perhaps also of less rigorous standards of achievement for children throughout childhood and adolescence.

Another questionnaire item asked: "Do you think that you were treated too severely or too leniently when you were a child?" The respondents were asked to check one of five categories in reply: too severely, rather severely, about average, rather leniently, or too leniently. Unfortunately, the number of students who answered this question was somewhat smaller than in the case of the question analyzed above, and no statistically significant differences were found. Nevertheless, the percentage differences were almost as great and were consistent with the above findings. That is, China-born Chinese parents appear to be considered more severe by their sons than are either Indonesian parents or Indonesia-born Chinese parents.

These findings may be considered to give fairly strong support to the general observation that Indonesian child-rearing practices are more permissive than are traditional Chinese methods. They are also consistent with the theory that child training among Peranakans has been considerably influenced by female ancestors of Indonesian extraction.

There is no direct or conclusive evidence to support that part of the hypothesis which states that greater leniency in child training results in less striving and anxiety for success in later years. But there is a certain amount of evidence that a generally easygoing personality is more typical in the groups where child training is more lenient than where it is more severe, whatever the cause may be. The writer was informed by a leading Indonesian doctor that the incidence of ulcers (often an indication of anxiety) is higher among Chinese than among Indonesians. Whether it is higher among Totoks than among Peranakans he did not know. But Chinese of both groups have told the writer that Totoks are more ambitious and have more business drive than Peranakans. The writer's own observations of the behavior of Indonesians, Totoks, and Peranakans also tended to corroborate these testimonies. We are speaking of averages and generalities. There are many exceptions—that is, easygoing Totoks and hard-striving Peranakans and Indonesians.

It must be emphasized that the evidence presented for the hypothesis is far from conclusive. Much careful research would be required to "prove" or "disprove" it. In any case, more lenient child training is not the only explanation for the decline in vocational striving among the Chinese. Other reasons, such as the weakening of obligations to the wider family, have been discussed above. But if it is true that more rigorous methods of child training tend to produce greater striving in business, then it must be expected that the characteristic perseverance of the Chinese will decline somewhat as child-rearing methods become more lenient.

An important factor in the lenient treatment of Chinese children in Semarang is the role of the Javanese nursemaid, or *babu*. Among 459 Chinese questionnaire respondents, 85 per cent answered "yes" to the question: "Did you have a *babu* to care for you when you were a child?" Fewer nursemaids are, of course, employed by families who do not send their children to high school; but it is probable that at least a majority of Chinese families in Semarang employ them. Among the high school respondents, fewer children of China-born fathers than of Indonesia-born fathers had a *babu;* the difference is not great, but it is statistically significant at the .05 level.[15] It is the common practice to put a child under the more or less constant care of a *babu* from about the time he learns to walk until he is old enough to go to school. Some children even sleep with their nursemaids when they are very small. The *babu* protects and entertains the child, but rarely commands or restricts. She makes almost no effort to discipline. At the slightest sign of grief or displeasure, she picks the child up and

[15] See Appendix IV for an explanation of the statistical levels of significance used in this study.

dandles and comforts him until he is happy again. If possible, a *babu* gives a child anything that he asks for. She often spends her own money for sweets or a toy. It is a common sight at mealtime to see a *babu* following a child around with a bowl of food and administering a spoonful whenever the child is willing to stop his play for a moment. This extremely permissive attitude is characteristic of Javanese child-rearing practices. But it is magnified by the role of the *babu* as a servant. As such, she is afraid to show any displeasure or impatience toward the child and is reluctant to require anything of him that would make him unhappy.

In addition to nursemaids, other servants are often employed by Chinese families. This minimizes the household responsibilities of children and may prevent them from acquiring certain work habits. This hypothesis was suggested by the remarks of a China-born professional man of Semarang, who also had a word to say about nursemaids:

As children in China we always had to work hard. First it was household work, and plenty of it. Then we had to help our fathers in their work. But our children nowadays won't touch hard work. Here we have servants to look after the work; and nursemaids look after the children. The nursemaids let them have their way in everything. I'd like to dispense with nursemaids. But we have to employ them. Otherwise we would be considered rather low.

The conclusion is that if leniency in child training is partly responsible for a declining business drive among the Chinese, the roles of the *babu* and the other servants may be as important in causing this change as are those of the parents.

The amount of space given to this topic must not lead to overemphasis of its importance. Hard work and perseverance are still very much in evidence among the Chinese of Semarang. The "decline" is as yet only slight. The example of a modern young couple, known to the writer, demonstrates that the traditional business drive of the overseas Chinese is not wholly a thing of the past.

Swie Ping Sam is a regular employee of one of the Semarang banks. But he does not confine his work to banking hours. In the afternoons and on weekends, he wholesales kerosene stoves, which he buys from a manufacturer in a neighboring city. Although a Peranakan, he knows the Chinese language, as well as Dutch and English, and he fills his evenings with translation work and language tutoring. His wife, Swie Tan Lo, is equally busy. She helps in the stove business, even traveling to other cities to make sales. Having been born and educated in China, she also works on the Chinese-language translations and often prepares stencils in Chinese.

Recently Swie Ping Sam started work on a new project. In view of the fact that local glass factories make only second-grade glass (using broken glass and bottles as the raw materials), he and some friends decided to manufacture glass from sand. He obtained samples of high-grade sand from various parts of Java and selected the best. With guidance from the *Encyclopaedia Britannica,* he managed to produce some sample glass. Convinced of the possibilities, he and his friends then set about planning a glass factory. They encountered a great many obstacles, however, and were finally forced to drop the project. Nevertheless, with this kind of perseverance and ambition, Swie Ping Sam and his wife may someday join Semarang's "Cadillac crowd."

Summary

In this chapter it has been brought out that Semarang Chinese predominate in almost all fields of the city's economic activity. The internal structure of their business enterprises is usually characterized by small-scale operations, diversity of lines of business, instability, familistic personnel and ownership patterns, and informal organization. However, the beginning of a trend toward more Western-type business organization was noted. In the external relations of Semarang Chinese enterprises there was found a strong tendency to maintain traditional practices based upon family ties, personal contacts, and maximum independence; but new business orientations were seen to be emerging. Contractual relations are increasing at the expense of trust relations; extreme individualistic competition is being modified by a wider sense of obligation and various types of business co-operation; frugality, perseverance, and the willingness to work long and hard are less emphasized than formerly, at least among the Peranakans.

CHAPTER IV

Ethnic Group Relations

Racial and Ethnic Groups

The topic of this chapter is popularly called "race relations." The term "race" implies that the population group to which it is applied is characterized by physical traits which are clearly distinguishable from those of certain other population groups. Anthropologists have found that the division of mankind into "races" is possible only in the broadest and most general terms. In all groups which are supposed to be racially distinct there are many individuals who display traits characteristic of other "races," even where no miscegenation has taken place in recorded history. Few social scientists would object to categorizing the Chinese and Dutch as racially distinct; but whether people from China and the people of the Indonesian archipelago can properly be considered as separate races is debatable.

A leading anthropologist, A. L. Kroeber, has divided the people of the world into fifteen major races under the four categories Caucasian, Mongoloid, Negroid, and unclassifiable. He bases his classification on general differences in eight physical characteristics, such as texture of hair, shape of nose, and stature. His Mongolian group (to which most Chinese belong) differs in only two of these characteristics from the Malaysian group (to which most Indonesians belong), and both are therefore included under the general heading of Mongoloid or "yellow." [1] The differences between these two groups noted by Kroeber are also recognized by the Chinese and Indonesians: Chinese have *mata sipit,* or Mongolian eyes, and Indonesians tend to have a slightly darker skin color. Other differences are less noticeable and less consistent.

In any case, a small but significant number of Indonesians have one or more Chinese ancestors, and almost all Chinese Peranakans have one or more Indonesian ancestors. As a result, there are a great number of people in Indonesia whose "race" could not be determined by their physical characteristics. Therefore it would be misleading to speak of the Indonesian Chinese as a "race" separate from the Indonesians. When, however, language, culture, and self-identification are taken into account, the two groups are quite distinct. It is therefore proper to speak of them as "ethnic groups."

Relations with the Dutch

During the period of Dutch rule up to the turn of the century, it was government policy to keep the various ethnic groups as separate as possible. Some of the legal barriers placed between groups were very rigid, especially between the Dutch on the one hand and the Chinese and Indonesians on the other. The segregation of ethnic groups was enforced in the educational system, in the legal system, in restrictions on area of residence, in government employment, and even in language usage. Social barriers were no less rigid.

Before World War II, however, segregation regulations were gradually reduced, though by no means eliminated. Social exclusiveness declined, but only slightly. Semarang was more liberal than other cities in this respect. After World War I the Dutch schools admitted the children of a few prominent Chinese families, and various Dutch organizations accepted a few outstanding Chi-

[1] A. L. Kroeber, *Anthropology* (New York, 1948), p. 132.

nese as members. There was less segregation in hotels, restaurants, swimming pools, and public places than there was in other large cities. Chinese with a Dutch education and considerable wealth had friendly relations with certain Dutch families, including reciprocal entertaining at teas, parties, and receptions. But even this contact was on a rather superficial basis.

The collapse of Dutch power and prestige during World War II and the final establishment of an Indonesian government in Semarang in 1950 accelerated the decline of Dutch exclusiveness. In 1955, for example, the school for Dutch children had more Chinese pupils than Dutch. (This was a result of financial necessity.) The Rotary Club had a number of Chinese members. Even before the war, the Dutch *Societeit,* a club for social entertainment, drinking, dancing, and so on, had a few Chinese members. But it now has many more. One of them has been elected to the office of treasurer. The Dutch sports club, after bitter controversy, admitted its first Chinese member in 1954. In the Catholic churches of the city the Dutch and Chinese often worship side by side, but the lay organizations are segregated according to ethnic group, and there is little social mixing. There is even less contact between Chinese and Dutch Protestants—they have separate churches and church organizations. Although a number of Chinese attend the Dutch churches, the amount of social contact is small.

Between Chinese and Dutch businessmen and, in the large Dutch companies, between the higher Chinese employees and the Dutch personnel, there is often long and fairly close contact. This is probably the most important source of cordial and friendly relationships between members of the two groups. Concerning relations with the Dutch, a well-to-do, Dutch-educated Chinese lady told the writer:

We have many Dutch friends. In fact, our Chinese friends and relatives say we are too Dutch. We have to explain that we only make friends with the really good Dutch people. Most Dutch people adopt a superior attitude and certain unpleasant actions as soon as they get east of

Suez. But they are not all like that. We choose friends for their congeniality, of whatever race they may be. We like our Dutch friends because they are so frank and straightforward. With Chinese and Indonesians you must always observe many formalities.

There is a tendency for Dutch-educated Chinese of the highest socioeconomic level to adopt the Dutch attitude of superiority and exclusiveness toward Eurasians. When the average Chinese speaks of a "Dutch" friend, however, he is usually referring to a Eurasian. Unlike the children of the European-born Dutch, Eurasian children as a rule attend government or mission schools, where they mix with Chinese and Indonesian pupils. But even in mixed schools, friendships tend to follow ethnic lines.

Intermarriage with the Dutch

Another important indication of the nature of ethnic group relations is intermarriage and the attitudes which surround it. Intermarriage between Dutch and Chinese was almost unheard of in the nineteenth century. A fairly good idea of the situation in the twentieth century is gained from the marriage records in the Office of Civil Registration.[2] It was not until 1919 that Chinese were required to register their births, deaths, marriages, and divorces; but Europeans had been registering these for some time before that. Unfortunately, however, the category "Europeans" in the records includes Eurasians, and it is thus impossible to distinguish Dutch from Eurasians.

Of 62 European men who married in Semarang in 1900, only one married a Chinese. Six married Indonesians. Of 73 married in 1910, again only one married a Chinese. In 1920, 4 out of 121 married Chinese; in 1930, 7 out of 140; and in 1940, 3 out of 148. For the period from 1900 to 1942, therefore, no definite trend is discernible. For randomly selected years during this period, the average percentage of Dutch and Eurasian men who married Chinese women was about 2.5.

[2] For an evaluation of the reliability of these records, see Appendix II.

In the years 1946–1953 inclusive, the yearly percentage of European men marrying Chinese wives averaged 6.3. This rise from the prewar figure is statistically significant at the .01 level. The number marrying Indonesian wives also rose significantly— from 10 per cent to about 14 per cent in the postwar years.

In the prewar period, according to the registration records, there were only isolated cases of Chinese men marrying European women. In the postwar years 1946–1954, 1.0 per cent of all Chinese men who registered their marriages took Dutch or Eurasian wives. Since virtually all Chinese-Dutch marriages are registered, but many Chinese Chinese marriages are not, the real percentage of Chinese men who took European wives must be well under 1.0. Whereas 32 Chinese have married Dutch or Eurasian women in these postwar years, 77 European men have married Chinese, or a total of 109 Dutch-Chinese or Eurasian-Chinese marriages in Semarang in nine years.

The increased number of such marriages since World War II may be indicative of a general trend toward reduced prejudice between the two groups. Probably a more important factor, however, is the increased number of Chinese who are individually acceptable to the Dutch because of fluency in the Dutch language and familiarity with the Dutch way of life.

Nevertheless, although the number of intermarriages between Chinese and Europeans has increased in postwar years, it is still relatively insignificant. This is not surprising in view of the problems involved in such marriages and the attitudes of both groups toward them. In a conversation about mixed marriages, a well-to-do Chinese told the writer:

I don't approve of intermarriage. I don't say one race is better than another, but I think it is better to keep each race pure. Besides, mixed marriages create many awkward social situations.

I happen to know two mixed couples intimately. Just for an example: in one case the Dutch wife refused to let her husband visit his poorer relatives. You know, with us it is an obligation to do so, at least at New Year's time. Otherwise they would think us proud. But she wouldn't allow it. Both of the cases of intermarriage I know have worked out unhappily. But since the men were Catholic, divorce was impossible. The children were not accepted by either the Dutch or the Chinese community. And they were excluded from the Dutch schools here—this was before the war. So both families decided to go back to Holland, where racial feelings are not so strong. Besides, the husbands could get along well in European society, whereas the wives couldn't stand Chinese society here.

Some years ago my nephew fell in love with a Dutch girl. Their fathers were close friends. But the families on both sides opposed their marriage. We did too. The girl was finally convinced that it couldn't work out, so they were not married.

It may thus be concluded that although the barriers of prejudice, custom, and social exclusiveness between the Dutch and the Chinese in Semarang are gradually declining, they are still rather strong.

Relations with the Indonesian People

Whereas the average Chinese person in Semarang rarely has face-to-face relations with a European, he is likely to have contacts with Indonesians every day. The economic functions of the Chinese as middlemen and retailers bring them into business relations with many Indonesians, and this sometimes develops into a close *langganan* relationship. Indonesian farmers and peddlers come to Chinese homes every day with produce and homemade wares, and many of these, too, become *langganan*. This makes for smooth relations. But in the majority of contacts between Chinese and Indonesians, the Chinese are of higher socioeconomic status. As already noted, most Chinese families in Semarang have at least one Javanese servant. The relationship is intimate, but very unequal. This helps to perpetuate Chinese feelings of superiority and stereotyped ideas concerning Indonesians.

The number and frequency of situations in which the two

ethnic groups associate on a basis of equality are increasing, however. It has been brought out that Indonesians and Chinese are co-operating in more and more business concerns and trade associations, and that the stronger economic position of the Chinese in these situations is counterbalanced by the greater influence of the Indonesians in external relations, especially with government authorities. This kind of business association, however, usually does not imply close social contact. The writer was told that in a certain Semarang trade organization the Indonesian members, who are in the minority, are always put on committees and elected to top offices. Co-operation is good, and the relations between the two ethnic groups are cordial. But there is little social mixing. At meetings and gatherings there is a tendency for Chinese and Indonesians to cluster into groups along ethnic lines.

Chinese and Indonesians often co-operate closely in temporary organizations to achieve specific purposes. Street and ward committees for the celebration of national holidays, a joint committee of student organizations for the collection of funds for flood relief, and the committee for the 1955 Semarang municipal fair are examples of such co-operation.

In the field of sports and entertainment, the two ethnic groups usually have separate organizations. There are a few exceptions. The Ikatan Motor Semarang (Semarang Motor Club) and the local motorcycle club are mixed organizations. The Persatuan Kesenian Semarang (Semarang Art Society), which is primarily a social dancing club, also has a mixed membership. The weight-lifting and soccer sections of the largest Chinese social club, the Ta Chung Sze, have a number of Indonesian members. But they comprise only about 2 per cent of the total membership of the club. Doctors and lawyers of the two groups co-operate and associate together in professional societies, though the Chinese lawyers also have a separate organization. A prominent Chinese of the professional class, who has paid considerable attention to the problem of the position of the Chinese in Indonesia, told the writer: "It will be a long time before there are organizations in which Indonesians and Chinese mix freely together on a basis of genuine equality."

The majority of Chinese children attend exclusively Chinese schools. There are some Chinese pupils in a number of government elementary schools, however, and an even larger proportion in government high schools and technical schools. In the Protestant and Catholic schools, the majority of pupils are Chinese. Therefore there is a fair amount of social contact between Indonesian and Chinese children in many of the schools of the city.

In the questionnaire which the writer administered in various high schools in Semarang, the question was asked: "Do you have close friends from other races or nationalities? If so, from which races or nationalities?" In the Catholic and Protestant schools, which have a mixed student body, about 43 per cent of the Chinese respondents reported that they had close Indonesian friends. The proportion was slightly lower in all-Chinese schools, but the difference was not statistically significant. This may indicate that Chinese young people have a considerable amount of contact with Indonesian young people even outside school.

There are a very large number of small tailoring, dressmaking, and homecraft schools in Semarang. Teachers and pupils are all women, and in many cases Chinese and Indonesian women study and work side by side. The Jajasan Persatuan Sekolah Mode (Federation of Fashion Schools of Semarang) is an example. According to its president, Mrs. Soemantri, 87 fashion schools in Semarang are members of this federation, and about 30 per cent of their pupils are Indonesian women.[3] A list of 138 women who passed the examinations given by the Federation in November, 1954, indicates that at least half of these schools have a mixed enrollment of Chinese and Indonesian women. In all cases of mixing, however, the teachers were Chinese. Where teachers were Indonesian, there were no Chinese pupils.[4]

No doubt the most positive ethnic group relations exist in the

[3] *Sin Min,* May 3, 1955.   [4] *Ibid.,* Nov. 12, 1954.

kampung areas of the city, where the Chinese have gone farthest toward assimilation with the Indonesian people and where they are not markedly better off than their neighbors. Even here, close friendships tend to follow ethnic group lines, and in times of crisis many of the Chinese move away to seek the security of numbers in the old Chinese quarter. Nevertheless, relations between Indonesians and Chinese in these areas are generally congenial. An informant living on a *kampung* street where the majority of residents were Chinese gave the following information:

There are several Indonesian families living on our street. We have good relations with them. We sometimes visit each other—especially when there has been a marriage or a death in someone's family.

Two of the Chinese here have Indonesian wives. One of them is my neighbor. His mother was Indonesian too. . . . Yes, he keeps his Chinese name, but the children have Indonesian and Western given names. They are too young for school. I don't know whether he will send them to an Indonesian or a Chinese school. . . . No, I don't suppose his marriage was arranged by the two families. Perhaps they met at the theater or somewhere.

I have a number of good Indonesian friends, including a couple of soldiers and police. I am also on friendly terms with the *lurah* [ward headman] and occasionally visit him at his home.

We have always had good relations with Indonesians here. It may be different in other places, though.

Intermarriage with Indonesians

The number of mixed marriages between Chinese and Indonesians is much more difficult to estimate than the number of Chinese-Dutch intermarriages, but a survey of the registered intermarriages provides relevant statistics.

For randomly selected years between 1920 and 1944, 1.0 per cent of the Chinese men who registered their marriages took Indonesian wives. No trend was discernible. In the postwar years 1946–1954, this figure rose to 2.2 per cent. The rise, though small, is statistically significant at the .01 level. The number of registered Chinese-Indonesian marriages in Semarang reached a peak of 23 cases in 1947, declined to a low point of one such marriage in 1951, and increased again to 12 in 1953 and 11 in 1954. In view of the relatively small numbers involved, however, it is impossible to draw any conclusions about trends in these years.

Chinese men who wish to take Indonesian wives sometimes do so by nominal adoption of the Mohammedan religion. The marriage is then performed and legalized by a religious official, the *penghulu,* and may not be registered at the Office of Civil Registration, since the marriages of Islamic Indonesians are not so registered. Moreover, a Chinese man occasionally takes an Indonesian "wife" without any official marriage proceedings. When the probable number of such marriages is added to the registered marriages discussed above, the result indicates that only about 3 or 4 per cent of the women married by Chinese men in Semarang in recent years have been Indonesians. Even if 10 per cent of the unregistered marriages were of this kind, the percentage of Chinese men marrying Indonesian women could hardly have exceeded 5 per cent.

Among Indonesian men, only the marriages of Christians are registered with the Office of Civil Registration. Before the year 1948, cases of registered marriages between Indonesian Christian men and Chinese women were very rare. In the six years from 1948 to 1955, there were ten such marriages in Semarang. Again, no information is available about how many Islamic marriages were performed between Indonesian men and Chinese women. But it is quite certain that the percentage of Chinese women who marry Indonesians is much lower than the percentage of Chinese men. (When a Chinese man marries an Indonesian, the family usually remains "Chinese"; but if a Chinese woman marries an Indonesian, the family is considered "lost" to Chinese society. There is less concern for ethnic group solidarity among Indonesians; and when an Indonesian woman marries a Chinese, she and her family usually gain economically.) In summary, it is estimated that only about three out of every one hundred Chinese men and women in Semarang marry Indonesians.

As mentioned above, there is little close social intercourse between Indonesians and Chinese in Semarang today. This in itself reduces the chances that mixed marriages will occur. In addition, there are prejudices among both Chinese and Indonesians against intermarriage. Among 50 Chinese mothers interviewed in a survey carried out in connection with the present project,[5] 12 stated that they had no objections to mixed marriage; 5 said that they accepted mixed marriage, but with reservations; 30 were opposed to it; and 3 gave no opinion. Although no conclusive figures can be derived from such a small sample, these results corroborate the reports of other informants who stated that the older generation of Chinese today are as a rule opposed to intermarriage. The following are examples of the opinions given by the interviewed women when asked about this subject:

We see nothing wrong in intermarriage. One of our sons is married to an Indonesian.

I think it is basically all right. If a mixed marriage fails, it is the attitudes and behavior of the family and relatives that are to blame.

I'm not against mixed marriage. . . . No, not even in the case of my own children. I do think it is better for husband and wife to be of the same social and racial origins. But most important is good character and congenial personality.

I have no special objection to mixed marriage. But I'm afraid that in most cases the differences in tradition and customs cause a lot of difficulties.

When a Chinese girl marries a foreigner [i.e., a non-Chinese], it is really a pity. In the case of boys, it really doesn't matter.

[5] See Appendix III for a description and evaluation of this survey.

I'm rather opposed, because children inherit the undesirable characteristics of the parents. I'm afraid intermarriage leads to a lot of that.

These attitudes may now be compared with those of the younger generation. The following question was asked in the questionnaire given to high school students in Semarang:

Young man H and girl J worked in the same office and became close friends. They were both Indonesian citizens, but of different racial descent. Their friends, thinking that their relationship might end in marriage, advised them to break it off. What do you think they should do?

Among 174 Chinese students who answered this question, 71 per cent saw no objection to continuing the friendship, even though it might lead to marriage; 7 per cent indicated mixed feelings about it; 17 per cent favored breaking off the friendship and avoiding marriage; and 5 per cent expressed an undecided or neutral attitude. These results are not strictly comparable with those of the interview survey, but it is safe to say that the younger generation of today is far less opposed to mixed marriage than are their parents. Here is a sample of the students' replies to the question on intermarriage:

They should continue their friendship—even to marriage. It is no one else's business.

Love is the most important thing. They need not pay any attention to the opinions of their friends. The opinions of their parents, perhaps.

If they really love each other, racial difference is no obstacle. Moreover, both are Indonesian citizens, and their marriage would have a beneficial effect—that is, in helping to eliminate discrimination between native Indonesians and others.

Each one should once again carefully consider the results which might follow, because they are of different races and certainly their characters and dispositions are different also. They must consider also the possible effect on their children. If they love each other, and dare to take the consequences, let them marry. But if they have any doubts, better not.

H should tell the girl frankly that they should have no idea of marriage, but should remain friends.

If possible they should end their friendship in order to maintain the honor of their respective races. One of them should leave the office, and they should keep away from each other.

If I were H, I would not get married in this case, because the peoples of Asia are still generally under the influence of their ancestors and it is therefore best to marry within one's own group.

Because Indonesian society is still rather old-fashioned, it would be best for them to drop their friendship.

Don't carry it on. Love between races is love based on pure lust, and is not good for one's family.

By far the most common reply to this question was that if the two "really" love each other they should get married. Many students added the proviso of parental consent. In the above selection of replies, a disproportionately large number of negative replies has been included in order to show the range of reasons given. The feeling of racial superiority was often implicit in the replies, as in some of these, but it was never stated directly.

This questionnaire item about friendship and possible marriage between persons of different ethnic groups or "races" was also answered by 311 Indonesian high school students. Among these, 68 per cent saw no reason to break off the friendship, even though it might lead to marriage; 3 per cent indicated mixed feelings about it; 25 per cent were in favor of breaking off the friendship and avoiding marriage; and 4 per cent expressed an undecided or neutral attitude. In these results, the Indonesian respondents appear to be slightly more prejudiced against mixed marriage than are the Chinese. The difference is statistically significant at the

.05 level. But the present writer believes this finding may be spurious in that the Chinese, being a minority group, are probably much less willing to express prejudiced attitudes than are Indonesians.

These figures corroborate the reports of informants, who agreed that the younger generation in both ethnic groups is more tolerant toward mixed marriage than are older people. If this fact is considered along with the fact that an increasing number of Chinese and Indonesians are attending coeducational high schools and universities together, it may be concluded that a gradually increasing rate of mixed marriages is to be expected.[6] This trend could be reversed, however, if for political or economic reasons the relations between the two ethnic groups should become seriously strained.

Ethnic Group Prejudices

The Chinese often consider themselves superior to Indonesians in ability, intelligence, and energy. They believe that the traditional culture and the historical achievements of the Chinese far surpass those of the Indonesian people, and that this is due to superior native endowment. For example:

A certain Chinese family once employed two chauffeurs. They were given equal wages and presumably the same duties. One of them, how-

[6] This is contrary to the trend suggested by Gouw Giok Siong in his book on mixed marriage, *Segi-Segi Hukum Peraturan Perkawinan Tjampuran* (Djakarta, 1955). In this otherwise scholarly and important study, Mr. Gouw misinterpreted the statistics which he gathered in a survey of the incidence of intermarriage in different cities of Indonesia. The figures are inadequate for any but the most tentative conclusions in any case, but one must note that, when his figures for all cities are taken into account, there appears to be an erratic but slightly increasing trend in the number of marriages between Chinese and Indonesians. Mr. Gouw may have good reasons for surmising that intermarriage between Chinese and Indonesians is decreasing, but his figures do not support the claim, except in the cases of three of the thirteen cities surveyed.

ever, was always passing off the hardest and dirtiest work onto the other. (In Indonesia, "chauffeurs" are also responsible for auto maintenance.) When asked why he did not do his share of the work, this chauffeur replied: "I'm a Chinese. He's not." The well-educated Chinese who told the writer this story commented: "Of course that is wrong. We shouldn't feel superior. But we do."

In addition to these superiority feelings, many Chinese are suspicious of and even hostile toward Indonesians or their government, because of strained relationships in the years of the Japanese occupation and the revolutionary war. Twice during these troublous times, Chinese communities in various parts of Java were attacked by the local people. Houses were looted or burned, and many Chinese were killed or injured. In Semarang itself there were no serious incidents, but Chinese refugees poured into the city with tales of atrocities and economic ruin. Once stable government was established, there was no more of this kind of violence. But the new government's legal and economic regulations and especially the actions and attitudes of local officials have often seemed discriminatory and antagonistic to the Chinese.

On the Indonesian side, too, there is hostile feeling, and even the majority of Chinese recognize that there is considerable reason for it. The Chinese had a privileged position in the colonial society. They owned and managed almost the entire internal trade and commerce of the nation and were considerably better off than the average Indonesian. Most of them had settled permanently in Indonesia, and had Indonesian mothers or grandmothers; but they clung to their own ways and looked down on their fellow Asians. Many of them had sympathized with the Dutch during the revolutionary war and had co-operated with, or at least failed to oppose, Dutch forces. Others felt allegiance only to China. And most of those who were neither Dutch co-operators nor Chinese patriots were indifferent to the Indonesian struggle for independence. Only a few had actively supported the Indonesian cause. For these various reasons, very few Indonesians now have friendly feelings toward the Chinese as a group. A government official told the writer:

We don't like the Chinese—for economic reasons, mostly. They're very sharp. Even the poor ones—they too will be rich someday. When the Japanese came, our people killed and looted the Chinese in many places. But they built up their position again during the occupation. When the revolutionary war against the Dutch broke out, we attacked them again. Now they have again restored their economic power. And their wealth comes from us.

We distrust them because they are opportunists. They will do anything for profit. When the Dutch were here, they supported the Dutch. And they would do it again if the Dutch came back. They supported the Japanese—anything to protect their money.

If they say they are loyal Indonesian citizens—or that they were born here, will die here, and consider this their homeland—this is true only so long as it is in their economic interests.

We may mix with them, treat them as friends, and so on, but we always feel a distance, a distrust.

These feelings are probably more bitter than those of the average Indonesian. In the daily relations between the two ethnic groups, such attitudes rarely appear. The increasing number of friendly and co-operative interrelations has been noted. Certainly the feelings of mutual hostility have abated a great deal since revolutionary times. If discrimination against the Chinese is not made official policy, ethnic group relations will no doubt continue to improve. But there is much latent hostility, and this can flare into violence on occasion. For example, the following incident was reported in an Indonesian-language Chinese newspaper in Semarang:

An Indonesian string and lampwick peddler was passing along one of the streets in the old Chinese quarter when a Chinese child began to tamper with his wares. In trying to push the child away, the peddler knocked him down. This angered the parents of the child, who were nearby. The father ran over and struck the peddler in the face, so that his nose was injured and began to bleed. The peddler retreated, calling for help.

Some Indonesian *betjak* men hurried to the scene and took up the quarrel with the child's parents. Their numbers grew rapidly, and as they became more menacing the Chinese family withdrew into their house for refuge. Within a few minutes there were hundreds of angry *betjak* men in front of the house, threatening to attack the family within. At this point the local police arrived, but they failed to disperse the crowd even by shooting their guns into the air. The mob continued to grow, until the military police and a unit of motorcycle police arrived and cleared the street. All traffic was blocked off for two and a half hours, and the police patrolled the street until late that night.[7]

Summary

In most places and at most times, contacts between the two ethnic groups are smooth and even congenial. Co-operative relations and mixed organizations are increasing in number, but so far they usually do not involve close social intercourse or genuinely equalitarian relations. At the same time, there still exists considerable prejudice, mutual suspicion, and latent hostility.

[7] *Kuangpo,* Jan. 18, 1955.

CHAPTER V

Chinese Community Structure

Speech Groups

All but a very small fraction of the Chinese in Indonesia come from southeast China, especially from the provinces of Fukien and Kwangtung. Within that area the pronunciation of the Chinese language differs greatly from region to region. These different ways of speaking Chinese are usually called "dialects." From a linguistic point of view, however, the major "dialects" may properly be considered as separate spoken languages, since they are often mutually unintelligible. Therefore Skinner's term "speech group" will be used, rather than the less accurate and somewhat misleading term "dialect group," to designate major linguistic groupings of overseas Chinese.[1]

In some parts of Southeast Asia, the Chinese communities are organized largely along speech-group lines. That is, the different speech groups have separate organizations; and social contact, trade apprenticeship, the selection of business or marriage partners, the lending of money, and many other activities tend to occur mostly within speech groups and not between them. There is even a considerable degree of occupational specialization

[1] G. William Skinner, *Chinese Society in Thailand: An Analytical History* (Ithaca, N.Y., 1957), p. 35.

according to speech group. This type of social organization was found to exist in Chinese communities in Sarawak [2] and in Chinese society in Bangkok.[3] In Semarang, however, speech groups are not nearly so important. The major commercial, charitable, ceremonial, social, and recreational organizations draw members from all groups. There are a few speech-group associations, but these find support only among the Totok minority.

One of the reasons for the relatively small emphasis on speech groups in Semarang is that the majority of Chinese there are Peranakans who speak little or no Chinese of any "dialect." Separated from their homeland communities by several generations, they tend to lose their regional loyalties too. The recent immigrants usually learn Indonesian, Javanese, or both quite quickly, because it is necessary in the major occupation among them, trade. (The different Chinese spoken languages are more universally used and longer perpetuated in Chinese communities where there is a large majority of Totoks or where the major occupations do not require command of the native language, as in agricultural, fishing, plantation, or mining communities.) In addition, Chinese schools in Semarang teach only the national dialect, Mandarin, and most educated people can at least understand it. For these reasons, there is no linguistic necessity for separate speech-group organizations. Furthermore, the Chinese nationalist movement which grew up after the turn of the century did much to remove speech-group distinctions and stimulate co-operation and unity in the Chinese community.

In the questionnaire and interview surveys initiated by the writer, respondents were asked to state their speech group or their ancestors' place of origin in China. It was found that many Semarang Peranakans did not know the answers to these questions. In some cases, a woman knew her own family's place of origin in

[2] T'ien Ju-k'ang, *The Chinese of Sarawak: A Study of Social Structure* (London, 1950), *passim.*
[3] Skinner, *op. cit., passim.*

China but did not know that of her husband's family. It might be assumed that she would be even less likely to know or care about her neighbors' homeland origins. It is a Chinese custom to have the name of the family's home district in China engraved on every tombstone; but this practice is often omitted today, because either knowledge or interest is lacking. These are indications of the declining importance of speech-group distinctions, at least among Peranakans.

Until very recent times, Chinese parents in Indonesia have played the dominant role in choosing marriage partners for their children. Interview and questionnaire results indicate that they have shown a strong preference for spouses of the same speech group. Among 28 interviewed families in which the speech group of both husband and wife was known, only 4 represented marriages between different speech groups. In the questionnaire replies there were 75 cases in which the speech group of both parents was known. Among these, 93 per cent of the marriages were between spouses of the same speech group. This figure is probably somewhat misleading, however. In the first place, there may have been a significantly larger proportion of mixed speech-group marriages among the parents of the students who did not know their parents' speech groups. Secondly, because of a very high numerical preponderance of persons of the Hokkian group, many of the intragroup marriages between Hokkians may result from chance rather than preference. Finally, the postwar generation of young people are taking a very active role in selecting their own spouses, and love, congeniality, and personal attributes are becoming much more important criteria for selection than any of the traditional criteria such as speech-group membership. It seems likely that the preference for marriage partners of the same speech group still exists, especially among Totoks, but it is undoubtedly declining fairly rapidly.

The Hokkian speech group came through the port of Amoy from the central and southern parts of the province of Fukien.

They were the earliest settlers in Indonesia. Other speech groups did not come to Java in significant numbers until the turn of the century. This fact is reflected in the questionnaire replies. Among the fathers of respondents the Hokkians comprise over 95 per cent of all who were born in Indonesia, but only about 30 per cent of those born in China. Among all 222 fathers whose speech group was known, 72 per cent were Hokkian. The members of this speech group are found in all occupations. They have no regional or speech-group organization.

Probably the next largest group in Semarang is the Hakkas. About 10 per cent of the questionnaire respondents who knew their family origins said that their fathers were of this group. In China, they are found in inland areas of southern China, mostly in northern Kwantung and southwestern Fukien. The majority of the Hakkas in Semarang originate from one county in Kwang-tung—Mei Hsien. It is probable that they came to Semarang earlier than other speech groups, except the Hokkians, for there seem to be more Peranakans among them. A disproportionately large number of the grocery and household-wares (glassware, hardware, and so on) stores in Semarang are owned by Hakka people. Many of these stores are found on Pekodjan Street, and there is a concentration of Hakkas residing in that part of the Chinese quarter. The Hakkas have a dialect-group association for mutual aid, the Ke Su Kung Hui. Participation in this organization is increasing, and there are plans for a new club building.

The Cantonese group in Semarang may equal the Hakkas in numbers. Only 6 per cent of the respondents who identified their family origins reported that their fathers were Cantonese; but the difference between this and the Hakka percentage could be due to sampling error alone. These people have come from Canton, Macao, and the surrounding areas. They are found in many occupations, but they tend to specialize in small industry, especially carpentry and the furniture business. The Semarang Cantonese have an active regional association, the Kwong Shui Hui Kwoon.

Economic co-operation and financial assistance are probably its most important functions, but it aids its members in other ways too. For instance, it is a semiofficial representative of the Chinese consulate general and can help members arrange passports and travel papers. In 1954 the association completed a fine new building, including a hall for weddings, meetings, and programs. Designed partly as a social club, the building has its own outdoor basketball field. Even before the official opening of the new headquarters, however, the main building of the provincial government of Central Java burned down, and Chinese organizations were asked to provide temporary quarters for various government departments. The building of the Kwong Shui Hui Kwoon now presents a curious sight on national holidays. Its name appears over the main entrance in bold Chinese characters, but a large sign in front says: "Provincial Department of Finance." High above, the five-star red flag of the People's Republic of China flies beside the Indonesian red and white ensign.

Another fairly large speech group in Semarang is the Hoktjia group. These people come from the Fu-ch'ing area between Foochow and Amoy. Among the questionnaire respondents who knew their family origins, about 6 per cent had Hoktjia fathers. Many Hoktjias are in the textile trade. They have an active regional association, the Yu Yong Kung Hui, which performs the same functions as that of the Cantonese.

Other South China speech groups which are represented in Semarang are the Teotjiu, Henghua, Hainan, and Hupeh groups. The number of questionnaire respondents whose fathers were from these five groups came to less than 4 per cent of the total.

Henghua people are from the county of P'u-t'ien, between Amoy and Foochow. In Semarang this group numbers only about five or six hundred. The great majority of them are in the trishaw-renting business, and many have bicycle shops besides. In fact, most of the bicycle dealers in Semarang are of Henghua origin, and they dominate the Semarang bicycle dealers' association.

Otherwise they have no regional association in Semarang. The speech of Henghua people is very similar to that of Hokkian and Hoktjia people. The three are often grouped together under the name "Min-nan," to distinguish them from those who originate from farther north in the same province.

Immigrants from Hupeh province form a very small but interesting group, the only distinct group which speaks a Mandarin dialect. Most of them are dental artisans, and, indeed, Hupeh people have a near-monopoly of this profession througout Indonesia. Without Western medical-dental training, the dental artisan uses traditional techniques and treatments, but modern dental equipment. A major part of his work is the insertion of purely decorative gold fillings, popular among Chinese and Indonesians alike. The Hupeh people in Semarang have no regional organization as such, but their professional association, the Chung Djawa Ya Yeh Kung Hui (Central Java Association of Dental Artisans), fulfills the same functions. This association has 190 members throughout Central Java.

In summary, although speech groups are by no means the most important organizational basis of the Chinese community, they still account for a certain degree of occupational specialization, and they channelize mutual aid and social relations to an important (but decreasing) extent, among Totoks at least.

Totoks and Peranakans

Speaking of the relations between Totoks and Peranakans, a Totok intellectual told the writer: "There is something like a clear line between us." Indeed, this line is one of the clearest social boundaries in the Semarang Chinese community. It is based upon linguistic, social, cultural, educational, and ethnic differences between the two groups. Hitherto the difference between the two has been spoken of as a matter of birthplace. Actually this is the least important aspect of the difference and is not an infallible basis for distinction between the two groups. Virtually all Peranakans were born in Indonesia. But not all Totoks were born in China. Originally, almost all Indonesia-born Chinese had Indonesian mothers or grandmothers. The language spoken in their homes was mostly Malay or a local language such as Javanese. They were Peranakans. But in the twentieth century, especially since World War I, more and more Totoks have brought their China-born wives to Indonesia. And many of the Indonesia-born children of these marriages are considered to be Totoks, in spite of their birthplace.

A certain occasional guest at a Peranakan home in Semarang is called "Mr. Totok" by the servants and is considered a Totok by his hosts. Yet he was born in Sumatra. When asked why he was a "Totok" though not born in China, his hosts told the writer: "Because he is like the Totoks. They are quite different from us. They speak Chinese, and their manners and customs are different." The various differences between Totoks and Peranakans should now be given further attention.[4]

The term "Peranakan" implies a mixed ancestry. In a very few cases Peranakans may have no Indonesian ancestors. But the great majority have them, and Peranakans are usually considered to be "racially" different from "pure-Chinese" Totoks. For instance, a Peranakan told the writer, with obvious pride, that his grandfather was a Totok. He went on to say, however, that since his grandmother was born in Indonesia, she must have had an Indonesian mother or, at the least, grandmother. Like many other

---

[4] The term "Baba" or "Babah" is synonymous with "Peranakan," but is perhaps slightly less frequently used. Similarly, Totoks are often called "Singkeh." This term is based upon two Chinese words meaning "new guest." Literally, the word "Singkeh" emphasizes the recent arrival of a Chinese immigrant, whereas "Totok" emphasizes his "pure" Chinese descent; in practice, the two words are used interchangeably. The term "Singkeh" is not used in Chinese speech among Totoks. In fact, there is no simple Chinese word for the Totok group. The term "Hua Ch'iao" applies to all persons of Chinese descent living overseas; and the phrase "Ch'iao-sheng-ti" applies quite literally to those born overseas.

Peranakans, he accepted the belief that Indonesian "blood" is inferior and that it is the mixture of Indonesian blood which makes Peranakans less capable businessmen than Totoks.

The assumption of "racial" difference and "racial" inferiority is, of course, contrary to the trend of modern scientific thought and knowledge in this field. In the first place, there is no evidence to support a belief in inherent racial differences in ability.[5] Secondly, the assumption that such characteristics as "business ability" or "perseverance" can be inherited biologically has found no support at all in psychological research. And finally, there is no evidence that race mixture produces inferior progeny. A recent authoritative work on racial and cultural minorities summarizes scientific knowledge on the biological aspects of miscegenation in these words:

1. Race mixture does not produce biologically or mentally inferior offspring.

2. Race mixture tends to produce offspring which exceed their parental groups in vitality, stature, and fertility.[6]

It is true that Peranakans sometimes differ from Totoks in physical appearance. For instance, they may have a noticeably darker skin color. But if there are differences in ability or personality between them, it must be assumed that these are based not upon biological inheritance but upon cultural learning. Nevertheless, the assumption of the "racial" inferiority of Peranakans is still a part of the system of prejudices which creates social distance between Totoks and Peranakans.

Educational differences between the two groups are also a source of estrangement. In the first place, Peranakans are generally better educated. Among the fathers of the high school questionnaire respondents, 82 per cent of the Totoks had had no more

[5] George Eaton Simpson and J. Milton Yinger, *Racial and Cultural Minorities* (New York, 1953), pp. 55–59.
[6] *Ibid.*, p. 53.

than an elementary school education, whereas only 41 per cent of the Peranakans had had this little education; 2 per cent of the Totok fathers had had more than a junior high school education, whereas the figure for Peranakan fathers was 26 per cent. These differences are statistically significant at the .01 level. They result from the fact that educational opportunities have been considerably greater in the Indonesian Chinese communities than in China itself.

The difference in type of education received by Totoks and by Peranakans was even more important than the difference in amount. Many Peranakans attended the Dutch-Chinese Schools established by the government, and others attended private Chinese schools with a more or less modern curriculum. Of the Totoks who received an education, some came to Indonesia early enough to attend these same Chinese schools; but most got their schooling in China, some in government schools and some in old-fashioned schools which taught only the Chinese classics. Among the fathers of the questionnaire respondents, all but one of the educated Totoks had attended Chinese schools only, either in China or in Indonesia. On the other hand, half the Peranakans had gone to the Dutch government schools. There is a tendency among Dutch-educated Peranakans to consider Chinese schools inferior and generally to look down on Chinese education. Conversely, Totoks consider Dutch-educated Chinese to have become "Dutch-minded" and to have lost their "Chineseness."

Today educational differences between the two groups are diminishing somewhat. Immigration has virtually ceased, so the number of China-educated Totoks is gradually decreasing. The high school students who have recently gone to China to continue their education do not expect to return. Young people who consider themselves Totoks are receiving as much education as the children of Peranakans. In most Chinese schools both Totok and Peranakan children are well represented. Many Peranakans, however, send their children to government or religious schools where there are very few Totoks. There is one Chinese school, the Chung Hua Hui School, in which no Chinese language is taught; very few of its pupils have Totok parents. The main Kuomintang school includes only a small proportion of Peranakans. Further details about the distribution of Totok and Peranakan children in Semarang schools will be given in Chapter VIII.

Cultural differences between the two groups are widely felt among the Chinese themselves, but are difficult for the outsider to observe. They consist partly in manners and mannerisms, and in these each side tends to see the other as rather crude. In addition, Peranakans are often said to be somewhat more "old-fashioned" in their ways. In the questionnaire results, there is some evidence on this score. In support of the contention, for instance, the proportion of daughters (as compared to sons) who are given a high school education is lower among Peranakans than among Totoks. This difference is significant at the .05 level. There was a higher proportion of family-arranged marriages among the parents of Peranakan respondents than among Totoks (about 84 per cent and 71 per cent, respectively); and more Peranakan than Totok parents want to take responsibility for the selection of their children's marriage partners (about 40 per cent and 31 per cent, respectively). These differences, however, are not statistically significant, probably because of the relatively low number of cases.

Among the non-Christians of the two groups, about 60 per cent of Peranakans, but only 46 per cent of the Totoks, maintain family altars for ancestor worship. This difference, significant at the .05 level, is at least partly due to the fact that the ancestor tablets of many Totoks are kept by their families in China. According to one informant, having no responsibility to maintain a family altar often results in a less traditional attitude toward ancestor worship.

With regard to religious preference, Peranakans are not more traditional. In the questionnaire results there are higher percentages of Catholics and Protestants among the Peranakan respondents and their parents than among the Totoks. But this difference between Peranakans and Totoks is statistically significant (at the .05 level) only in the case of Catholicism among the respondents themselves. Among the non-Christian parents and children of both groups, a slightly higher proportion of Totoks than of Peranakans adhere to the traditional Chinese religions; but the difference is not statistically significant. In both generations considerably more Totoks than Peranakans adhere to the Buddhist religion. Among the parents of respondents, there are few Totok Taoists, but somewhat more Peranakans embrace this religion. The differences with regard to Buddhism and Taoism are significant at the .01 level.

Totoks and Peranakans are said to differ with regard to their business practices. Although the writer found evidence of certain differences in this respect, as discussed in Chapter III, there is no doubt that opinions about these differences have been exaggerated on both sides by prejudice and rivalry. For instance, a Peranakan businessman told the writer:

Totoks are better businessmen because they are bigger gamblers and because they don't care about respectability. They'll take all kinds of insult and degradation at the hands of government officials. Most Peranakans prefer to withdraw from a situation where discrimination is apparent or where only obsequiousness will achieve one's goal. So Totoks have developed better relations with government officials and Indonesian business "partners." Then too, there are more Totoks who are willing to resort to bribery and sharp practices in order to get favors from the government or put across business deals. It's hard for Peranakan businessmen to compete under present conditions.

Totoks are convinced that Peranakan businessmen are inherently less capable and less hard-working. They ascribe part of their own success as a group to a higher degree of mutual aid. It is true that there is more financial assistance given among Totoks, at least among those of the same surname or the same native district in China. But most Totoks have an exaggerated view of their own ability as compared to Peranakans, as well as a mistaken belief that it is based upon inherited "racial" differences.

It is widely believed that Totoks are better off economically than Peranakans. The writer found conflicting evidence on this question, at least for Semarang. Among the fathers of questionnaire respondents, 19 per cent of the Totoks were reported to own automobiles, as compared to 23 per cent of the Peranakans. This difference was not statistically significant. The occupational distribution of the two groups was also roughly the same, though a higher percentage of Peranakans was found in white-collar jobs. The difference in this respect was significant at the .05 level, but was not great. About one-fifth of Semarang's 60,000 Chinese are Totoks. Whether the proportion of Totoks among wealthy businessmen is actually greater than this, and their proportion among the poorest class less, was impossible to determine conclusively. Peranakan businessmen certainly hold a dominant position in Semarang trade and commerce. At the other end of the socio-economic scale, the *kampung* Chinese are mostly Peranakans, but there are many perhaps equally poor Totoks in the byways of the Chinese quarter. Since most people in the lowest-income group cannot send their children to high school, they are not represented in the questionnaire results, and any measure of the proportions of Totoks and Peranakans among them is lacking.

The Indonesian government's policy of placing restrictions on Chinese business is based upon the contention that in comparison to Indonesians the Chinese are in a relatively strong economic position. No one can deny this claim, but many Peranakans assert that it is only the Totok Chinese to whom this argument can properly be applied. They maintain that the Peranakan group as a whole is little better off than the Indonesian people. For example, the following newspaper article appeared in the Chinese New Year supplement of a Semarang newspaper:

If the situation in the large cities, in the towns, and even in the smallest villages is carefully investigated, it will be apparent that the economic position of the Peranakan Chinese, most of whom are Indonesian citizens, is steadily declining.

When one enters the splendid buildings which adorn the main streets or the stores and businesses found everywhere, one finds that the number owned by Peranakans is very small. Along the busy streets of the business sections the stores operated by Peranakans can often be counted on the fingers of one hand.

Furthermore, if one enters the narrow *kampung* streets, where the surface of the road turns to mud when it rains, it will be clear that most of the tiny poor-looking houses are the homes of Peranakan families. The majority of them live scattered throughout the *kampung* areas, together with the common people of Indonesia.

Their livelihood is from their labor; they are workers in offices, stores, and factories; peddlers of cigarettes, candy, and soft drinks; or small shopkeepers. Not a few of their womenfolk have to do toilsome labor in order to add to the meager incomes of their fathers or husbands. . . .

Because Peranakans lack credit opportunities and because they are still considered to belong to the "economically strong" group, much of their potential economic strength remains frustrated.[7]

In view of the vested interests which may lie behind such reports, the present writer remains highly skeptical of them. In the absence of conclusive evidence to the contrary, however, the popular belief that Totoks are generally somewhat better off than Peranakans cannot be rejected.

Another social difference between Totoks and Peranakans is in the size of their families. According to the questionnaire respondents, the average number of children in the families of their parents' generation was 5.5 among Totoks and 6.6 among Peranakans. Upon settling in Indonesia, however, Totok men raised families (of the respondents' generation) averaging 7.7 children; the average number of Peranakan children in this generation

[7] *Kuangpo,* Jan. 22, 1955.

declined to 5.7. The differences between Totoks and Peranakans and between generations within each group are all significant at the .01 level. There was also a difference in family size contingent upon whether Totok men married Totok women or Peranakan women. Where both father and mother were Totoks, the average number of children was 8.1; where the mother was Peranakan, the average was 7.0. However, this difference was not statistically significant, probably because of the relatively low number of cases.

In order to interpret these results, an effort was made to analyze the separate effects of education and socioeconomic status on family size. This will be reported in detail in Chapter X. Tentative conclusions are, however, as follows. The decline in family size among Peranakans was primarily due to the effects of an increased amount of education, especially among women. The relatively small size of the China-born families, on the other hand, was due to a depressed economic condition. Once their economic well-being had been substantially improved in Indonesia, Totoks raised larger families, as was customary among the elite in China. They had had little modern education, and the traditional large family was still their ideal.

The questionnaire respondents were asked: "If you get married, how many children would you like to have?" The sons and daughters of Totoks did not differ significantly from Peranakans in their replies to this question. The average number of children wanted in each group was between four and five. This is significantly lower than the average actual number in the respondents' own families.

Probably the sharpest difference between Totoks and Peranakans is linguistic. Indeed, the distinguishing mark of a Peranakan is his inability to speak one of the "dialects" of China's coastal provinces. The "mother tongue" of the Peranakan is Indonesian, a local language such as Javanese, or even Dutch; that of the Totok is Hokkian, Cantonese, or one of the other types of speech of the

China coast. Totoks, of course, have had to learn Indonesian, and sometimes even Javanese, for business purposes. The Indonesian spoken by both groups is somewhat different from the Indonesian taught in government schools, and is sometimes called "market Malay." The children of both Totoks and Peranakans learn North China Mandarin speech in Chinese schools. During the Japanese occupation, many Peranakan young people and adults spent some time studying Mandarin, and adult classes are still carried on. There is thus considerable overlapping of language abilities, and Totoks and Peranakans are almost never at a loss to communicate. But their language preferences are quite different.

Table 3. Distribution of language usage in families of different parentage *

Languages of daily conversation	Both parents China-born	Only father China-born	Neither parent China-born
Chinese	96%	65%	16%
Indonesian	33	51	81
Javanese	7	16	19
Dutch	0	0	22
Number of families	(75)	(43)	(198)

* All differences in this table are significant at the .01 level except in the case of figures in the center column which differ with corresponding figures in the other two columns by less than 30 per cent.

Questionnaire respondents were asked: "What are the languages of daily conversation in your family?" Table 3 shows the distribution of replies to this question. The Chinese which is used in Totok families is mostly coastal speech of one type or another. In Peranakan families it is either a smattering of coastal words and phrases or Mandarin.

These results show the extent of the overlapping of language abilities. They also indicate why the great majority of Peranakans never attain fluency in Chinese and why many Totoks do not master Indonesian—for it is often only the language of the home

which a person learns to speak with ease and fluency. The combination of preference for one's own language and reluctance to
reveal one's deficiency in other languages constitutes one of the
most important obstacles to social relations between Totoks and
Peranakans. A Peranakan teacher told the writer:

I know very few Totoks. Actually we have very little social contact
and almost no close friendly relations. Before the war, I was an officer
of the Association of Chinese Teachers [Chinese Onderwijzersbond].
We tried to bring the Totok teachers into our organization. But it
proved impossible. We invited them, but they didn't come. Anyway,
we would have had serious language difficulties if they had.

Similarly, a Totok intellectual told the writer that many Totoks
prefer not to go to Chinese doctors because they are all Dutch-
educated Peranakans. Instead these people patronize Dutch
doctors or traditional Chinese medical practitioners. Of course,
the social distance created by language differences is greatest between Totoks and Dutch-educated Peranakans, because the latter
usually speak Dutch among themselves and few Totoks understand any Dutch at all.

The social barrier between the two groups is also apparent in
the selection of marriage partners. Among 169 China-born fathers
of questionnaire respondents, 34 per cent had Indonesia-born
wives; among 292 Indonesia-born fathers, only 2 per cent had
China born wives. These figures should not be interpreted as an
indication that the attitudes of Peranakans are more exclusive
than those of Totoks. Although such may be the case, the very
small proportion of Peranakans who married China-born wives
must be largely accounted for by the fact that very few unmarried
or unengaged women emigrated from China. Many Totok men
were married before they left China and therefore had no chance
to marry Peranakans. But others who came to Indonesia unmarried returned to China to get married, or "imported" a China-
born wife, rather than marry a Peranakan. Then too, some of

those who married Peranakan women have other wives and children in China as well. In any case, informants agreed that there has been considerable preference for marriage within the Totok and Peranakan groups rather than between them. Educated Peranakan women, especially, were said to be reluctant to marry Totoks.

According to the questionnaire results, among Totok men, those who took Peranakan wives were generally better educated than those who took Totok wives, but were about equally well to do. Among Peranakan women, those who married Totok men had considerably less education than those who married Peranakans, but they had more education than Totok women. Apparently some Totok men consider education more important than birthplace and native language in choosing a wife. This is an indication of the importance of education in limiting social participation.

Totoks and Peranakans join together in more or less co-operative and equal relations in community organizations established for specific (usually utilitarian) purposes in line with the interests of both groups—for instance, in many of the business and trade associations, welfare and religious organizations, school boards, teacher associations, and student organizations. Where there is a mixed membership, the language used is Indonesian, though sometimes Chinese translations are given. Meetings and publications of the Sianghwee, for example, are often bilingual. Some associations have two secretaries, one for the Chinese language and one for Indonesian.

In organizations in which the basic purposes directly or indirectly involve close social relations, the active members are usually either almost exclusively Totok or predominantly Peranakan, depending upon the language generally spoken at meetings. The speech-group associations for mutual aid and recreation, for example, have almost no Peranakan members. The Hwa Joe Hwee Kwan, a social club of rather well-to-do people, has few Totok members. The membership of the Ta Chung Sze, which is intended to be a community-wide social and recreational club, is 20 per cent Totok; it used to have several Totok officers, but they withdrew because of language difficulties. One of the ceremonial and funeral societies, the Perkumpulan Indo Tionghoa, is exclusively Peranakan. Others are mostly Totok. The Buddhist-Taoist-Confucianist religious society, Sam Kauw Hwee, attracts mostly Peranakans. The major Chinese Protestant churches are divided along language lines. The Tiong Hoa Kie Tok Kauw Hwee (Chinese Christian Church) is exclusively Peranakan. The Hwa Kiauw Kie Tok Kauw Hwee (Overseas Chinese Christian Church) is Totok. The services of the latter are conducted in the Hokkian dialect, often translated into Mandarin; but its women's association has weekly meetings using the Indonesian language, because so many of the wives of Totoks are Peranakan. The Catholic Church is not divided in this manner; it has relatively few Totok members, and sermons are usually given in Dutch or Indonesian. The two Chinese priests in Semarang are recently arrived Totoks, and their main duties are educational.

As for the trend in Totok-Peranakan relations, there is little doubt that prejudices, differences, and social exclusiveness are disappearing. This is largely owing to the fact that immigration has virtually ceased. Within a few generations there will be no China-born group in the Chinese community, if present immigration policy is continued. This will have the effect of minimizing the present social and cultural differences. In addition, there is now a large number of Peranakans who have been educated in Chinese-language schools, and these persons are generally well accepted in both groups.

A new distinction is emerging which may become as important as that between Totoks and Peranakans today—that is, the distinction between Chinese who are Indonesian citizens and those who are Chinese citizens. It seems likely that this new dividing line, with the different loyalties which it implies, will form the basis for continuing differences in language and education, and for new prejudices and social exclusiveness. Today, however, the distinction by birthplace and language is still more important than the distinction by citizenship.

In summary, it may be said that there are still linguistic, educational, social, and cultural differences between Totoks and Peranakans. As a result, there exist considerable prejudice and social distance between the two groups; this is reflected in the selection of marriage partners and in organizational participation.

Social Prestige

According to tradition, the four main occupations in Chinese society were ranked in descending order as follows: (1) scholars, (2) farmers, (3) artisans and laborers, and (4) merchants. The "scholars" were, in practice, the landowning gentry, because few people in other occupations could afford the time and leisure required to master classical literature and calligraphy. Since these arts formed the basis of the civil service examination system, government positions from top to bottom almost always went to the educated gentry. Official position and landownership were at least as lucrative as trade, so the gentry as a class was as wealthy as the urban merchant class. Nevertheless, education and government position were of much higher prestige value than mere wealth, and merchants and traders never won the respect accorded to the scholarly gentry.

The special nature of Chinese emigration was responsible for turning the social prestige scale upside down in Chinese communities overseas. The gentry did not emigrate. Until well into the twentieth century, there were virtually no Chinese scholars in Southeast Asia. Almost all the immigrants were illiterate farmers, laborers, and petty merchants. Their purpose was to make money, and wealth became practically the sole criterion of success and social position. The sons of wealthy overseas families were sometimes given a meager classical schooling, but this contributed little to their social rank. The traditional Chinese reverence for learning was not lost, but if anyone had taken the time to achieve scholarly distinction, he would have lost out in the race for business success.

In the twentieth century, education is of growing importance in social ranking in Semarang, especially among Peranakans. In part, this is a reflection of the traditional value attached to education. Diplomas and degrees command a certain amount of respect. They are hung or placed in prominent places in homes and offices, listed on calling cards, and mentioned in introductory conversation. The Dutch title "Doctorandus," usually abbreviated "Drs.," is roughly equivalent to our M.A., but is considered quite a distinction. It is even listed after names in the telephone directory.

It is difficult to disentangle and compare the prestige values of education and wealth in the Chinese community today. For one thing, Chinese schools give many commercial courses, and education is often considered as a means to business success. Furthermore, those with the highest academic degrees—doctors, lawyers, and engineers—come from well-to-do families and generally have very high incomes. Virtually all of them have cars, one of the most important outward signs of membership in Semarang's wealthy class. Thus education often appears linked with monetary success.

Nevertheless, education is not a prerequisite to high social standing. Many of the influential and respected Chinese of Semarang have little or no formal education. But almost without exception they are wealthy men. The conclusion is, therefore, that wealth is a much more important determinant of social ranking than is education.

There is a growing number of educated people (especially among the lower-income professionals, such as teachers and newspapermen) who reject wealth as a measure of social worth. But the continuing strength of the wealth prestige system is demonstrated by the fact that these same people rarely fail to adopt deferential manners in the presence of the wealthy. This is a result of the fact that wealth means social power, whereas education does not.

Occupation is even less important in determining social prestige, except insofar as it is a sure indication of wealth. Doctors, lawyers, teachers, and carpenters, for example, can be rated socially, because their approximate income levels are known. But most Chinese in Semarang are traders and businessmen, and the members of this occupation may be found at all levels of the social scale. Similarly, white-collar workers range from minor clerks to very highly paid cashiers.

With wealth as the primary determinant of social prestige, the outward signs of wealth become very important in the judging and the demonstrating of social status. As already mentioned, a car is one of the most significant prestige symbols, since only a very small minority can afford the luxury of a private car. The price of a new Ford, Plymouth, or Chevrolet is roughly four times the total annual income of the highest-paid non-European employee of a Western firm—a department manager, for instance—and six to eight times the annual income of a high school principal. One can build a large bungalow at a mountain resort for less than the cost of a new car. But bungalow owners drive to the mountains in their own cars, and thus bungalows, too, are a sure sign of wealth.

There are numerous other prestige symbols. Electric refrigerators, which are usually kept in the living room or dining room, are often visible from the street. One's travels abroad, like one's educational achievement, are frequent conversation openers. And there are many other forms of conspicuous luxury spending. The writer was informed of an Arrow-shirt wearer who made a practice of loosening and pulling back his collar far enough for the label to be seen; a remark such as "Gee, it's hot here!" would serve both to excuse and to draw attention to his action.

There are a certain number of wealthy Chinese who do not care for modern luxuries or who are too frugal in their habits to spend money on them. But most of these join with the others of their class in a more traditional and socially beneficial way of demonstrating business success—the public presentation of large donations to charitable causes. At least a dozen schools, two orphanages, a large hospital, and several clinics are supported wholly or in large measure by the voluntary contributions of Semarang Chinese. When the Tiong Hoa Hwe Koan opened a secondary school in 1919, Major Oei Tiong Ham contributed 15,000 guilders and a piece of land for the construction of a new building; and Mrs. Tan Bian Ing gave 10,000 guilders. In 1955 half a dozen *kretek*-cigarette manufacturers contributed funds for a nurses' residence for the Semarang Chinese hospital. Three leading Chinese firms used to distribute cash to the poor at New Year's time. It has been noted how generously the Semarang Chinese contributed to various patriotic funds and relief drives between the world wars. They still contribute to patriotic funds and relief drives, but usually for Indonesia, not China.

Contributions to almost all such causes are given a maximum of publicity—in publications, announcements, and signs or special plaques. Usually the majority of contributors are ordinary people who give small amounts. For instance, in a publication of the Semarang Confucian Society (Khong Kauw Hwee), the names of 250 contributors to its educational work are listed. The amount donated by each person is also given, and these amounts range from 80 sen (about 7 cents U.S.) to 1,000 rupiahs (about $90). The great majority of contributions ranged from 10 to 25 rupiahs. There were only nine contributions of 500 rupiahs or more. It is clear that social prestige is not the only motive for charitable giving. Nevertheless, it remains an important method of demonstrating wealth and business success.

Social Stratification and Social Mobility

Discussion of the social ranking system in the Semarang Chinese community raises the question: are there distinct class groupings based upon this system? The answer to this can be approached in various ways—through self-identifications, social participation, cultural differences, or economic functions.

It is not difficult to divide the Chinese community into groups according to economic criteria. A very small laboring class and a larger group of white-collar employees are completely dependent for their jobs and incomes upon the dominant Chinese business class and the European corporations. Most of the lower-income professionals are likewise dependent, for they are employed by school boards, foundations, and corporations managed by businessmen. Only people of the small upper-professional group have independent incomes—but their most important clients are businessmen.

This type of analysis is useful in understanding the distribution of power in the community. Since the formal organs of government are in Indonesian hands and therefore external to the Chinese community, influence and power within the community are a virtual monopoly of successful businessmen. There are no politicians deriving independent power from popular followings. The implications of this situation will be explored further in a subsequent section on leadership.

Although it is possible to divide the community roughly into owners and employers on the one hand and employees on the other, and to ascribe power to the former group, there are virtually no elements of a "class struggle" in the community. A large proportion of employees are sons or relatives of their employers and therefore feel a much closer bond with them than with other employees. In any case, almost the entire employee group accepts the values of the business group: they seek and respect monetary success, and hope someday to join the business class themselves.

A high degree of occupational and social mobility also acts as a deterrent to intergroup conflict. Many employees do, in fact, become independent businessmen. And it is not uncommon for not-so-successful businessmen, and for sons or brothers of successful businessmen, to accept jobs as employees in the big trading companies, especially the European firms. Many such employees have an independent business on the side, as in the example given near the close of Chapter III. Professional people, too, often engage in business as a side line. The writer is acquainted with a free-lance journalist who runs a restaurant, another who operates a bookshop, a writer and correspondence-course teacher who has a small publication business, and several regular teachers who have other business side lines. At least one of the leading Chinese school principals of Semarang is an ex-businessman, and another recently resigned from his post in order to go into business.

Within families, very different occupations and occupational levels may be found. In one family, for example, the brothers and brothers-in-law are engaged in the following occupations: plantation employee; family-store manager; government employee with a business side line; farm-produce merchant; owner of a store, a small rubber factory, and some real estate; clerk and middleman; owner of an iron-goods store and dealer in cars and motorcycles.

Intergeneration mobility is also quite marked. In 43 families covered in the interview survey, 9 of the family heads were in the same occupation and line of business as their fathers; 16 were at roughly the same occupational level, but in different lines; and 18 were at different occupational levels. Of the last, 8 were in higher-income occupations than their fathers—for instance, the white-collar worker's son who is a doctor, the small businessman's son who is a big businessman, and the laborer's son who is a teacher. On the other hand, 10 were judged to be in lower-income occupations than their fathers—for instance, a farm-produce merchant's son who is a clerk in a trading company and a building contractor's son who is a teacher.

Finally, vertical mobility is still very common in the Chinese community. As previously mentioned in connection with the instability of Chinese business enterprise, there is a considerable amount of rising and falling of family fortunes. Since the Japanese occupation, a fairly large group of *nouveau riche* has appeared in Semarang, while many of the old family fortunes have collapsed.

Occupational and social mobility serve to hinder the emergence of distinct socioeconomic classes and class consciousness. There are few specifically employee organizations. The Semarang Association of Cashiers (Semarangsche Kassiers Vereeniging) is an example, but it maintains close co-operative relations with employers and even receives donations from them. The occupational solidarity which it demonstrates is not class solidarity.

The nearest thing to class consciousness in the Chinese community is the somewhat vague awareness of three groups: a small group of "wealthy" people at the top, a somewhat larger group of *kampung* Chinese at the bottom, and the "ordinary" people between. This division is not primarily based upon a difference between employers and employees, but upon different degrees of economic well-being. Perception of the size and boundaries of each group varies from person to person. Some would say that the *kampung* people are very numerous; others would include only a small number in that category.

There is greater awareness of two other lines in the community —that is, between relatively well-educated people and others, and between Totoks and Peranakans. Educated people tend to look down upon less well-educated people and to prefer to associate with persons of equal education. And similar social barriers are found between Totoks and Peranakans.

Thus there are three grouping criteria among the Chinese: wealth, education, and birthplace. Although wealth is the most important factor in determining social prestige and social power, the other two factors are equally or even more important in determining group identification and social participation.

Several organizations which perform business or community leadership functions, including the Chung Hua Tsung Hui (a local federation of Chinese associations) and the Sianghwee, have both educated and uneducated Totok and Peranakan members and officers. In contrast to these, many (but not all) social and recreational clubs and ceremonial and funeral societies have a membership representative of a wider range of economic levels, but are more affected by educational and Totok-Peranakan distinctions. Friendships, social relations, and marriages are also limited at least as much by educational and Totok-Peranakan differences as by socioeconomic level.

In the socioeconomic stratification, as in the education scale, social participation is limited not so much by distinct lines between groups as by relative distances. That is, there is no exclusiveness between fixed groups, but people in any position in either scale prefer not to have close social relations or friendships with people too far "below" them. A teacher, for instance, may feel excluded from social contact with the very wealthy class. He has few interests in common with them and feels uneasy in their presence. On the other hand, he does not enjoy the company of uneducated people and has few friends among *kampung* Chinese. He finds most of his friends (and almost certainly his wife) among the educated people of the middle class. A businessman of the middle class with less education than the teacher has somewhat more social access to wealthy people, but only to those with equal or less education. He might also have more friendly contacts with *kampung* people. In general, there is less exclusiveness between the middle group and the *kampung* people than between the wealthy class and others.

The questionnaire included the following item: "What considerations do you think are most important in choosing a marriage partner?" Respondents were asked to check three out of a list of ten possible "considerations." Among 322 Chinese high school students answering this question, 97 per cent checked "mutual love," 86 per cent checked "good family," and 40 per cent checked "education." Other items such as "religion" and "family consent" were all checked less frequently. "Income" was considered important by a smaller number of respondents (5 per cent) than any other item except "astrology" (compatibility of horoscopes). The differences between these percentages are all statistically significant at the .01 level. The factor of "good family" is no doubt judged partly by economic criteria; but the low interest in "income," as compared to "education," indicates the importance of the latter as a determinant of social relations, at least in theory. In practice economic considerations may well play a more important part in the selection of marriage partners for these young people than they now realize.

Educational achievement was certainly an important factor in the choice of marriage partners among the parents of the questionnaire respondents. Among 129 couples, in 70 cases husband and wife had roughly the same amount of education; in 41 cases the husband had slightly more; and in 6 cases the wife had more. (The product-moment correlation between the level of education achieved by husbands and that of their wives is .83.) The questionnaire data gave no comparable information about the relative economic status of marriage partners. But since education is not highly correlated with economic status, the above results indicate that educational level is an important independent factor in the selection of marriage partners.

Thus, in spite of a great deal of social mobility and "looseness" in the stratification system of the Chinese community, there is some group identification, and this forms the basis for distinctions in social participation.

Cultural Differences between Socioeconomic Groups

A certain amount of information on cultural differences may be derived from the questionnaire results. In order to provide a rough indication of socioeconomic status, the respondents were asked whether their families owned cars or motorcycles. In analyzing the socioeconomic differences, respondents were divided into three categories: those whose family owned a car; those whose family owned at least one motorcycle or motor scooter, but no car; and those whose family did not own any motor vehicle. In the analysis which follows, the last group will be called "non-owners."

It was recognized that this was at best a very rough categorization. Some very wealthy people do not have cars. Some small businessmen have cars for business purposes. Nevertheless, it was the best measure of economic status that could be obtained. The replies to the question on father's occupation were of little help because the two most frequent answers, "trade" and "employee," cover such a wide range of socioeconomic levels.

The identification of a motorcycle-owning group was intended only as an intermediate category for analytic purposes. In most cases where differences between car owners and nonowners were evident, the motorcycle owners were found to be between the two. However, in testing the hypothesis that car owners tend to be more modern in their practices than nonowners, an unexpected, though understandable, finding was made. With regard to social dancing and close friendship with persons of the opposite sex, children of car owners did not differ from children of nonowners; but children in motorcycle-owning families appeared to be considerably more "modern" than either. The number of students who answered these questions was rather small, and the differences are not statistically significant. But this result is reported here because it fits with the observations of the writer that it is the young people of the moderately wealthy group, especially of the *nouveau riche,* who most eagerly emulate the way of life portrayed in the moving pictures. With car unattainable, motorcycles and leather jackets (in spite of the tropical weather) have become the outward symbol of this group. Beyond these unconfirmed observations, however, the writer obtained no further information about the nature of the group.

In China various investigators have found that family size varies directly with socioeconomic level; that is, the more well to do the family, the more children there will be.[8] There is no evidence of this in the questionnaire data. Families who do not own a motor vehicle have an average of 6.4 children, as compared to 6.0 in the car-owning families. This is close to the maximum averages found in China. Presumably, this is an indication that the poorer families in the questionnaire sample are still well enough off to be unaffected by the poverty checks to fertility which exist in China. In addition, it may well be that the modernist preference for smaller families is more prevalent among car owners than among non-owners, because of the greater amount of modernist schooling among the former.

With regard to the religious preferences of the fathers of questionnaire respondents, there are more Catholics and Protestants and fewer adherents of traditional Chinese religions among car owners than among nonowners. The differences, however, are not quite great enough to reach statistical significance. Among the non-Christians of both groups, it is found that a larger number of car and motorcycle owners maintain family altars for ancestor worship than do nonowners. This difference is significant at the .05 level. This may be an indication that the continuity and welfare of the family are more important to well-to-do people than to others. It may also be partly due to the expense of ceremonial paraphernalia and offerings.

With regard to education, the average number of years of schooling among car owners was about two years more than the average among nonowners. (The difference was not statistically significant, because of the low number of replies to this question.) Slightly more car owners than nonowners were reported to have had a high school education. A few car owners had attended a university, whereas none of the nonowners had. Several of the car owners, however, had had no education at all. Although these results indicate a low correlation between economic status and education,

[8] Olga Lang, *Chinese Family and Society* (New Haven, 1946), pp. 147–150.

the relationship would undoubtedly have appeared greater if *kampung* people had been properly represented. In spite of a liberal policy of differential school fees and scholarships in the Chinese and mission schools, not many *kampung* people can afford to let their children attend high school.

All of the Chinese secondary schools in Semarang include students from wealthy, middle-income, and fairly poor families. The only Semarang school in which the Chinese students are almost exclusively from wealthy families is the Dutch community school, where Chinese students form a majority of the small student body. The Chinese schools vary, however, in the proportion of wealthy students attending. The proportion of students who come from car-owning families is considerably lower in the two most pro-Peking high schools than in the three other Chinese high schools and two Catholic high schools. (These differences are significant at the .01 level.) The Protestant high school is intermediate in the proportion of well-to-do students.

Thus the demographic and cultural differences between the wealthy group and the large middle group in the Chinese community are not very great. Corresponding differences between these and the *kampung* group are undoubtedly greater, but the questionnaire survey did not include a significant number from the *kampung* group. In general, however, it may be said that their way of life is less affected by modernist trends and more influenced by Indonesian culture than is that of the other two groups.

Summary

Chinese society in Semarang may be presented as divided horizontally by lines of prestige and power and vertically by lines of group identification. The horizontal lines are based upon socio-economic distinctions and educational achievement. The vertical lines are based upon the Totok-Peranakan distinction and upon type of education (Chinese or Dutch). None of these "lines" is fixed or distinct. They are social boundaries which are drawn at

different points by different individuals and which are frequently
crossed in friendships, social contacts, and even marriages.

In spite of their flexible nature, the social boundaries within
the community mark off a number of fairly distinct groups. The
kampung group is at the base of the socioeconomic pyramid. Distinctions of birth and education are not important in this group.
Above this level, the pyramid is divided vertically between Totoks
and Peranakans, but there is an intermediate group which has
social access to both sides—Peranakans who have been educated
in Chinese schools. On the Totok side of the pyramid there are
further vertical lines marking off speech groups, but these are
of diminishing importance. Within all vertical groupings there
are distinctions based upon wealth and educational achievement.
One of the most distinct social groups delineated by such factors
is composed of well-to-do Peranakan professional and business
people who have had Dutch higher education and whose way of
life has become more Dutch than Chinese. This is a rather small
group. Parallel to it, at the top of the pyramid, there are social
groupings of wealthy Totoks or Peranakans whose educational
achievements are much more modest. The bulk of the community
falls into an intermediate socioeconomic category which is again
divided by the vertical lines of speech group, birthplace, and type
of education, and by horizontal lines of relative wealth and educational achievement.

In this chapter the analysis has been almost entirely structural.
Very little attempt has been made to discern changes, since practically no data were available on the social structure at earlier
times; therefore no analysis of change processes has been possible.

CHAPTER VI

Organizations

In this chapter various types of organizations will be discussed; those which are typical or important will be described in detail. Information concerning the following types of organizations is presented in other chapters: trade and professional organizations, religious groups, speech-group associations, and student, teachers', and women's organizations. Nevertheless, a general picture of the organizational structure of the community will be made apparent in this chapter.

Sports Clubs

Participation in sports is rather widespread in the Chinese community and is the main preoccupation of many young people. An illustration of its importance may be seen in the fact that a Semarang association originally organized primarily to promote the use of Mandarin speech has gradually become almost exclusively a sports club; today many of its members do not or cannot speak Mandarin.

Probably the majority of organizations in the Chinese community have sports sections. In addition, there are a number of clubs devoted wholly to sports. Although traditional Chinese shadow-boxing has been practiced ever since the Chinese arrived in Indonesia, participation in modern sports did not begin until the establishment of the Chinese modernist schools in the first decade of this century. But the sports facilities which the schools have been able to offer have fallen far short of the demand, even to this day; and there are still very few public facilities. Therefore, many sports clubs have been organized to fulfill the need.

The first sports association in Semarang was a soccer club organized as a branch of the Hwa Joe Hwee Kwan in 1911. In 1917, it became an independent organization under the name "Union." It is still an active club today, with branches for badminton, pingpong, billiards, soccer, tennis, and Chinese shadowboxing.

In the twenties and thirties, a modernist youth organization, the Hua Chiao Tsing Nien Hui, was organized in many Indonesian cities. Its main purpose was to provide all kinds of sports facilities. It still exists in many places, but the Semarang branch was disbanded during the Japanese occupation. In 1954 there was talk of re-establishing it; but a suitable club building could not be found, and many former members had already joined other sports clubs. In addition to organizations with facilities for several sports, there are clubs for specific sports, such as basketball, badminton, tennis, and swimming.

Social Clubs

The so-called "social clubs" range from small, private gambling clubs to large public associations for recreation of all kinds. The earliest of these was the Boen Hian Tong, organized in 1876 as a Chinese music society, with an exclusive membership of wealthy and prominent men. It soon became a mutual-aid society, however, and today is primarily a funeral society. It still counts some of the wealthiest and most influential Chinese of Semarang among its members and officers.

Another important social club is the Hwa Joe Hwee Kwan, founded in 1904. Its members are mostly well-to-do, middle-aged

Peranakan men, though it has a youth section too. Before the war it was known primarily as a gambling club. Public gambling is now illegal, however, and the club has turned to other forms of recreation. It provides a hall and rooms for games, meetings, weddings, receptions, and parties. It organizes picnics and outings. In 1955, it arranged a four-day group tour through East Java and, on another occasion, chartered a bus for members who wanted to attend a religious festival at a temple in a neighboring town. In addition, it supports various community welfare activities.

There are a number of informal music clubs in Semarang, both for traditional Chinese music and for modern popular music. The dancing club mentioned in an earlier chapter, the Persatuan Kesenian, holds weekly dances (Western-style social dancing) and occasionally presents a demonstration by semiprofessional ballroom dancers.

The Sin Shen Yu Ie Hui, a dramatic society, was established in 1954. Its stated purposes are to give training in dramatic arts, to hold picnics and outings, and, by giving dramatic performances, to collect money for charitable causes. The proceeds of its first play were given to the Confucian Society's charity school, the Chinese orphanage, and the Semarang Red Cross organization.

The largest social club in Semarang is the Ta Chung Sze. It was established in 1946 by the merger of half a dozen social and sports organizations. It provides facilities for chess, pingpong, billiards, badminton, tennis, soccer, and weight lifting. A swimming section has special hours reserved for it at the municipal pool. The club owns a brass band of twenty-eight pieces, but its dance-band section is more popular. Its library is one of the best in Semarang. It has a very active drama section, which arranges lectures on dramatic arts and presents amateur plays. In 1954 it gave a four-act play, "Harta Kimura" (Kimura's Treasure), which was written by an officer of the club, Sie King Poon. Half of the proceeds went to the Semarang Chinese hospital.

Mutual-Aid Societies

In this category are included speech-group associations (discussed in the previous chapter), brotherhoods, and ceremonial and funeral societies. Of those existing in Semarang today, the Hoo Hap Hui and the Sam Ban Hien are the oldest, having been founded in 1899 and 1900 respectively. These were brotherhoods organized along the lines of the secret societies in China and were without doubt connected with them. The officers and most of the members were Totoks. Members were ranked according to the dues they were able to pay—from the wealthy leaders, who provided the main financial support, down to the underworld strong men, who paid no dues at all. The latter served as guards and henchmen and were sometimes sent on missions of blackmail, extortion, or even murder. The two brotherhoods maintained a bitter feud, and fights between them were common, even on public ceremonial occasions.

In recent years the nature of these organizations has changed greatly, in the main as a result of community revulsion against the secrecy and violence of their former activities. The two brotherhoods joined in a "pact of peace." Two prominent members of each society became members of the other, as a symbol and guarantee of friendship. There are still a few businessmen who employ illegal or strong-arm methods against their enemies. But instead of turning to the low-ranking members of their brotherhoods, they hire Indonesian veterans of the revolutionary war—a practice which leaders and authorities of both Chinese and Indonesian communities greatly regret.

One of the major functions of the Hoo Hap Hui and the Sam Ban Hien today is to provide ceremonial services. In this they are joined by two other societies, the Fang Gie Hong and the Hauw Gie Hui. These organizations provide professional ritual directors and all kinds of paraphernalia for weddings (which are often held in their own clubhouses), funerals, and public ceremonies. Each one owns both a monstrous dragon, which is carried on poles and manipulated dramatically by a trained team of over a dozen men, and a magnificent lion outfit, in which two men perform all kinds of stunts and antics. These fabulous beasts appear in parades, religious processions, and public festivities. For the most part, the four ceremonial societies maintain a strict political neutrality. They take part in the August 17 celebration of Indonesia's Independence Day, the October 1 celebration of the birth of the People's Republic of China, and the October 10 celebration of Kuomintang China's national day.

Along with several others, these four organizations are also funeral societies. Chinese funerals involve very heavy expenses, and most Chinese want to assure that they and their families will have as fine funerals as they can possibly gather money for. The funeral societies provide a kind of insurance system for this purpose. Each time a member dies, all other members contribute a fixed amount toward funeral expenses. In 1955, for instance, members of the Perkumpulan Indo Tionghoa donated one rupiah for each funeral, and the family of the deceased received about 3,000 rupiahs.

Political Organizations

There are three important political associations in Semarang, which generally represent the three national orientations to be found in the Chinese community. The partisans of the Nationalist Party of Chiang Kai shek maintain an active branch of the Kuomintang. The pro-Peking group has organized the Sin You She. Many of the Chinese who profess no tie to either Chinese government, but consider Indonesia as their country, are members of BAPERKI (Badan Permusjawaratan Indonesia), which takes an active part in Indonesian national politics. The main purposes of this organization are to defend the constitutional rights of minorities and to promote their incorporation into Indonesian society as loyal, equal, and recognized partners in the body politic. Through petitions, public protests, and meetings with government officials, BAPERKI opposes discriminatory measures against Indonesian citizens of foreign descent. It also puts forward candidates for election to government bodies. BAPERKI is primarily a Chinese organization, concerned with the problems of the Chinese minority. But it also has a token number of native Indonesian and Arab members. In the Semarang branch the officers, though not all the members, are Chinese.

The national organization of BAPERKI is generally regarded as being favorably disposed toward Communist China. In Semarang, as elsewhere, pro-Kuomintang members dropped out for this reason. However, through personal acquaintance with several of the officers of the local branch, the writer became convinced that in 1955 the majority of Semarang members and officers (including all the top officers) felt no loyalty to Peking and were not Communist-minded. They favored some developments in Communist China and were critical of others.

National parliamentary elections were held in Indonesia a few months after the writer's departure. BAPERKI is reported to have polled 11,236 votes in the municipality of Semarang. The writer estimates that there were not more than 25,000 eligible voters among the Chinese; and about half of these were women. In view of the fact that a large proportion of Indonesian Chinese are apathetic toward local politics, it seems likely that the figure for the BAPERKI vote is very near to the total number of Chinese who voted. In other words, Chinese voters were overwhelmingly in favor of BAPERKI.

Whereas BAPERKI is open only to Indonesian citizens, the Kuomintang and the Sin You She include very few Chinese of Indonesian citizenship. These organizations appeal primarily to those who consider themselves citizens of either Nationalist or Communist China, but their influence extends to others as well. Through meetings, speeches, national-day celebrations, and publications, they seek to win or to increase the loyalty of Semarang

Chinese for the Taiwan or the Peking government. In addition, they have organized schools which promote their respective political viewpoints. The Sin You She also gives free evening courses in Mandarin.

Community Leadership Organizations

"Community leadership organizations" are those organizations which act as spokesmen for the interests of the Chinese community, which serve as intermediaries between the community and the government, and to which members of the community turn for help and guidance when in need.

The earliest of these was the Kongkoan. This was the headquarters of the Chinese community officers appointed by the Dutch. It was established in 1835 by Captain (later Major) Tan Hong Yan as an office where people could seek information or help in legal affairs, relations with the government, and other matters. At first this office was situated on the Tan family property, but in 1837 Major Tan Hong Yan had a special structure built next to the major temple of the community, the Tay Kak Sie. The new building was given the name Tjie Lam Tjay, which may be translated as "Guidance Office." Gradually the functions of the Chinese officers, who were referred to as "the Kongkoan," were separated from those of the Tjie Lam Tjay office, and the latter became a separate organization in about 1872. The officers of the Kongkoan gave help or direction in legal matters, police affairs, tax-assessment problems, and other relations with Dutch businessmen or officials. Chinese births, marriages, and deaths were registered at the Kongkoan. The Tjie Lam Tjay, on the other hand, took responsibility for supervising temples and religious affairs, burying those who died destitute, and managing graveyards.[1] The Kongkoan was abolished along with the institution of Chinese officers in 1931. The Tjie Lam Tjay still exists, but it is of little importance as a community leadership organization today.

[1] Liem Thian Joe, *Riwajat Semarang* (Semarang, c. 1933), pp. 101–102.

Long before the end of the Kongkoan, its leadership and function as spokesman for the Chinese community were challenged by the Sianghwee, which had been established in 1907. As noted in Chapter II, the Sianghwee was the primary link between the Semarang Chinese and the government in China. It also gradually took over the Kongkoan's position as intermediary between the Chinese community and the Dutch colonial government. In addition, it took an active lead in the internal affairs of the community. For example, when the Tiong Hoa Hwe Koan school ran into financial difficulties in 1908, the Sianghwee took over the responsibility for its support; it was still financing the school when the high school branch was established in 1919. During a severe cholera epidemic in 1910, the Sianghwee hired two traditional Chinese medical practitioners to direct the campaign against the disease in the Chinese quarter; it paid the daily wages of people hired to care for the sick who could not otherwise afford them; it indemnified families who had to burn the belongings of family members who had died; and it contributed 3,000 guilders to the Dutch Chamber of Commerce for its anticholera work in other parts of the city. On numerous occasions the Sianghwee collected contributions for charitable causes—for the Semarang Chinese poorhouse and home for the aged, for the victims of volcanic eruptions, and even (at the invitation of the Dutch Resident in 1924) for destitute Germans and Austrians.[2]

The Sianghwee began to withdraw from its community leadership activities in 1934, when it called together the representatives of all Semarang Chinese associations in order to establish a separate organization, the Hoa Kiauw Kioe Kok Houw Wan Hwee, for the collection of relief and patriotic funds to be sent to China. Today the Sianghwee is exclusively a commercial organization. It is regarded as representative of "big businessmen" rather than of the community as a whole.

[2] *Boekoe Peringetan, 1907–1937, Tiong Hwa Siang Hwee, Semarang* (Semarang, 1937), pp. 14–17.

During their occupation of Indonesia, the Japanese merged all Chinese organizations into one central association for each town or municipality. These organizations, called the Hua Ch'iao Tsung Hui (Overseas Chinese Central Association), were responsible for maintaining order in the Chinese communities, collecting contributions for the Japanese war effort, and enforcing the decrees of the military regime. They also conducted the recreational and welfare activities of the various organizations which had been disbanded.

After the Japanese surrender, most of the old organizations were re-established. But the Semarang Chinese found a continuing need for the co-ordinating activities of the Hua Ch'iao Tsung Hui, and the community solidarity which it had symbolized was increased by postwar events. It was therefore reorganized as a federation of organizations, under the name Chung Hua Tsung Hui (Chinese Central Association). Almost all Chinese organizations in Semarang affiliated themselves with it. Associations with the same name and purpose were also set up in other cities and towns.

In October, 1945, British military forces arrived to accept the Japanese surrender and to "maintain order." They remained for over a year, while the Dutch built up enough military strength to re-establish their control over most parts of the archipelago. During the period of British military government in Semarang, the Chung Hua Tsung Hui served as the official representative of the Chinese community; and under the succeeding Dutch government this intermediary function was largely maintained.

Two historical events have lessened the importance of the Chung Hua Tsung Hui as a community leadership organization in the years since 1946. The first was the establishment of the People's Republic of China and the withdrawal of Chiang Kai-shek's government to Taiwan. This caused a political split and an internal struggle for control in many overseas Chinese organizations. A large number of organizations in Semarang today have

Peking-oriented (though usually not pro-Communist) leaders, including the Chung Hua Tsung Hui. In another large group of organizations the leaders have maintained enough neutrality to hold a membership representative of all points of view; most of these have remained affiliated with the Chung Hua Tsung Hui. Pro-Kuomintang individuals and organizations, however, no longer recognize the leadership of the Chung Hua Tsung Hui. In addition, there are many Chinese who do not like either Chinese government and have therefore become indifferent to China-oriented organizations.

The second historical event which lessened the community leadership function of the Chung Hua Tsung Hui was the final establishment of an independent Indonesian government throughout the archipelago. In Semarang, an all-Indonesian government took over from the Dutch authorities in early 1950. Chinese fears of looting and massacre quickly subsided, and the need for community solidarity and mutual aid diminished greatly. The majority of Chinese in Semarang then became Indonesian citizens. Many of them have taken the position that Indonesian Chinese should not set themselves apart by forming exclusively Chinese organizations. Some have objected to the Chung Hua Tsung Hui on these grounds, calling it a "state within a state."

Nevertheless, the Chung Hua Tsung Hui is recognized by government authorities and sometimes acts as an intermediary between the government and the Chinese community. This was dramatically illustrated by the following incident. When the Semarang headquarters of the provincial and residency governments was destroyed by fire in December, 1954, government officials visited various private and public buildings in an effort to find temporary quarters for various offices. They decided that parts of four Chinese association buildings should be requisitioned for this purpose. The associations, however, were reluctant to give up the space, and they called upon the Chung Hua Tsung Hui to hold a meeting of all Chinese organizations to discuss this problem. In an effort to smooth over the tense situation, the Resident then held a press conference in which he outlined the needs of the government for temporary quarters and the reasons for the selection of certain buildings. He expressed his regret that in the confusion of the emergency situation he had neglected to request the help of the Chung Hua Tsung Hui, but had gone directly to various Chinese associations instead. He promised to deal through the Chung Hua Tsung Hui in future relations with the associations involved.[3] Thus the Chung Hua Tsung Hui was brought in as intermediary. In the end, however, the government got its way.

At about the same time, foreigners throughout Indonesia were required to register with the police. The Chung Hua Tsung Hui set up an office to help foreign Chinese fill out the required forms and to instruct them as to where and how to submit them. In connection with the visit of President Sukarno to Semarang in the same month (December, 1954), the Chung Hua Tsung Hui put an announcement in the newspapers requesting that all citizens of the People's Republic of China fly both Chinese and Indonesian flags for two days.

Like the Kongkoan of former days, the Chung Hua Tsung Hui also gives advice and guidance in all kinds of legal matters and relations with government authorities. A young Peranakan businessman (who, incidentally, displays only the Indonesian flag on festive occasions) told the writer: "We need the Chung Hua Tsung Hui. Whenever we are in any sort of trouble, we go there for advice."

Other activities of the Chung Hua Tsung Hui may be learned from the following newspaper summary of the annual report of its 1953–1954 officers:

The Chung Hua Tsung Hui has twenty-seven member organizations. From these organizations it receives contributions of 435 rupiahs

[3] *Sin Min,* Dec. 17, 1954; *Kuangpo,* Dec. 17, 1954.

per month, and from 506 individual supporters it receives an average of 991 rupiahs per month. In December, 1953, the Chung Hua Tsung Hui received from the Semarang municipal government an allocation from taxes of 2,250 rupiahs to be used for the poor and destitute; and in July, 1954, the Semarang students who left for China in order to attend universities there gave a contribution of 500 rupiahs for our social welfare fund.

Contributions given out by the Chung Hua Tsung Hui were 2,750 rupiahs for the Foundation for the Boys' Orphanage at Tanah Putih, Semarang; 1,000 rupiahs for the Arrangements Committee of the Chinese Boy Scout Jamboree in Semarang; and 203 rupiahs for other social welfare aid—a total of 3,953 rupiahs.

In addition to its regular daily work, the Chung Hua Tsung Hui, by calling together the Assembly of All Associations [Kok Sia Thoan], established the Committee for the Celebration of the National Day of the People's Republic of China on October 1, 1953; the Semarang Overseas Chinese Committee for the Celebration of Indonesia's National Day on August 17, 1954; and the Semarang Overseas Chinese Committee for the Aid of Victims of the Eruption of Mount Merapi. The last was able to collect 24,685.50 rupiahs and 97 pieces of used clothing, which were turned over to the Central Committee for Mount Merapi Victims in Semarang on March 10, 1954.

At the end of July, 1954, the assets of the Chung Hua Tsung Hui totaled 22,695.82 rupiahs; from this sum 16,000 rupiahs were lent to Mr. Liem Kiauw Jok, and 5,500 rupiahs to the Foundation for People's Housing (to be repaid in 1956). In addition to one typewriter and other office equipment, the Chung Hua Tsung Hui owns one automobile, a Pontiac.[4]

The Kok Sia Thoan (Assembly of All Associations), mentioned in the preceding paragraphs, has no constitution and no regular officers. It is a meeting of delegates from all Semarang Chinese organizations, called together by one of the community leadership organizations in order to discuss business of concern to the whole community. The earliest record of this institution

[4] *Sin Min,* Sept. 1, 1954.

which the writer found concerned a meeting called in 1907 by the Sianghwee at the initiative of an officer of the Tiong Hoa Hwe Koan. The meeting was held at the Kongkoan; and officers of the Kongkoan as well as those of the Sianghwee, the Tiong Hoa Hwe Koan, and the Tjie Lam Tjay played an active part. The purpose was to take action on a decision of the government to close its poorhouse and old-age home for Chinese. It was resolved to send a delegation to the Dutch Resident to request reconsideration of the decision and, in the event that the government was determined to end its support of these institutions, to organize a private foundation for their support. The government stood firm, and from that time the Chinese have operated their own welfare institutions.[5]

There are records of seven meetings of the Kok Sia Thoan between 1916 and 1935, but without doubt it was called together much more frequently than that. Three of its prewar meetings will serve as examples of its functions. In 1916, when the new republican government in China was in serious financial difficulties, delegates from at least ten organizations attended a Kok Sia Thoan called by the Sianghwee. On this occasion the assembly established a special organization to collect funds for the support of China's treasury. In 1923, on the initiative of the Sianghwee, the Kok Sia Thoan was assembled in connection with the celebration of the twenty-fifth anniversary of Queen Wilhelmina's coronation. A contribution of 7,400 guilders was allotted to the Dutch celebrations committee of Semarang, and 5,000 guilders was put aside for street decorations, processions, and festivities in the Chinese community.[6]

In 1924, a meeting of the Kok Sia Thoan was called to protest the municipal government's plan to fill in a stagnant pond in the Chinese quarter. The local Chinese had a geomantic conviction that the pond was necessary to the continuing prosperity of their community. Recognizing the problem of malaria control, how-

---

[5] *Boekoe Peringetan*, p. 14.   [6] *Ibid.*, pp. 13, 17.

ever, the Kok Sia Thoan requested the government to leave the pond, but to repair it and to clean it periodically. Their request was granted.[7]

Before the war, the officers of the Tjie Lam Tjay (in charge of community religious affairs, graveyards, and paupers' burials) were elected at periodic meetings of the Kok Sia Thoan. In recent years, however, the Kok Sia Thoan has shown no interest in the Tjie Lam Tjay, which has had to become a self-perpetuating committee.

During the period of the writer's stay in Semarang, the Kok Sia Thoan was called together twice by the Chung Hua Tsung Hui. On one occasion, thirty-three organizations planned and joined in committees to arrange celebrations for Indonesia's Independence Day on August 17, 1955; on the other occasion, twenty-two organizations formed committees for the celebration of the national day of the People's Republic of China on October 1, 1954. Among those significantly absent from the latter were the Sianghwee, the Betjak Bond Semarang (Association of Trishaw Owners), the Fang Gie Hong (one of the ceremonial and funeral societies), the Chinese English School, the Ta Chung Sze (social club), and the Union (sports club). Catholic and Protestant organizations did not take part in either meeting. The Chung Hua Hui School (a Chinese school in which the language of instruction is Indonesian) and the pro-Kuomintang schools did not join the planning committees, but they were represented in the parade for Indonesia's Independence Day.

On December 10, 1954, Semarang newspapers announced that the Ta Chung Sze was calling together the Kok Sia Thoan for the purpose of discussing the government's intention of requisitioning office space in the buildings of Chinese organizations. The chairman of the meeting was the head of the Ta Chung Sze, and the discussion was lively. However, a prominent member of the Chinese community asserted that the meeting could not be con-

[7] Liem, *op. cit.*, pp. 262–263, 270–271.

sidered the Kok Sia Thoan because too few organizations were represented there. Accordingly, the only action taken by the meeting was to request the Chung Hua Tsung Hui to call the full Kok Sia Thoan immediately for further discussion of the problem.[8]

This incident illustrates several characteristics of the Kok Sia Thoan. Theoretically, any organization may summon it; and it is customary for the head of the summoning organization to act as chairman. Apparently, however, if the Kok Sia Thoan is called together by the Chung Hua Tsung Hui it can be expected to gain more support than if any other organization today calls it. In any case, the various organizations are not obligated to send delegates to a meeting of the Kok Sia Thoan, and they usually do so only if the subject under discussion is of direct interest to their members. If too few organizations are represented, a meeting cannot be considered the Kok Sia Thoan.

General Characteristics of Semarang Chinese Organizations

Socially active Chinese often deplore the lack of interest in organized activities among the members of their community. Dutch scholars and businessmen, on the other hand, exclaim over the number of Chinese organizations, and ascribe to the Chinese a propensity for organization. Actually, the Chinese are probably little different from most other peoples in the numbers who do or do not like to participate in organizations, and in the number of active participants who deplore the inactivity of the others. Nevertheless, Chinese organizations in cities such as Semarang are relatively numerous. This is partly because of the diversity of groups in the community. For instance, different language and speech groups form the basis for separate organizations; and differences in political orientation multiply the number of student and teacher organizations and even sports clubs. In addition, welfare functions which in many places are carried out by state

[8] *Sin Min,* Dec. 11, 1954; *Kuangpo,* Dec. 15, 1954.

and municipal governments must be fulfilled by community organizations in Semarang—as provision for schools, orphanages, old-age homes, and cemeteries.

It is characteristic of most Chinese organizations that they serve many functions. The diversity of the activities of the speech-group associations and the prewar Sianghwee has been brought out. Another example is the Hwa Joe Hwee Kwan, which has social, recreational, ceremonial, religious, and welfare activities. There are relatively few organizations whose activities are limited to one specific field, such as some of the smaller sports clubs.

It is also typical of Chinese organizations in Indonesia that they are local in nature. Even trade associations (such as the Sianghwee) whose economic self-interests were pressing them to co-operate with their counterparts in other cities were very slow to join national federations. Attempts to establish a national federation of Chinese schools have repeatedly broken down. Funeral societies, women's organizations, social clubs, and welfare societies are organized on a local basis. Confucian societies from various parts of Indonesia recently formed a national federation, but the Semarang Khong Kauw Hwee (Confucian Society) did not take part. There are exceptions—for example, church synods and conferences, national student associations, and sports federations. But it would seem that the Chinese associations of Semarang generally prefer to stand alone.

The tendency of Chinese organizations to serve multiple functions and to avoid ties with other organizations may be viewed as another manifestation of a continuing preference for face-to-face trust relations, rather than contractual relations, as discussed in Chapter III. The brotherhoods were a prime example of organizations which sought to fulfill a wide range of functions within the context of close personal relations and loyalties. Organizations such as the Hwa Joe Hwee Kwan continue to do so today, though to a lesser extent. The main function of the funeral societies could be carried out by large-scale private insurance companies, but the Chinese prefer the local society with its personal relations and multiple services.

Another important reason for the preference for the small, local society is that it assures the members more control over its policies and more knowledge of its affairs. Almost all Chinese organizations have annual or biennial membership meetings for a review of past activities, the formulation of new policy, and the election of officers. Sometimes a supervisory board is established to see that the regular officers act according to the rules and purposes of the organization and carry out the policies laid down in general meetings. In many associations the members have the right, through petition, to call a general meeting or demand new elections if they do not approve of the actions or inaction of their officers.

Officers of Chinese associations are usually elected by secret ballot in one of two ways: either a chairman is chosen, who then appoints his own "cabinet" of officers, or a group of officers is chosen, who then distribute the various posts among themselves. The funeral and ceremonial society Fang Gie Hong is an example of the former. An annually elected chairman appoints the following officers: vice-chairman, secretary, treasurer, adviser, executive secretary, committee head, and five committee members. The financial policies of the society are laid down at the annual membership meeting.

Another funeral society, the Boen Hian Tong, has the second type of election, occurring every two years. The outgoing officers nominate a slate of some two dozen candidates. At a general meeting, each member votes for twelve of these on a secret ballot. The twelve candidates receiving the highest number of votes then hold a meeting to assign the various offices among themselves. The Sianghwee and the Chung Hua Tsung Hui also use this system, though in the case of the latter it is a joint meeting of old and new officers which determines the assignment of posts.

The formal structure of Chinese organizations is thus seen to be quite democratic. Members are assured of a voice in selecting officers and determining general policy. In addition, there are usually regular means of controlling and checking on the actions of officers. The extent to which this formal structure assures representative and capable leadership will be discussed in the next chapter.

Summary

The nature and functions of various Semarang Chinese organizations, including sports clubs, social clubs, brotherhoods, ceremonial and funeral societies, political organizations, and community leadership organizations, have been outlined. Other types of associations are described in other chapters. Among the changes that have taken place are the proliferation of sports clubs, the transformation of secret brotherhoods into peaceable ceremonial and funeral societies, and the succession of community leadership organizations. These changes have been ascribed to such factors as new community orientations and values, changing government policies, wartime necessities, and political division within the community. In spite of the changes noted, several general characteristics of Semarang Chinese organizations were apparent: multiple functions, preference for local independence, and a generally democratic formal structure.

CHAPTER VII

Leadership

Chinese Officers under Dutch Rule

Between the years 1672 and 1931, Dutch authorities put the leadership of the Semarang Chinese in the hands of appointed officers chosen from the community itself. Beginning with a captain, the system was progressively elaborated until, by the beginning of the twentieth century, there were a major, a captain, five lieutenants, and sixteen *wijkmeesters* (neighborhood heads) for Semarang. This system was comparable to the "indirect rule" by which the Indonesian population was governed through regents and lower territorial officials. As noted in the previous chapter, the Chinese officers as a group were called the "Kongkoan," although this name actually refers only to the office where these officers dealt with community business.

The primary function of the Chinese officers, as far as the Dutch were concerned, was to maintain peace and order in the Chinese community. In matters of custom, religion, marriage, and divorce, they were given complete authority to make decisions. They registered births, marriages, and deaths, and witnessed the swearing of important oaths. In certain matters, especially the enforcement of the opium monopolies, the officers' own guards were empowered to make arrests and even to imprison offenders, at least temporarily, in the Kongkoan.[1] When Chinese became involved with the police or courts for civil or criminal offenses, the Kongkoan officers were usually consulted by the authorities. Their unofficial judicial power was very great, because in almost all cases of disputes or disturbances among the Chinese themselves the arbitration of a Chinese officer was preferred to court settlement.

The government occasionally turned to the Chinese officers for advice in matters of direct concern to the Chinese. The Kongkoan officers also acted in an advisory capacity on the tax commissions. Their role in helping to assess for tax purposes the income and property of their compatriots was no doubt a major factor in their power within the community.

The Kongkoan was also the channel through which the regulations and orders of the government were directed to the Chinese community. In 1920, for example, when the government decided to suppress certain nationalist and left-wing Chinese organizations in the Indies, the prohibiting decrees were issued through these Chinese officers.[2]

Three major prerequisites were necessary to become a Chinese officer: wealth, connections with Dutch officials, and influence in the Chinese community. Or these, wealth was a prerequisite to the other two. The following excerpts from a book by a Chinese traveler, who visited Semarang in about 1784, will serve to suggest the importance of wealth, as both cause and result of official position. They will also illuminate other characteristics of Chinese officers and public attitudes toward them:

Our rich merchants and great traders, amass inexhaustible wealth, whereupon they give bribes to the Hollanders, and are elevated to the ranks of great Captain, Lieutenant, Commissioner of insolvent and intestate estates, or Boedelmeester, Secretary, and such like appellations; but all of them take the title of Captain. When the Chinese quarrel or fight, they represent their cause to the Captain, before

[1] Liem Thian Joe, *Riwajat Semarang* (Semarang, c. 1933), p. 160.
[2] *Ibid.,* p. 247.

whom they make a low bow, without kneeling, and call themselves his "juniors." The rights and wrongs, with the crookeds and straights of the matter, are all immediately settled, either by imprisonment or flogging, without giving the affair a second thought. . . .[3]

The power of the Captain in Batavia is divided, and the profits of the situation are uncertain; but the authority of the Semarang Captain is fixed, and his profits more regular in their returns. The boiling of the sea to make salt, and the cultivation of the fields to produce revenue, are all the perquisites of the Captain. Thus it is that a person who fills this office, can amass stores of wealth.[4]

The present writer does not know how common direct bribery was in obtaining appointments. But the giving of expensive gifts to Dutch officials at the New Year and other times was customary among wealthy Chinese.[5] And certainly would-be officers had to be able to pay large sums of money to the government for the tax monopolies which were farmed out to them.[6] On the other hand, these monopolies were a source of great profits to the officers. It is said that Major Oei Tiong Ham, who held the opium monopoly for Semarang, Solo, Jogjakarta, and Surabaja in the years 1890–1903, netted a total profit of 18,000,000 guilders from it.[7] Kongkoan officers neither received nor needed a salary from the government.

As noted above, not only wealth but business connections and acquaintances with Dutch officials were essential prerequisites to appointment as a Chinese officer. Occasionally such connections took precedence over wealth. In the appointment of the last major of the Semarang community, for instance, the authorities passed

[3] Ong Tai Hae, *The Chinaman Abroad; or, A Desultory Account of the Malayan Archipelago, Particularly of Java* (English trans., Shanghai, 1849), p. 4.

[4] *Ibid.,* pp. 8–9.   [5] Liem, *op. cit.,* pp. 74, 149–150.

[6] For a discussion of the monopoly tax-farming system, see George McTurnan Kahin, *Nationalism and Revolution in Indonesia* (Ithaca, N.Y., 1952), pp. 10, 12–13.

[7] Liem, *op. cit.,* p. 181.

over men of greater wealth and prominence and picked Tan Siauw Liep, a well-to-do merchant who had come to Semarang penniless and had developed contacts with the Dutch as he built up his business. In 1901 he became one of the five lieutenants; within a few years he was made captain; and in 1909 he was appointed to the post of major.

In the matter of making the acquaintance of Dutch officials and winning their confidence, friends and especially relatives of Chinese officers had a great advantage over all others. It was not uncommon for officers to use their influence to obtain appointments for their friends and relatives. In any case, those with sufficient wealth and influence to qualify for appointment were likely to be found among a small number of top-ranking families. And given the tradition of family-arranged marriage and the control by Chinese officers over all marriages in the Chinese community, most top-ranking families were likely to have marital alliances with the families of the Chinese officers. Probably in the majority of cases, therefore, nepotism and social structure combined to keep appointments within families and kin groups.

The most striking example of this occurred in the family of Tan Tiang Tjhing, who became the first major of Semarang in 1829. His three sons were all appointed lieutenants, and one of them rose to the position of major. Three sons of the latter and two sons-in-law became lieutenants; and among these, two achieved the rank of major. There were thus nine officers in three generations of one family.

In most cases, the Dutch authorities were careful to select Kongkoan officers who already had good reputations and considerable influence in the Chinese community. This intention was very apparent in the appointment of Oei Tjé as captain, about the middle of the eighteenth century. According to early records, Oei Tjé was a chinaware merchant who was not very wealthy, but was very highly esteemed in the Chinese community. For one thing, he could read and write Chinese. He was always ready to help people to write business or personal letters to China; and he often entertained friends and acquaintances with the stories that he had read in Chinese classics and novels. He was well-liked for his simple, honest, and straightforward disposition. Finally, he was a clever and just arbiter of disputes, and many people also took their personal and family problems to him for advice. His popularity was proved in the following incident. Some years after his appointment, he was imprisoned by the government because he was unable to render account of certain tax moneys. Believing that he was innocent, but was protecting others by his silence, the Chinese community won his release by taking up a voluntary collection to pay off the missing sum.[8]

There is no doubt that the Kongkoan officers received considerable respect and honor in the Chinese community—at least until the beginning of the present century. With the rise of the Chinese nationalist movement and the growing importance of the leadership of the Sianghwee (the Chamber of Commerce), the popularity and prestige of the Chinese officers declined sharply. As noted in previous chapters, in the twentieth-century struggle against the restrictions and disabilities put upon them by the Indies government, the Chinese community looked to the leaders of the Sianghwee as their champions. The Kongkoan officers, on the other hand, being dependent upon the government for their positions, were sometimes regarded as "tools of the Dutch." However, they retained much of their power and importance because they were able to obtain favors from the government and occasionally even benefits for the whole community. Probably for this reason, the Sianghwee itself in 1914 sent a delegation to the Resident to oppose the abolition of the institution of Chinese officers.[9]

[8] The writer considers this story fairly reliable, because it appears in two independent, early sources: Ong, *op. cit.*, pp. 26–27, and early Kongkoan records, as reported in Liem, *op. cit.*, pp. 41–44.

[9] *Boekoe Peringetan, 1907–1937, Tiong Hwa Siang Hwee, Semarang* (Semarang, 1937), p. 16.

In its own dealings with the government, the Sianghwee did not use the Chinese officers as intermediaries. The government, too, sometimes bypassed them and went directly to the Sianghwee. In 1921, for example, upon the occasion of the visit of the Governor General to Semarang, the government asked the Sianghwee to arrange welcoming festivities in the Chinese quarter. A generation earlier, this certainly would have been the duty and privilege of the Kongkoan officers. In the present case, the Sianghwee called a meeting of representatives of all community organizations, the Kongkoan among them. The meeting appointed a welcoming committee which included Major Tan Siauw Liep along with thirteen other prominent merchants.[10]

In January, 1931, after the death of Captain Liem Kiok Liam and the resignation of Major Tan Siauw Liep, the government abolished the Kongkoan and the institution of Chinese officers. For the next ten years, the Chinese community was ruled directly by the municipal government through three Chinese *wijkmeesters,* or neighborhood heads, who were salaried officials. One or two representatives of the Chinese were also appointed to the municipal council, but these were recognized leaders only of that part of the Peranakan group which favored entering Indies politics.

Recent Community Leaders

Since World War II, leadership in the Chinese community of Semarang has become increasingly dispersed. At most times during the past, there were at least one or two leaders who had prestige and influence in all sectors of the community. Today, however, there are no leaders acknowledged by the whole community. An examination of certain individual leaders of the past twenty-five years will provide the background needed in order to analyze the changing basis of leadership in a later section of the chapter.

It has already been noted that the community leadership func-

[10] *Ibid.,* p. 17.

tions of the Sianghwee began to decline even before the Japanese occupation. Nevertheless, in the last decade before the war, the Sianghwee leaders were still the most respected and influential men in the community. Two of these were outstanding. One was Tan Tek Peng, whose name first appears on the governing board of the Sianghwee in 1923. In 1935 he was elected chairman, and throughout the thirties he took a leading part in the various activities of that organization. Unlike most of the Chinese leaders of the time, he was not an independent businessman, but held top managerial positions in the Oei Tiong Ham Concern of Semarang. One informant described him as the "real leader" of the Chinese business community until the time of his transfer to Djakarta after World War II.

Thio Thiam Tjong, on the other hand, was both business leader and leader in community affairs. When the highest officers of the Sianghwee withdrew in 1929, he became head of the committee given the task of reorganizing the association. He was chairman of the revived Sianghwee from 1931 to 1934 and remained active in its affairs until he left Semarang after the war. In addition, he was an officer or participant in numerous community organizations. For instance, he has been a member of the board of the Chinese English School for many years and was once its chairman. He was one of the leaders of the 1927 Chung Hwa Congress, a conference which brought together prominent Dutch-speaking Chinese from different parts of Java to discuss means of improving the position of the Indies Chinese. After the outbreak of the Sino-Japanese War, he took a major part in organizations which mobilized financial and moral support for the struggle against Japan in China. During the Japanese occupation of Indonesia, therefore, he was imprisoned, along with other Chinese leaders. It is said that even under severe pressure from the Kempeitai he refused to give information about others connected with the China aid funds, but insisted upon taking full responsibility himself. During the period of Dutch reoccupation after the war, he was called to Djakarta to become the personal adviser of Governor General Van Mook. Since then he has spent little time in Semarang, although he has remained active in Chinese affairs in Djakarta.

Mr. Thio was the last widely accepted leader of the Chinese community in Semarang. The extent of his popularity was due partly to personal characteristics: courage, ability, public-spiritedness, financial generosity, and, as one informant put it, "willingness to help the underdog." It was also due to his ability to bridge the gaps between various groups in the community. As the successful owner and manager of a thriving business inherited from his father, he had the respect of the business community. Having attended a university in Holland, he not only won the general prestige of a higher education, but also gained the recognition of the rather exclusive group of well-to-do, Dutch-educated Peranakans. Unlike most leaders belonging to the latter group, however, he was popular among Totoks as well. For one thing, he took an interest in things Chinese and visited China every few years. More important was his strong support of the movement among Indonesian Chinese to help China in its struggle against Japan. Thus on all sides he was considered a "champion" of the Chinese community.

Tan Tjien Lien is a man whose leadership might have been comparable to that of Thio Thiam Tjong, had there not arisen new divisions within the Chinese community itself. He may be considered a contemporary leader, for he was the chairman of the Sianghwee during most of the period of the writer's stay in Semarang.

Tan Tjien Lien is a fourth-generation Peranakan. His great grandfather, a Hokkian from Amoy, settled in Sumatra. His father established a gold and jewelry shop in Semarang and was wealthy enough to send him to St. Stephen's College in Hongkong for his high school education and then to St. John's University in Shanghai, where he studied economics. Thus he speaks and writes

English and Chinese, as well as Indonesian. From Dutch-educated relatives he has also acquired a working knowledge of Dutch. With this background, Mr. Tan, like Mr. Thio, is well suited for bridging the gaps between the major segments of the Chinese community; he can "get along well" with Totok and Peranakan alike.

During the period of his studies in Hongkong, Tan Tjien Lien was baptized as a Christian. Today he is a member of the newly established Baptist church in Semarang. His five children are all receiving a Christian education. Because of the high degree of religious toleration in the Chinese community, religious affiliations are of no consequence in the selection of leaders. Mr. Tan's membership in a Christian church, therefore, does not jeopardize his popularity among non-Christians.

Mr. Tan went into business in 1937 as a life insurance agent. In 1947 he founded the Union Trading Company, which handled mainly farm produce and tobacco. On business trips to Europe and Japan in 1950 and 1952, he made arrangements to export vanilla, kapok, and other produce to Holland and castor oil and kapok oil to Japan. In 1952, he founded the Semarang newspaper *Kuangpo*, a pro-Kuomintang organ. He is still chairman of its board of directors.

Mr. Tan rose to a position of community leadership in the troublous years following the Japanese surrender. During the "Allied occupation" of Semarang in 1946, the British authorities dealt with the Chinese community through the Chung Hua Tsung Hui (Chinese Central Association), successor to the Japanese-sponsored Hua Ch'iao Tsung Hui. As a member of the executive committee of this organization, Mr. Tan won a reputation for courage in his blunt and uncompromising dealings with the British authorities on behalf of the Chinese community. During the revolutionary war and the anti-Chinese outbreaks that followed, many prominent Chinese were reluctant to take leadership positions because of the uncertainty of the situation and the possibility of jeopardizing their future. Mr. Tan, however, accepted the post of chairman of the Chung Hua Tsung Hui in 1948 and held it until after the transfer from Dutch to Indonesian municipal government in 1950. In that year, he was elected chairman of the Sianghwee, and he retained this position until mid-1955. He became vice-president of the country-wide federation of Sianghwee organizations in 1952 and president of the Semarang Kapok Producers Association at about the same time.

Tan Tjien Lien has also been active in community organizations as a member of the Semarang Rotary Club, a member of the board of the Semarang Chinese hospital and of the Chinese English School, and an officer of the Peranakan political party, BAPERKI. In 1953, he became the president of the school association which managed Semarang's three pro-Kuomintang schools.

As brought out in the previous chapter, after the establishment of the People's Republic of China and the withdrawal of Chiang Kai-shek's government to Taiwan, internal dissension arose in many of the Chinese organizations of Semarang. Completely unwilling to compromise with what he considered to be "red influences," Mr. Tan withdrew from the board of the Chinese English School and from BAPERKI. He also lost his position first in the Chung Hua Tsung Hui and then in the Sianghwee. With a shift in power to the neutralists and Peking sympathizers in the Chung Hua Tsung Hui, pro-Kuomintang officers either withdrew or were voted out. The Sianghwee, in this period of conflict, had to remain neutral, for its nature required the co-operation of all important businessmen. Therefore it could not retain a strongly pro-Kuomintang chairman. Thus Tan Tjien Lien's position as a community leader came to an end with the rise of political divisions in the Chinese community.

The present chairman of the Chung Hua Tsung Hui is Liem Siauw Tjong. Like Mr. Tan, he is a fourth-generation Peranakan of Hokkian extraction. His father was an employee of one of the business houses of Semarang. Educated in a government-operated Dutch Chinese school, Mr. Liem is fluent in the Indonesian and

Dutch languages and knows some English as well. Since 1921 he has been an employee of the most important insurance company owned by Indonesian Chinese, now named "Lloyd Indonesia." Through experience and reading, he has made himself an expert in all matters pertaining to insurance. He holds the position of "attorney" (a top managerial post) in the Lloyd Indonesia, N.V., and in two affiliated concerns, and represents these companies on the local commissions of the Council of Fire Insurance Companies in Indonesia, the Accident Underwriters' Association in Indonesia, and the Marine Underwriters' Association in Indonesia.

Mr. Liem does not adhere to any particular religion, although he maintains a family ancestral altar. He is the father of seven boys and a girl. He has sent all of them to the Chung Hua Hui School in Semarang; three of them are now working or studying in Holland, and a fourth is studying law at an Indonesian university.

Since World War II, Mr. Liem has been very active in community organizations. In 1946 he helped to found the Ta Chung Sze, a social and sports club, and became its first president. He serves on the board of another social club, the Hwa Joe Hwee Kwan. He was once head of one of the mutual-aid societies (primarily a funeral society) and is now the head of another, the Boen Hian Tong, which is the oldest and probably the most distinguished of such societies in Semarang. Formerly a member of the board of the Chinese hospital, he is on the boards of both the Chinese English School and the Chung Hwa Hui School. He is also chairman of the parents' association of the latter.

Mr. Liem was asked by the present writer, "To what do you attribute your success as a leader?" In reply, he outlined his philosophy of work as follows:

1. Give serious attention to all matters, however small, and carefully consider all possible consequences.

2. Work to the best of one's ability, and take full responsibility.

3. Do not make high-sounding promises, for what is promised must be fulfilled.

4. Be honest and straightforward.

5. Consider and try to understand criticism, and respect the opinions of others.

6. Behave correctly and respectfully, especially toward older people.

7. Carry to full completion all work or responsibilities undertaken.

It is to the credit of Mr. Liem that he has a wide reputation for most of these qualities, as well as for public spirit, ability, and a simple way of life. In fact, Mr. Liem comes as close to being a generally recognized community leader as is possible today. However, his leadership has limitations. Not having taken a partisan position in Indonesian or Chinese politics, Mr. Liem is in no sense a political leader. As he does not speak Chinese and is associated mostly with Peranakan organizations, he is not as close to the Totok community as some community leaders have been. In addition, he has not played an important part in the Sianghwee or in other commercial organizations. He is head of the most representative community organization, the Chung Hua Tsung Hui, but the community leadership functions of this federation have greatly declined since the period of war and revolution in the 1940's.

There are at least four or five other community leaders whose popularity rivals that of Mr. Liem. A fuller account of community leadership would include at least a dozen more names—for example, The Sien Tjo, a prominent leader both before and after the war; Liem Djing Tjie, a "self-made" businessman with unusually wide popularity for a Totok; and Ko Kwat Tiong, a lawyer with a reputation for exceptional devotion to community welfare. It would be impossible to rank such leaders in order of importance. Those chosen for special attention in this chapter are merely those who best illustrate the general trends and characteristics which are under consideration.

The Dispersion of Community Leadership

With this discussion of individual leaders as a background, a general outline of the trend toward dispersion of leadership which has taken place over the past fifty years may now be given. For each of five successive periods, the allocation of leadership in the following major areas will be considered.

1. *Administrative leadership:* participation in the actual day-to-day governing of the Chinese community.

2. *Political leadership:* leadership in organizations which attempt to influence the Dutch or Indonesian government, to support the government or people of China, or to give political orientation to the local Chinese.

3. *Commercial leadership:* leadership in business or commercial organizations or affairs.

4. *Organizational leadership:* leadership in community organizations, such as schools, charitable institutions, religious societies, and mutual-aid clubs.

Although information is inadequate for definite conclusions, it seems probable that during the eighteenth and nineteenth centuries, captains and majors had a virtual monopoly of all four types of leadership among the Chinese of Semarang. Most of the functions of government were administered by them. Through their connections with the government and their tax monopolies, they usually held a dominant position in commerce. Although there were relatively few community organizations, the Kongkoan officers took the lead in religious and charitable activities. So far as the writer knows, there were also few "political" currents in the Chinese community during this period. (The Semarang Chinese participated, however, in the revolt against Dutch authority in 1740–1741—under the leadership of Kwee An Say, the Semarang captain.[11]) It is probably correct to say that Oei Tiong Ham, who was appointed to the post of major in 1896, was the

[11] Liem, *op. cit.,* pp. 29–35.

last Kongkoan officer to hold a predominant position in community leadership of all kinds.

In the period 1900–1931, the Chinese officers retained administrative leadership. Commercial and political leadership, however, passed almost completely into the hands of the Sianghwee leaders. Organizational leadership was divided between the Kongkoan and the Sianghwee.

In the last ten years of Dutch rule, from 1931 to 1941, administrative leadership was in the hands of three Chinese *wijkmeesters,* or neighborhood heads. Commercial leadership remained the undisputed monopoly of the Sianghwee, but political leadership was divided according to new alignments within the community itself.[12] As already pointed out, however, the leadership of Thio Thiam Tjong to some extent bridged the differences within the community in this period.

During the Japanese occupation, from 1941 to 1945, all leadership functions were centralized in one organization, the Hua Ch'iao Tsung Hui. The Sianghwee was abolished, and many of its leaders were imprisoned. Other organizations were also disbanded. Therefore the Japanese-appointed officers of the Hua Ch'iao Tsung Hui were the community's only leaders. It is of interest to note in passing that with few exceptions these leaders were not accused of "collaboration" with the enemy. The consensus was that they had no alternative but to serve and that they utilized their positions and their abilities in the best interests of the Chinese community. Some of them are still elected to positions of leadership today.

In the period from the end of the war to the "transfer of sovereignty" in 1949, Semarang was ruled first by a British military administration and then by the Dutch-sponsored federal government. The Hua Ch'iao Tsung Hui was reorganized as a federation

[12] For a detailed discussion of political alignments in this period, see Donald E. Willmott, *The National Status of the Chinese in Indonesia* (Cornell Modern Indonesia Project, Ithaca, N.Y., 1956), pp. 7–9.

of community organizations and called the Chung Hua Tsung Hui. It was the primary source of political and organizational leadership in the community, and it shared administrative leadership with government-appointed *wijkmeesters*. Commercial leadership was centered in the Sianghwee, as before.

In the period since 1950, administrative leadership of the Chinese community has been taken entirely out of Chinese hands. Indonesian *lurah* were substituted for the Chinese *wijkmeesters* in 1953, and the Chinese have come under the direct jurisdiction of various departments of the municipal and national governments. Thus the Chung Hua Tsung Hui has lost its administrative functions. Although it has become somewhat Peking-oriented (celebrating October 1 as a national day, for instance), many of its leaders, including its chairman, are nonpartisan. It therefore gives little political leadership. Of the three contemporary political organizations which were discussed in the previous chapter, only the Sin You She is a member of the Chung Hua Tsung Hui. Kuomintang sympathizers reject its leadership as too "red," and most BAPERKI members consider it too China-oriented.

The question of national identification has become so important in recent years that not only Totok leaders, but China-oriented Peranakans of either Chinese or Indonesian citizenship can have little influence or prestige with those members of the Peranakan community who identify themselves with Indonesia. Similarly, Peranakan leaders who make a point of their Indonesian citizenship are not popular among Totoks. The leaders of the Chung Hua Tsung Hui include persons of both Chinese and Indonesian nationality, but they attempt to remain publicly neutral on the question of citizenship. In the politics of national identification, then, the Chung Hua Tsung Hui provides no leadership.

In addition, the Chung Hua Tsung Hui has no commercial functions. This means that by and large it now provides only "organizational" leadership. Commercial leadership is still concentrated in the Sianghwee, but there are signs that its dominant position in this sphere is being weakened by government regulations which require Chinese collaboration with Indonesians in business enterprise. To some extent, Chinese business leadership is shifting into joint Indonesian-Chinese commercial and trade associations. Futhermore, Sianghwee leaders take less interest in community affairs than formerly.

Comparison of the lists of officeholders in the most important contemporary organizations bears out the above analysis. In 1955, all eighteen officers of the Chung Hua Tsung Hui held offices in other community organizations: schools, religious societies, clubs, and mutual-aid societies. Whereas four of them held offices in the Boen Hian Tong, four in the Tiong Hoa Hwe Koan School, three in the Chinese English School, and four in a sports club (the Perserikatan Olahraga Tionghoa), only two were officers of the Sianghwee, and only one was active in BAPERKI. On the other hand, of the thirty-four successful and unsuccessful candidates for the Sianghwee board in 1955, only a few were active in community organizations; for example, one was an officer of the Tiong Hoa Hwe Koan School, another was an officer of the Chinese English School, and a third was an officer of both of these, as well as of the Confucian Society and the Chung Hua Tsung Hui. Three others were officers of BAPERKI. Thus it is evident that organizational leadership is concentrated in the Chung Hua Tsung Hui and not in the Sianghwee.

In summary, whereas administrative, political, commercial, and organizational leadership have been concentrated in a few persons or organizations at times in the past, these different types of leadership are now separate and dispersed. That is, contemporary leaders in any one of these fields are rarely prominent in another field. Leaders in the organization field, especially those of the Chung Hua Tsung Hui, have gained the widest respect and recognition in the community. But the "all-round" leader with influence and prestige in the whole community is a man of the past.

Characteristics Important to Leadership

An attempt will now be made to assess the characteristics and personal qualities for which people are elected to positions of leadership in the Chinese community. This analysis is based on general information and opinions given by informants, personal information about various leaders, the writer's own observations and impressions, and a very rough and small-scale survey of characteristics of certain community leaders. In the survey, a sample group of twenty-five leaders was chosen from lists of the officers of twelve of the most important community organizations. Persons were included on this list either because they held chief executive posts in single organizations or because they were committee or board members in two or more organizations. Certain details about each of these leaders were gathered from informants. The size and method of choosing the sample group indicate that it cannot be considered representative of all officers of community organizations. Rather, it includes perhaps nine out of the twelve most prominent community leaders and a very small representation of the most active among possibly several hundred other officers of community organizations. The results of this survey are therefore no more than suggestive.

It has already been noted that wealth was a prerequisite to appointment as a Kongkoan officer in former times. Thio Thiam Tjong, the most prominent community leader during the 1930's, was also a very wealthy man. The recent head of the Sianghwee, Tan Tjien Lien, is considered fairly wealthy. Three-quarters of the sample group of leaders are private businessmen, all at least moderately wealthy. Two of the nonbusinessmen are also well to do.

There is therefore no doubt that wealth is an important characteristic of community leaders. This is owing in part to practical considerations. Direct, voluntary contributions are a major source of financial support for almost all Chinese organizations. It is not unusual for wealthy persons to be elected to positions of lead-

ership in the expectation that their contributions will thereby increase. In addition, it is advantageous to have a wealthy person
solicit the personal contributions of others. As a result, those
elected to office in community organizations are not always capable. At least one of the wealthy men in the sample group of
leaders is neither capable nor popular. Others are no more than
moderately able or well liked. However, wealthy men who hold
responsible positions but have no qualifications or inclination for
leadership are not expected to be very active. Others are given
only nominal leadership, in such positions as honorary president,
patron, or adviser. The situation has its parallel in the granting
of certain honorary degrees by many American universities.

On the other hand, the significance of wealth is not entirely
on the practical level. As brought out in Chapter V, wealth is a
predominant factor in social prestige, especially so when it is accompanied by sizable contributions to community welfare. The
rich men who are known to give large donations to social and
charitable organizations earn respect and a reputation for public
spirit. Presumably the prestige of such men is an important consideration among those who elect them to office, aside from the
expectation of financial support.

In his book on the Chinese of Sarawak, T'ien Ju-k'ang shows
how leadership in the community of Kuching is based on wealth
used as power.[13] With the backing of cliques of followers who are
indebted to them for personal loans and commercial connections,
the wealthiest men win the most important positions of leadership in the community. The present writer could find no evidence
of such use of wealth in Semarang today. In fact, even the prestige
value of wealth seems to have declined considerably. In this connection, it will be recalled that one recent and one contemporary
community leader, Tan Tek Peng and Liem Siauw Tjong, are
salaried employees of business firms; without benefit of personal

[13] T'ien Ju-k'ang, *The Chinese of Sarawak: A Study of Social Structure*
(London, 1950), pp. 68–79.

wealth, they achieved prominence through personal qualities of leadership.

The importance of government connections to the former Kongkoan officers was mentioned. In the last decades of Dutch rule, such connections were desirable for other community leaders, not only because of their practical utility, but also because of their prestige value. Today government connections are still a desirable qualification for leadership, but they do not have the importance they once had. Unlike the Dutch government, the Indonesian government is not highly respected by the Chinese community, and therefore acquaintance with officials does not bring prestige. Moreover, the activities of many organizations, such as religious groups and funeral societies, are so remote from government that nothing is to be gained by government connections. Nevertheless, the ability to obtain personal favors or group benefits from government officials is still very important for the officers of certain organizations, especially the Sianghwee and other commercial associations. Substantial help in the procurement of individual import or export licenses or of foreign exchange, for instance, is a task which is expected of the leaders of business associations. In other organizations, influence with the government is desirable, but not so important. An earlier chapter told how the leaders of the Chung Hua Tsung Hui became involved when the provincial government requisitioned rooms in the buildings of four Chinese associations. Whether their efforts had anything to do with the eventual return of these rooms, the writer does not know. On several occasions when central government regulations have been misapplied, Semarang leaders of BAPERKI have brought about changes in the policies of local government agencies toward the Chinese. This no doubt accounts for much of the popularity of BAPERKI among Semarang Chinese voters.

With regard to the question of what personal qualities are important for leadership in the Semarang Chinese community, to mention "intelligence" and "ability" would be correct, but misleading. It is necessary to be more specific. The kind of intelligence associated with achievement in formal education is not important, as will presently be brought out. Ability in business organization and financial matters is important, and it is not at all scarce in the Chinese community. What is scarce, however, is willingness to put much time and effort into fulfilling the responsibilities of leadership. Because of the diversity of the community, the number of organizations among the Semarang Chinese is relatively large. Therefore there is constant competition, not only for wealthy patrons, but for leaders who will spend the time and effort necessary for the success of each organization. The person who shows himself capable of taking and fulfilling responsibility in one organization is immediately subject to pressure to accept posts in other organizations; and the person who assumes leadership in several organizations, especially if they include schools and charitable institutions, earns a reputation for public spirit comparable to that of the wealthy contributor to numerous community welfare activities. For these various reasons, it is not surprising to find a considerable number of leaders who hold posts in four or more organizations.

Another personal quality important for leadership in the community is the ability to "get along with all kinds of people." As elsewhere, this is partly a matter of being likable, good-natured, and skillful in handling human relations. But among the Semarang Chinese, it is a matter also of maintaining positive relations with diverse groups within the community. Indonesian, Dutch, and several "dialects" of Chinese are languages used in ordinary conversation in different groups. A leader who can speak most of these can have much wider influence than one who does not. Similarly, and perhaps even more important, the leader who has learned the language of political neutrality or who actually has no partisan views has a great advantage. If a leader does not have a strictly neutral position on such questions as who should govern China or which country Indonesian Chinese should identify with, he is likely at least to show tolerance and respect for the opposite view. The inability of Tan Tjien Lien to maintain rapport with the pro-Peking group was one of the reasons why he was not re-elected to the chairmanship first of the Chung Hua Tsung Hui and then of the Sianghwee.

There are two considerations which apparently are not important in the selection of leaders in the Semarang community: religious prominence and advanced professional education. The monk of the Tay Kak Sie temple, the leading lecturers in the Chinese religious societies, and the Christian clergymen play no part in the leadership of organizations other than their own; and, with only a few exceptions, doctors, lawyers, engineers, and teachers do not hold leading positions outside of organizations directly related to their professions. Doubtless a major reason for this is lack of interest, among the people of these groups, in taking leadership. Doctors, lawyers, and engineers, whose wealth, education, and prestige should qualify them for leadership, usually find little congeniality with the members or officers of community organizations. Furthermore, they are less likely than businessmen to feel themselves part of the "Chinese community" or *sia hwee Tionghoa,* as it is called. Religious leaders and teachers lack not only interest, but wealth; and they have prestige only in limited groups. On the other hand, prominent leaders may be of any religious persuasion, and some of them have very little formal education.

Summary

The former Dutch-appointed Chinese officers had very wide official and unofficial powers in the Chinese community. Wealth, government connections, and popularity were the major prerequisites to their appointment. After 1900, the nationalistic leaders of the Sianghwee gradually supplanted the Kongkoan officers as the recognized leaders of the Semarang Chinese.

In 1931 the Kongkoan was abolished, and in the decade that followed, the leadership of Thio Thiam Tjong and Tan Tek Peng was especially outstanding. In the postwar years, Tan Tjien Lien rose to considerable prominence, but his community leadership came to an end with the growing political diversity among the Semarang Chinese. Today, leaders of the Chung Hua Tsung Hui, such as Liem Siauw Tjong, have achieved fairly wide recognition; but their influence is confined almost entirely to social and charitable matters, such as sports, religious affairs, private clubs, schools, and medical institutions.

The careers of these leaders illustrate the various changes which took place from the time when administrative, political, commercial, and organizational leadership were concentrated in the hands of a few people, to the present time, when leadership in these four fields is dispersed among many different individuals and organizations.

With regard to the qualifications for leadership today, wealth and government connections are of considerable, though somewhat diminished, importance. In addition to general ability and intelligence, willingness to accept and fulfill leadership responsibility and ability to "get along well" with different people and diverse political groups are desirable personal qualities for the Semarang Chinese leader. On the other hand, religious or educational distinction seems to be of little importance in community leadership.

CHAPTER VIII

Schools and Education

The Growth of Schools

Before the advent of modern schools in the first decade of the twentieth century, very few of the Semarang Chinese obtained any schooling at all. From time to time, small private schools were established by wealthy merchants, primarily for their own children. The teachers, who were usually brought from China, spoke and taught the particular coastal speech ("dialect") of their patrons. Discipline was extremely strict, hours were long, and holidays were few. The children learned to read and write and sometimes to calculate with an abacus. Their only textbooks were the Chinese classics, which they had to read again and again until they could recite them aloud from beginning to end.[1]

In 1904, the first Chinese school with a modernized curriculum was established in Semarang—the Tiong Hoa Hwe Koan School. Five years later, the government opened the first Dutch-Chinese School. In 1916 the Chinese English School was established. The cultural orientations of these early schools have been described in Chapter II. A few notes on educational developments during the 1930's will be added before the discussion of contemporary schools.

[1] Liem Thian Joe, *Riwajat Semarang* (Semarang, c. 1933), p. 179.

By 1930, there were several Dutch-Chinese Schools in Semarang, one of them a girls' school. These were all primary schools, with a curriculum identical to that of equivalent schools for Dutch children. An initial preparatory year was added, however, in order to give the pupils a sufficient familiarity with the Dutch language to follow instruction in Dutch. A Dutch-Chinese School of special interest was the Chung Hwa Hui School. This was established in 1929 by The Sien Tjo and other leaders of the Chung Hwa Hui, a politico-cultural organization of Dutch-educated Chinese professionals and businessmen.[2] Graduates of this school were permitted to take the entrance examinations of government secondary and higher schools, and some continued their education in universities in Holland. Unlike the other Dutch-Chinese Schools, the Chung Hwa Hui School was managed and financed privately by Chinese supporters. During the 1930's, at the request of the government, it took over the Dutch-Chinese girls' school and the preparatory classes for all Semarang Dutch-Chinese schools.

In the late 1930's, the Tiong Hoa Hwe Koan established secondary grades for the first time. The Chinese English School, a secondary school from the first, began to shift its cultural orientation at this time. History and geography were no longer taught from a British point of view, and more emphasis was given to Chinese language and literature.

During the Japanese occupation, these two Chinese-language schools were closed. The Chung Hwa Hui School was the only Chinese school that remained open, and it did not teach the Chinese language. Nevertheless, a large number of people, young and old, Totok and Peranakan, utilized the forced idleness of the occupation period for the private study of Mandarin Chinese. The postwar years saw the re-establishment of Chinese schools and the rapid growth of Protestant and Catholic mission schools. The

[2] For further information on the Chung Hwa Hui, see Donald E. Willmott, *The National Status of the Chinese in Indonesia* (Cornell Modern Indonesia Project, Ithaca, N.Y., 1956), pp. 8–9.

expansion of existing schools and the establishment of new ones is continuing today. For example, the Chung Hwa Hui School opened a new classroom building in 1954, and an extension of the Chinese English School was completed in the following year. A new Catholic school, the Yu Te Shueh Hsiao, began classes in 1955. It was the first Christian Chinese-language school.

Distribution of Chinese Pupils among Semarang Schools

Chinese children attend at least fifty different schools in Semarang today. This number includes Chinese-managed schools in which all the pupils are Chinese, mission and church schools in which varying proportions are Chinese, and government schools in which usually only a small proportion are Chinese. An accurate assessment of the distribution of Chinese children among these various schools is impossible, since comprehensive statistics are not available. Rather than omit the subject altogether, however, the writer will venture certain estimates. These are based upon fairly accurate statistics for some schools, partial or rough information for others, and mere considered guesses for the rest. Therefore they are only suggestive and should be regarded with some skepticism.

In the first place, the writer estimates that there were over 12,000 Chinese children attending school in Semarang in 1954–1955. Of these, roughly 8,500 were in primary grades, and almost 3,600 in secondary grades. The writer considers it likely that about 5 per cent of the pupils in primary grades and about 15 per cent of those in secondary grades were from families who reside outside Semarang. If this is approximately correct, Semarang pupils accounted for about 8,000 of those in primary schools and about 3,000 of those in secondary schools.

Education is not compulsory in Indonesia, primarily because there are not yet a sufficient number of schools and teachers. In the Semarang Chinese community there are some children for whom even an elementary education is not available. On the basis of municipal statistical records, the writer estimates that in Semarang there were about 8,500 Chinese children of primary school age (6–11) and about 6,000 of secondary school age (12–17) in 1955. Thus it appears that at least several hundred Chinese children of primary school age were not attending school, whereas only about one-half of the appropriate age group were attending secondary schools. The proportion in secondary schools was probably considerably less than one-half, however, because many of the students then in attendance had had their studies interrupted in the years of war and revolution and were over the age of seventeen.

The great majority of children of school age who were not in school must have been girls, for although almost half the pupils in primary schools were girls, this proportion dwindled to a third or a quarter in upper secondary grades. With the exception of Catholic schools and the government household science schools, all Semarang schools attended by Chinese are coeducational. However, practices in coeducational schools vary from quite rigid segregation to rather unrestricted mixing of the sexes in the classroom, in play, and in extracurricular activities.

Chinese children are distributed among the following types of schools: Chinese-managed Chinese-language schools; Chinese-managed Indonesian-language schools; Christian schools; and government schools. One school, the Chinese English School, falls into two of these categories: some instruction is in Indonesian, some in Chinese; and in the higher grades, students are actually divided between a Chinese section and an Indonesian section, with separate classes and curricula, according to their aspirations for future work or study. The students of this school will therefore be divided between the first two categories mentioned above.

In 1955, the Chinese-managed Chinese-language schools included the Sin You She School (pro-Communist), the Tiong Hoa Hwe Koan School (Peking-oriented), half of the Chinese English School (also Peking-oriented), and three pro-Kuomintang schools. There were almost 6,000 pupils in these schools, that is, roughly half of the Chinese children attending school in Semarang. Most of the teachers were either Peranakans who had had their higher education in China or Totoks.

In the category of Chinese-managed Indonesian-language schools are the Chung Hwa Hui School and half of the Chinese English School. Although the former does not offer any course in the Chinese language, all but two or three of its pupils are Chinese. In 1955, the total number of pupils in this category of school was about 1,500, or approximately one-eighth of all Chinese children attending school in the city. The Chung Hwa Hui School has several Dutch and Indonesian teachers on its staff, in addition to Chinese Peranakans educated in Indonesia.

Christian schools include a number of Catholic schools, a Seventh-Day Adventist school, and perhaps a dozen other Protestant schools. In a few of these schools, all the pupils are Chinese; in the others, the proportion of Chinese varies from high to very low. The writer has little accurate information about the number of Chinese in these various Christian schools. Possibly the number in 1955 somewhat exceeded 3,000—about a quarter of all Chinese pupils attending school in Semarang. In the Catholic schools, many of the teachers, both clergy and laymen, are Europeans. In the Protestant schools, however, almost all teachers are Indonesians or Chinese Peranakans.

There are eight or nine government secondary schools and perhaps twice as many government primary schools which are attended by Chinese students. On the basis of information concerning only a few of these schools, the writer believes that there were well over 1,000 Chinese pupils in government schools in 1955, possibly more than 10 per cent of all Chinese pupils in the city.

Two schools which do not fit into any of the categories discussed above are the school for Dutch children and the school of the Confucian Society. The latter, which had about 170 pupils, will be described in the next chapter. Several dozen Chinese students were attending the Dutch school in 1955.

Although the pattern of school attendance partly reflects the political and cultural orientations of the Chinese community, it is undoubtedly true that the pupils of the various schools are much less partisan nationally, religiously, and politically than are the respective school staffs. In the next chapter it will be shown that the majority of students in politically oriented schools are probably apolitical. In most schools there are even a certain number of students whose families are opposed to the general outlook of the staff. The writer knew a strongly pro-Kuomintang businessman who was sending two of his children to a Peking-oriented school. This occurs because other factors are often more important in the choice of schools than is religion or politics, such as proximity, academic standards, school fees, or lack of accommodation in a preferred school.

A number of educational institutions outside the school system under discussion should be noted in passing. Many Chinese children attend Chinese-language or Indonesian-language kindergartens, most of which are connected with Chinese-managed or Christian schools.

Since World War II, there has been a nationwide adult literacy campaign in which free, public courses in reading and writing the Indonesian language are taught by volunteer teachers. In the Chinese community of Semarang, classes have been held at the Kwee family temple, in the hall of the Perkumpulan Indo-Tionghoa (a mutual-aid society), and perhaps in one or two other places. The Sin You She society has organized free courses in Mandarin Chinese.

A number of individuals and small, private schools give instruction in languages, typing, shorthand, and commercial subjects. Several dozen women dressmakers operate small schools in their homes, and a local federation of such schools regularly gives standard examinations in designing, cutting, and tailoring clothing of all kinds. There are similar schools for embroidery work and fancy machine stitching. Finally, the government operates an adult education program, which offers courses leading to advanced diplomas in various subjects. In all these institutions, a substantial number of Chinese take part.

Totok and Peranakan Children in Semarang Schools

An analysis of Semarang municipal statistics indicates that in 1955 about 3,500 Chinese children of school age (6–17) had Totok fathers. On the basis of estimates of the total number not attending school, it seems likely that almost 1,000 Totok children of school age had either left school or had never had an opportunity to enter. Of the Totok children who were attending school, probably only a few dozen were in government schools, about 200 in Christian schools and Chinese-managed Indonesian-language schools, and about 2,300 in Chinese-language schools. If these estimates are approximately correct, children of Totoks comprised about 45 per cent of the Semarang pupils of Chinese-language schools in 1955.

The writer estimates that among over 8,500 Peranakan children attending school in the city about one-third were in Chinese-language schools, one-third in Christian schools, one-sixth in Chinese-managed Indonesian-language schools, and one-sixth in government schools.

Differences in citizenship and national outlook do not correspond exactly to Totok-Peranakan lines. This is especially true in the Chinese-language schools, in which many of the pupils are Peranakan children who lost their Indonesian citizenship in the option period, 1949–1951. Conversely, in Christian schools there are a certain number of Indonesian-born children of Totoks who claim Indonesian citizenship. Among the respondents in the questionnaire survey, students claiming Chinese citizenship comprised 85 per cent of those in Chinese-language schools, 22 per cent of those in Chinese-managed Indonesian-language schools, and 2 per cent of those in Christian schools. The corresponding percentage for government schools was probably even lower than for

the Christian schools. If the percentage given above for questionnaire respondents in Chinese-language schools is nearly representative of all pupils in these schools in 1955, it means that a
substantial majority (perhaps over two-thirds) of Peranakan children in these schools were claiming to be Chinese citizens. This
would be almost one-quarter of all Peranakan students.

It has been pointed out in an earlier chapter that differences and
distinctions between Peranakans and Totoks are gradually disappearing. This is especially true of those of school age. Many
young Peranakans now know the Chinese language, and virtually
all children of Totoks know enough Indonesian for practical purposes. In the Chinese-language schools there is much mixing of
the two groups. And citizenship is not a matter which draws a
sharp line between Peranakans and Totoks.

Different Curricula and Their Purposes

With but few exceptions, the curricula of Semarang schools are
designed primarily to prepare pupils for a continuation of their
studies in higher schools if they so desire. Therefore, curricula
are adjusted to the entrance requirements of various institutions
of higher learning. This makes for diversity. The one requirement which all schools must meet is the government regulation
that the Indonesian language must be taught a specified number
of hours each week in each grade.

The Chinese-language schools endeavor to make their curricula
comply with the standards of the respective departments of education in Peking and Taiwan. Many standard Chinese textbooks
are imported for this purpose. Some of these have been banned
by the government Inspectorate of Foreign Education, which ex-
ercises increasingly careful supervision over the curricula and textbooks of Chinese schools. The Kuomintang schools have not yet
established higher secondary grades and therefore have had no
graduates seeking university entrance. But each year several

hundred students of the Peking-oriented schools take the same matriculation examinations that are given in schools in China. In 1955, about fifty students from Semarang schools went to China to continue their education there. They do not expect to return to Indonesia. Eighteen graduates of one Semarang school were studying in seven institutions of higher learning in different parts of China in 1955.

The curricula of the Chung Hwa Hui School and the Indonesian section of the Chinese English School comply with the standards of the Department of Education of the Indonesian government, and students take the regular matriculation examinations set by that department. Academic standards are high in both schools, but the Chung Hwa Hui School has had an especially outstanding record in the government examinations. Although students of the Chung Hwa Hui School spend more time on European languages than is required by the Department of Education, students of the Chinese English School probably carry a heavier burden of additional work, since they spend considerable time in their Chinese studies.

The Christian schools fit their curricula to the standards of the Indonesian Department of Education with very little modification. Few of them teach the Chinese language, even as an elective. Chinese graduates of most Christian secondary schools, as well as those of the Chung Hwa Hui School and the Chinese English School, may continue their studies in the government universities and professional schools of Indonesia. At least several dozen students from these various schools were in Indonesian institutions of higher learning in 1955. A few had been able to attend universities in Holland, and there were at least three or four Semarang Chinese in American and Canadian universities. Several graduates of Semarang Christian schools were attending the Protestant theological college in Jogjakarta.

None of the Chinese schools provides specialized training for teachers, but there are both Catholic and Protestant teacher-training schools in Semarang. Like the government normal schools, these are of secondary school level.

In the regular government primary and secondary schools there are very few Chinese. However, the proportion of Chinese students is higher in the specialized secondary schools: two technical schools, a nautical school, and a household science school for girls. In the 1955 graduating class of the last, over one-fifth of the students were Chinese.

The government's Public School VI is of special interest. It is an "experimental school" for Chinese children of Indonesian citizenship. In 1955, there were 106 boys and 75 girls in attendance. The curriculum is the same as in other government elementary schools, except that the Chinese language is offered as a second language, and courses include material on Chinese history and culture. The aim of the government is to see whether it can provide a type of education which will attract Chinese of Indonesian citizenship away from foreign Chinese schools. In 1955 it was still too early to evaluate the success of this program, but several difficulties were already apparent. For instance, it was the opinion of an Indonesian official that the school did not have sufficient financial resources to enable it to maintain a standard of teaching equal to that in many Chinese schools.

Organization and Financing of Schools

The Chinese schools of Semarang are managed by boards of six to ten members or more. Each board is elected periodically by the members of a school organization consisting of numerous subscribers, many of whom are parents of pupils in the school. The primary responsibilities of school boards are fund raising, financial supervision, appointment of staff, and decisions on overall policy. One exception to this pattern is the Chung Hwa Hui School. It is managed by a self-perpetuating foundation, the five officers of which are assisted and advised by a parents' association.

Most of the teachers in Chinese schools belong to teachers' associations. Those of the three pro-Kuomintang schools have formed the Oversea Chinese Teachers' Orthodox Association. Many of the teachers in the Christian schools and the Chinese-managed Indonesian-language schools belong to the Perserikatan Guru Tionghoa (Chinese Teachers' Association). This was organized by Dutch-educated teachers in several cities before World War II. Its membership is still largely Dutch-speaking.

In each school there is some kind of student government or at the least student committees for such activities as sports, recreation, and publications. These student organizations also play an important part in various fund-raising activities. In addition, there is a national association for Chinese secondary school students of Indonesian citizenship, the Chung Lien Hui, which has an active branch in Semarang. It arranges tours and outings, organizes festivals and sports events, campaigns for various charities, and endeavors to promote good relations between Indonesians and Chinese of Indonesian citizenship.

The Chinese-managed schools of Semarang are completely self-supporting. They receive no subsidies from the government. A major part of their income is derived from school fees, which are often graduated according to the wealth of the family. Donations from parents, patrons, and alumni are a second major source of income. In addition, bazaars or "Fancy Fairs," dramatic performances, concerts, and programs of various kinds are used to raise money, especially for particular projects, such as the addition of new laboratories or classrooms. Advertisements in commemorative books or in programs for special events are another common source of supplementary income. According to one Chinese school principal, large grants and donations are extremely rare.

The Christian schools are financed in various ways. Most of them charge school fees. Many of the primary schools receive government subsidies, and in some cases these cover the major part of the school budget. Those which do not receive subsidies are supported by local churches. Most Christian secondary schools are partly subsidized by the government, though the extent of the assistance is less than in the case of primary schools. Protestant secondary schools which receive no government subsidies are partly supported by the Pengampu Sekolah-Sekolah dan Asrama-Asrama Kristen (Fund for Christian Schools and Boarding Houses).

In government primary schools, pupils pay no tuition; but in government secondary schools and universities, students pay substantial fees. There is an extensive system of government scholarships, but these involve commitments to a period of service after graduation, and very few Chinese take advantage of them.

Summary and Conclusions

The educational facilities available to the Chinese community in Semarang have been expanding at a relatively rapid rate. However, there is still a small but significant number of children who do not attend school. Among those attending in 1955, probably about one-half were in Chinese-language schools, one-eighth in Chinese-managed Indonesian-language schools, one-quarter in Christian schools, and one-eighth in government schools. These estimates are, however, based on insufficient information and must not be regarded as accurate. Although most of the schools have specific religious, political, or national orientations, a significant proportion of the students in each school do not share the partisan views of the staff in these matters.

In 1955, a great majority of the children of Totoks were attending Chinese-language schools, where they were only slightly outnumbered by children of Peranakans. Probably about two-thirds of the children of Peranakans were attending Indonesian-language schools, but of those who were in Chinese-language schools, the majority claimed to be Chinese subjects. Differences of birthplace, language, and education between Totoks and Peranakans are disappearing especially rapidly among young people of school age.

The curricula of Chinese-language schools in Semarang complies with that of the school system in either China or Taiwan. Many Semarang students have gone to China for higher education. Christian schools and Chinese-managed Indonesian-language schools have adjusted their curricula to the national system of education in Indonesia.

The Chinese schools of Semarang are managed by periodically elected school boards and are self-supporting. Christian schools, most of which have Indonesian as well as Chinese pupils, often receive government subsidies.

From the material presented in this chapter, several conclusions seem justified:

1. The rapid expansion of the school system and the substantial fees and donations which parents contribute to the schools are indications that the Chinese community places a relatively high value on education.

2. Although the school system which has developed tends to minimize differences between Totoks and Peranakans, it undoubtedly intensifies differences in national orientation.

3. Among the Chinese pupils in Semarang schools, the great majority of those who are Indonesian citizens are receiving an education consistent with the requirements and aims of the Indonesian national school system; on the other hand, foreign Chinese are receiving an education more suitable for life in China than in Indonesia.

CHAPTER IX

Religion and Magic

Religious Orientations

With regard to religion, the Chinese in Semarang display certain attitudes generally characteristic of the Chinese everywhere. But in some respects their religious orientations are very different from those of the nonemigrant Chinese. Similarities will be discussed first.

The religious tolerance of the Chinese has often been noted.[1] It is based not merely upon indifference to the religion of others, but upon a genuine respect for all religions and a feeling that everyone has a right to his own convictions. This attitude is characteristic of the Semarang Chinese too. It is common to find members of one family professing different religions, yet accepting the fact without conflict and often without concern. The following are some examples of religious tolerance in family situations. The cases are taken from the interview survey, but names have been changed in order to preserve anonymity.

Mr. Tjan Ting Lo and his wife are Buddhists of the intelligentsia. They also carry out the rituals of ancestor worship. But in seeking the

---

[1] Olga Lang, *Chinese Family and Society* (New Haven, 1946), pp. 290–291.

182

best possible education for their children, they have decided to send them to Catholic schools. Mrs. Tjan told the interviewer that they realize this may mean that their children will adopt Catholicism.

A produce merchant and his wife adhere to traditional Chinese religion; they maintain a family altar and the appropriate rituals. They send their daughter to a Catholic school and their son to a Protestant school.

Mr. and Mrs. Ho Ming Swan say that they have no religion. They send their children to the most pro-Peking school. At New Year's time, however, they carry out the ritual of ancestor worship when visiting relatives, and Mrs. Ho sometimes accompanies friends or relatives to the temple for worship.

Mr. Lee Ping Kow maintains a family altar and sometimes goes to the temple to worship or pray. Mrs. Lee is a Catholic and is determined to raise her children as Catholics. She accompanies her husband to the temple, but does not herself pray. The children do not attend a Catholic school. Incidentally, Mrs. Lee enjoys *mahjong* (the well-known Chinese gambling game) and is a believer in magic.

Questionnaire respondents were asked: "Do you ever have differences of opinion with your parents? If so, concerning what problems?" Only about 8 per cent of those replying to this question mentioned religion as a point of disagreement. Yet about 40 per cent of the respondents claimed religious preferences different from their parents. Similar results were obtained in an extensive questionnaire survey in China before World War II.[2]

Another indication of religious tolerance is to be found in the fact that a large number of the questionnaire respondents are of the opinion that it is not important for marriage partners to have the same religion. The following question was asked:

What considerations do you believe to be most important in choosing a marriage partner? Please make circles around the three considerations below which you think most important, and cross out the ones you do not consider important:

2 *Ibid.*, p. 290.

mutual love	education
good family	ideals
household abilities	proper horoscope
same racial descent	religion
consent of families	a good income

About half the Christians, but almost no non-Christians marked "religion" as important. None of the Christians, but over half the non-Christians considered it unimportant. On the whole, only horoscopy and income were considered important less often than religion. "Ideals" were considered important more than twice as often.

Even among Christians, who are taught in the Semarang churches that it is wrong to marry non-Christians, such inter-marriage often occurs. Among the parents of the questionnaire respondents, over 40 per cent of the Catholic women and about 35 per cent of the Protestant women were married to non-Christians; the percentage of Christian men married to non-Christians was about 10 per cent in the case of both Catholics and Protestants. The higher proportion of women who married non-Christians is largely owing to the fact that there were considerably more Christian women than men. The shortage of men was more marked among Catholics than among Protestants. Most relevant here is the fact that in spite of a surplus of Christian women about a tenth of the Christian men were married to non-Christian women. No doubt some of these marriages were family-arranged. Nevertheless, they indicate tolerance on the part of the families at least.

Religious tolerance is evident also in the admission policies of Semarang schools and in Chinese parents' selection of schools for their children. The schools attended by Chinese in Semarang admit pupils of all religions. It is recognized that religious schools may convert their pupils to their particular religions, yet Chinese of all religions are found among the parents of the pupils of Christian as well as non-Christian schools. According to the questionnaire results, even in the case of Christian schools, about 75 per cent of the parents of Chinese pupils profess traditional Chinese religions or no religion at all. About 8 per cent of the respondents in non-Christian schools had Christian fathers; almost 10 per cent of the respondents in Catholic schools had Protestant fathers; and about 4 per cent of the respondents in Protestant schools had Catholic fathers. In some of these cases, the mothers' preferences were being followed; but the religious tolerance of the fathers is evident.

Closely associated with religious tolerance is the equally common Chinese characteristic of religious eclecticism. Many Chinese not only respect all religions, but adopt beliefs and practices from several at the same time. This was evident in China, where, for centuries, elements of animism, ancestor worship, Confucianism, Taoism, and Buddhism were combined in the faith and rituals of the majority of the people. The same is still true of a large section of the Chinese community in Semarang. This eclecticism is also exemplified in the modern Sam Kauw Hwee (Three Religions Society), the purpose of which is to promote an integration of Confucianism, Buddhism, and Taoism compatible with modern life. The following examples of eclecticism are taken from the interview survey:

All Christian families interviewed still celebrate the Chinese New Year's festival, and some visit family graves on the traditional festival day of Tjing Bing; many non-Christian families, on the other hand, celebrate "Santa Claus Day." The meaning of these holidays is, of course, altered to fit the religious views of each family.

Mr. Wan Han Kie, a professional man, has been a member of a Protestant church for a number of years. Yet he still occasionally prays at the temple, and at New Year's time he "pays his respects" in the traditional way before the ancestor altars of relatives and friends.

Mrs. Kwik Pan Ik claims no particular religion, but carries out ancestor worship and occasionally goes to the temple. When in serious trouble, however, she sometimes "prays to God in the Catholic way." She was educated in Catholic schools.

Mrs. Kan Tjoe Sie is a devout Catholic. She once had a serious illness, which was cured through the agency of a temple god. She still goes regularly to the temple to make offerings and express her gratitude in the traditional way.

Chinese eclecticism has led also to the adoption of beliefs and practices from the Indonesian people. For example, Chinese sometimes follow the Javanese custom of burning a certain type of incense at the door in order to ward off evil spirits. Javanese holy places, especially the graves of eminent rulers and religious leaders, are often visited by Chinese. In such cases, Chinese usually offer flowers, in the Javanese manner, rather than using incense sticks. In praying to these local spirits, Chinese worshipers often ask for wealth, health, or children. The following case will illustrate this type of eclecticism.

On the annual "birthday" of a temple god in Welahan, not far from Semarang, thousands of Chinese from all parts of Central Java and many from more distant cities join in worship and festivities there. The writer accompanied thirty-four members of the Hwa Joe Hwee Kwan in a bus chartered by their club. The group included fifteen women, and ages ranged from about thirty-five to over sixty.

The god at Welahan is famous for his healing powers, and members of the Hwa Joe Hwee Kwan group joined the crowds giving thanks for past cures or praying for new ones. Many also gave food offerings, which were brought from home or bought at the temple. One member of the group presented a live goat.

After two hours at Welahan, our group took a four-hour side trip to the mountain shrine-tomb of Sultan Muria of Demak, an early Islamic ruler. The shrine, situated on a high peak, is a strenuous half-hour climb from the end of the motor road. Yet the majority of our group, including several men and women over sixty, walked to the top. There they bought flower offerings, drank or washed in holy water, and knelt and prayed before the tomb of Sultan Muria. The writer was told that the Sultan's spirit was supposed to be very potent and that "you can pray to become wealthy."

The Hwa Joe Hwee Kwan officer who organized and led the excursion was a Catholic. He did not participate in the worship at either place.

A practical, this-worldly approach to religion is another characteristic of the Chinese which is also found in the community of Semarang. Most Chinese do not expect mystical experience from their religion and show little interest in theological or metaphysical doctrines. Religion is expected to define one's duties and responsibilities and to provide a way of obtaining supernatural aid in achieving concrete ends. Even ancestor worship focuses the worshiper's attention much more upon proper behavior and family responsibilities in this life than upon hopes and expectations with regard to future life.[3] Material on rituals, legends, astrology, and morality appears in the Chinese press in Semarang, but mysticism and metaphysics are virtually never discussed.

Agnosticism is often associated with this practical, nonmystical approach to religion. It ranges from the intellectual agnosticism of many Confucian scholars to the doubts of ordinary people about the potency of certain gods. Very few Chinese have dogmatic beliefs about the supernatural. The writer asked a member of the Hwa Joe Hwee Kwan excursion group whether he believed in the efficacy of petitionary prayer to the spirit of Sultan Muria. "I really don't know," was the reply, "but there is no harm in trying."

The following translation also illustrates this point. It is the last verse of a song written in Indonesian by a Confucianist Peranakan. The song is intended to be taught to children for their edification.

> I don't know whether God in Heaven
> Really loves men boundlessly.
> But I can tell with certainty
> That parents love their children so.[4]

Among the differences between the religious orientations of the Chinese in Semarang and in China, the most striking is in

[3] Marion J. Levy, Jr., *The Family Revolution in Modern China* (Cambridge, Mass., 1949), pp. 249–250.

[4] K. T. M., "Kenang-Kenangan," in L. T. Y., *Oepatjara Hoe-Soe dan Song-Soe (Pernikahan dan Kamatian), Menoeroet Pikiran dari Saorang Khong Kauw* (2d ed.; Tjitjoeroeg, 1949), p. 61.

the degree of religious interest and participation. The present writer has spent many years in China. Upon arriving in Semarang, he was struck by the number and elaborateness of family ancestral altars visible from the street as one walks through the Chinese quarter, and also by the number of temples and the amount of public support which they must receive in order to be in such good repair and upkeep. In 1955, the main pavilion of the Sam Po temple was replaced, at great expense, by a much grander one. And for a population of 60,000 Chinese, community religious festivals are marked by unusually elaborate and expensive celebrations and processions. On the other hand, even before the establishment of the Communist regime in China, many temples there were in a state of extreme disrepair, a number had been converted into schools, and some had been abandoned. It would be difficult to say whether or not the amount of interest and participation in traditional religious activities among the common people of China was declining before the rise of communism. Certainly a very large proportion of the educated and nationalist-minded middle class had lost interest.[5] In Semarang the corresponding proportion has been much lower. It is not at all uncommon to find students and professional people who devoutly participate in traditional religious activities.

There is no doubt that the observance of traditional religious customs is declining in Semarang; but the decline has been more gradual than in China itself. Whereas in China the rejection of traditional religious beliefs by the intelligentsia usually signified a more or less complete loss of interest in religion, in Semarang the decline of traditional customs has been accompanied by new religious interests. With the founding of the Tiong Hoa Hwe Koan organizations in the early years of the present century, there was a considerable revival of interest in Confucian teachings. Today the Semarang Khong Kauw Hwee (Confucian Society) is a thriving organization. In recent years the Sam Kauw Hwee (Three Re-

[5] Lang, *op. cit.*, pp. 162, 290; Levy, *op. cit.*, p. 343.

ligions Society) has grown into a nationwide organization of considerable importance. In addition, both Catholicism and Protestantism have spread very rapidly in the Chinese community. The result is that religions of various kinds hold a much more important place in the life of Semarang Chinese today than they did in China even before the establishment of the Communist regime there.

Table 4. Comparative distribution of religious preferences of high school students in Semarang (1955) * and China (1936) †

Religious preferences	Non-Christian schools		Christian schools	
	In China	In Semarang	In China	In Semarang
Christian	3%	19%	33%	56%
Chinese religions	12	22	17	5
No religion	85	59	50	39 ‡
	100%	100%	100%	100%
Number of replies	216	298	224	226
Number not answering	44	119	52	15

* Based on the writer's questionnaire survey (see Appendix I).

† Based on a questionnaire survey conducted in eight high schools in five cities of North, Central, and South China, as reported in Olga Lang, *Chinese Family and Society* (New Haven, 1946), pp. 360–362.

‡ This figure is significantly different at the .05 level from the figure in the adjacent column. All other figures in corresponding adjacent columns are significantly different at the .01 level.

Further evidence for this conclusion will be found in Table 4, in which the religious preferences of high school students in Semarang are compared with those of high school students in China. The figures for China are taken from the results of a questionnaire survey carried out by Olga Lang in 1936. Too much confidence should not be placed in the exact proportions shown in the table, because it is not known just how representative the two samples are. Furthermore, the question about religion may have been presented in a different way in the two questionnaires. But the differences are sufficiently great to lead to the conclusion that they are not due merely to sampling error, questionnaire variability, or both.

According to Table 4, there is a considerably higher proportion of Christian students in Semarang in both Christian and non-Christian high schools. Although the proportion of Christian students in China may have increased slightly in the ten years following 1937, it should be noted that even in the Christian schools at that time (which had almost certainly been in existence as long as had Semarang Christian schools in 1955) the proportion of students who were Christians was significantly lower than in Christian schools in Semarang today.

In order to compare the prevalence of Chinese religions in the total high school population of both areas, it is necessary to take into account the fact that there were perhaps a dozen times as many non-Christian as Christian high schools in China, whereas Chinese students in non-Christian high schools in Semarang outnumbered Chinese students in Christian high schools by little more than two to one. The figures for Christian and non-Christian schools may be combined by correcting for their relative numbers, and the proportion of all high school students who adhere to Chinese religions is then found to be about 5 per cent higher in Semarang than it was in China. Since the trend among students in China over the intervening period has certainly been away from traditional religion, it seems safe to say that Chinese religions are more widely adhered to among Semarang students today than among students in China even before the establishment of the People's Republic.

Two cautions concerning these results must be added. In the first place, as will be seen in Table 4, there was an unusually high number of students in Semarang non-Christian schools who gave no answer to the question on religion. If it was generally a matter of chance whether or not this question was answered, the percentages shown are approximately correct. However, it seems likely that the majority of those who did not answer failed to do so because they had no religious preferences to report. Even if it is assumed that all of those who did not answer belong in the "no religion" category, the results are still significantly different as before, except in the case of Chinese religions, where the difference becomes less and is significant only at the .05 level.

In the second place, caution is required in generalizing these results. Table 4 is based upon the questionnaire replies of high school students and cannot be taken to represent the general populations from which the students come. Compared to the students, there are fewer Christians and probably fewer persons with no religion in the older generation, both in Semarang and in China. Groups with less education, in both places, would probably also include fewer Christians and persons of no religion than does the student group.

Aside from Table 4, the figures for Semarang students may be compared with those for students in China in another way—that is, by comparing the difference in religious preferences between fathers and sons in each group. This will give an idea of the inter-generational religious trends in both places. On the basis of the figures obtained by Olga Lang,[6] it is calculated that in the Christian high schools surveyed in China about 30 per cent of the students reported that their fathers had no religion and about 50 per cent claimed no religion themselves. On the other hand, about 52 per cent of the Chinese students in Semarang Christian schools reported that their fathers had no religion, but only about 39 per cent of them had no religion themselves. Thus, in Christian schools, the trends are for students in China to be less religious than their parents and in Semarang more religious than their parents. A similar analysis shows that in non-Christian schools about 30 per cent of the students in China are "less religious" than their parents, as compared to only about 10 per cent in Semarang.

These results give support to a general conclusion that in the

[6] Lang, *op. cit.*, pp. 360–362.

Semarang Chinese community there has been much more interest in religion, both Christian and traditional Chinese, than among people of equivalent education in China. The reasons why specific religions have attracted followings among the Semarang Chinese will be discussed in succeeding sections of this chapter, but at this point one reason why religion in general has been of greater interest and importance than in China will be dealt with.

In both China and Indonesia, Western civilization had a great impact on the Chinese, through war, diplomacy, government action, education, missions, and personal contacts. This has had the effect of undermining complacency about the traditional ways of doing things and has brought into question many traditional beliefs. The Chinese nationalist ideology which grew up was only a partial solution to the doubts and problems raised in the minds of thinking people. In China, the modernist intelligentsia, drawn mostly from the lower gentry and the urban population, turned their interests and energies toward political, social, and economic problems and their solutions. They saw Chinese society as backward, and they were determined to modernize and industrialize the country. Thus they were attracted to secular ideologies such as democracy, communism, socialism, and fascism. A large number of the intelligentsia had experienced deprivation themselves, and this probably encouraged radical thought.[7]

In Indonesia, on the other hand, there was no urge to change the social or economic structure. The Chinese were comparatively well off and were generally satisfied with the colonial economy (which, to a large extent, still exists). Therefore the problems of personal relations and personal orientation raised by modernist currents were more important to the Semarang Chinese than social or economic problems. Those who were perplexed by these problems tended to seek answers in religion rather than in secular ideologies.

The two Chinese newspapers in Semarang give considerable

[7] *Ibid.*, pp. 317–318, 334–335; Levy, *op. cit.*, pp. 343–344.

attention to religion, both in news items about religious activities and in articles on religious topics. The right-wing *Kuangpo* devotes somewhat more attention to church news and regularly publishes short Christian sermons. The chairman of its board of directors is a Christian. The left-wing *Sin Min* emphasizes Chinese religion, with quite frequent articles by leaders of the Confucian Society or the Three Religions Society. But both papers attempt to give fair coverage to all religious positions. In 1955, for instance, the *Sin Min* published long, favorable articles about several Semarang churches; and the *Kuangpo's* Chinese New Year's issue contained a number of articles on Chinese religions. On the other hand, social ideologies are almost never discussed in the newspapers.

It is significant that the various Christian churches in Semarang are all conservative. They engage in social service, but they do not subscribe to the "social gospel" of liberal Christianity—that is, to the idea that it is the responsibility of every Christian to join in concrete social action for the purpose of reforming the unjust institutions of society. It appears that the Catholicism, Dutch Calvinism, and American fundamentalism of the Semarang churches are well suited to the individualistic religious interests of the local Chinese. This is in great contrast to the situation in China, where the majority of the members and leaders of the Student Christian Movement, as well as a small but significant minority of other Christians, were deeply concerned not only with social service but with social reform.

Similarly, the revival of interest in Chinese religions in Indonesia, as symbolized in the Confucian societies and the Three Religions Society, is indicative of the fact that the perplexities facing the local Chinese are individual rather than social. These religions, as taught in Indonesia at least, emphasize personal righteousness and "peace of mind" for the individual. They do not attempt to give answers to social or political problems and are not expected to do so.

Note should be taken of the exceptions to the general line of argument here. In the Christian high schools of Semarang, about 39 per cent of the Chinese students claim no religion; the corresponding percentage in non-Christian schools is about 59 per cent. Some of these young people believe in ancestor worship or temple prayer, but do not consider that these involve "religion." The majority of them, however, have no religious convictions at all.

Many young people, though probably only a minority, have become proponents of Marxism or of Sun Yat-sen's Three Principles of the People. Among the older generation, a small minority has likewise found satisfaction in secular ideologies. But on the basis of experience in both China and Semarang, the writer has concluded that among persons of comparable education and social position the proportion who adhere to secular ideologies is very much smaller in Semarang than in China.

In summary, it may be said that, although many of the attitudes toward religion which are found in China are also characteristic of the Semarang Chinese community, local conditions have been such as to create a much greater interest in religion in Semarang than in China. For those seeking answers to the perplexities of the modern world, social ideologies have had the greatest appeal in China, whereas individualistic religions have been found more satisfying in Semarang.

Definitions of Religion and Magic

In the discussion of the various types of religion in the Chinese community of Semarang, use will be made of a distinction sometimes made by sociologists [8]—that is, the distinction between "religion" and "magic." Special definitions of these two terms will facilitate analysis and understanding of the functions of different

[8] See, for instance, Kingsley Davis, *Human Society* (New York, 1948), pp. 537–541, and Milton J. Yinger, *Religion, Society, and the Individual* (New York, 1957), pp. 41–42.

religions; but since they depart somewhat from common usage, it is important for the reader to keep in mind the particular meanings intended here. The two terms are defined as follows:

A *religion* is a system of beliefs and practices which (1) commands loyalty or reverence for certain deities, objects, or concepts, (2) provides sanction for certain social and individual moral standards, (3) attempts to give satisfying answers to major human perplexities, and (4) prescribes certain ceremonial or organizational behavior.

Magic is ritualistic activity intended to achieve concrete goals through the agency of nonempirical or supernatural forces or powers.

It should be noted that under these definitions religion does not necessarily involve belief in supernatural powers which can be induced, through prayer or ritual, to aid men in gaining desired ends. Such beliefs are here considered magical. Nevertheless, religious systems usually include magical beliefs, and religious ceremonial often includes magical ritual. In practice, there is no strict dichotomy between religion and magic. The distinction is primarily an analytical one.

Many Chinese in China and a few in Semarang maintain that Confucianism is not a religion, because it has no dogmas about the supernatural. Confucius sanctioned older forms of religion, especially ancestor worship, but his teachings were primarily ethical and somewhat agnostic. Thus it may be doubtful whether Confucianism is a "religion" in the popular sense. According to the definitions here it is certainly a religion, but a religion with virtually no magic connected with it, at least in its original form. It pays little attention to deities, but it involves loyalty and reverence for certain principles and institutions and also for Confucius himself. Similarly, Buddhism as taught by its founder contained very little magic. It might well be argued that the great religious prophets of all ages have paid little attention to magic—

that is, to means of gaining concrete, practical ends through super-natural intercession. Instead, their emphasis has been upon morality and devotion—or purely "religious" ideas, according to the present definition. Nevertheless, almost all religions, as popu-larly practiced today, include many magical elements. It is interest-ing to note that among the religions found in Chinese com-munities Confucianism contains the least amount of magic and popular Taoism probably contains the most. The amount of magic in Christianity usually falls somewhere between; it is found chiefly in petitionary prayer, but also in such elements as Catholic medals and fundamentalist faith healing.

As reported earlier, the questionnaire and interview surveys revealed a fairly large proportion of Semarang Chinese who claim to have "no religion." Many of these believe in ancestor worship and some pray at temples, at least occasionally. But they do not consider these activities "religious." About 42 per cent of the questionnaire respondents who said that they had "no religion" stated that they believe in ancestor worship. Under the definition as stated, however, ancestor worship must be regarded as a religion. Similarly, among the women of the interview survey who claimed to have no religion, about 33 per cent go to the temple to pray, at least occasionally. According to the definition, temple worship is largely magical, and the religious aspects are not so important. Temple worship is usually utilitarian and individualistic. It does not define one's responsibilities to other men. But to the limited extent that prayer to temple gods expresses emotional devotion or dutiful thanksgiving, it must be regarded as religious.

The functional significance of religion is quite different from that of magic. Religion serves emotional, and sometimes intellec-tual, needs—needs which are greatest in times of social transition or cultural confusion. Religion, in the sense defined, may mobilize and direct the energies of individuals, groups, or even whole so-cieties toward change; more often it supports existing institutions. Thus it may help either to integrate or to reintegrate a culture.

And religion usually contributes to solidarity and mutually beneficial morality within groups or communities. Magic, on the other
hand, is utilitarian and instrumental. It serves specific needs in
areas where empirical or scientific methods are inadequate. Psy-
chologically, it may function to reduce anxiety about such problems as sickness, business success, weather, the bearing of children,
and natural catastrophies. Where it involves group activity, it may
contribute to community solidarity; but among the Semarang
Chinese, at least, it is mostly individualistic.

Traditional Chinese Religion and Magic

Traditional Chinese religion and magic include such a wide
range of beliefs and practices, both in China and in Semarang,
that it is unrealistic to deal with them as a single religion. It is no
more realistic to divide them among the "three major Chinese
religions," Confucianism, Taoism, and Buddhism. A small minority of the Chinese in Semarang are willing to classify themselves
as adherents of one or another of these three religions. But even in
these cases, it is only a matter of emphasis; the three are almost
always found mixed together, though in different proportions.
Furthermore, there is a large body of common beliefs and practices which do not stem directly from any of the three.

In the description of traditional Chinese religion and magic in
Semarang, various elements which are present or absent, important or relatively unimportant, in the beliefs and practices of
different persons and families will be outlined. Individual cases
will be cited to show how the various elements may be combined
in different ways in practice.

Before ancestor worship, the worship of household gods, and
temple worship are discussed, it should be noted that certain basic
forms of ritual behavior are the same for all three. They consist
of the following major elements:

1. *The altar.* This varies from a simple table or shelf to elaborate and expensive shrines, according to the means of the family

or community. Household altars are usually placed at the back of the outer room of the house—whether it be a shop or a sitting room—or, in wealthy homes, in a special chapel. On every altar there is at least one incense urn. In addition, there are usually candlesticks, vases, and other ornaments.

2. *The offering of incense.* After lighting one or more incense sticks (usually three), the worshiper stands before the altar, holding them upright in his clasped hands. He then raises the incense before his face and lowers it a number of times, sometimes bowing slightly each time. While doing this, he prayerfully expresses his praise or respect, reports or asks for information, or requests advice or aid. Such prayers are usually said almost inaudibly or offered silently. An attitude of reverence is maintained, even if no prayer is offered. The ritual is complete when the incense sticks are placed upright in the altar censer.

3. *The prostrate bow.* In this ritual, known to the West as the "kowtow," the worshiper kneels before the altar and bows his head to the ground. This may be repeated a number of times, according to the situation. Usually the worshiper rises to a standing position after every third prostrate bow.

4. *Ceremonial food offering.* These offerings range from a few simple items, such as tea and rice, to the most lavish arrays of beverages, fruits, and prepared foods, dependent upon the occasion and the means of the family. When the offering is ready, the deities or ancestors' spirits are invited to partake, usually by prayer during the offering of incense. An intermediary deity called Toa Pek Kong (literally, Great Paternal Uncle) is often asked to summon the spirits to the feast, and he too is invited to join in. After a certain length of time—sometimes determined by the burning out of a large incense stick—it is assumed that the spirits have had their fill. The food is then eaten by the family or distributed to neighbors, friends, or visitors.

Virtually all the paraphernalia used in these basic rituals has symbolic meaning. For instance, altar candles signify uprightness and spiritual enlightenment; the ceremonial offering of wine symbolizes the purity of the worshiper in body and spirit; a certain type of cake is a token of long life.[9] Many who carry out these rituals are not aware of the symbolic meanings of the various objects, but in any case they treat them with respect or reverence.

Ancestor Worship

According to traditional Chinese belief, a person's spirit, after death, lives on in a world of spirits. Beliefs about this afterlife vary from indefinite notions of an eternal but shadowy existence to very concrete pictures of a series of courts of justice and diabolical torture chambers for the condemned. But whatever the concept of life in the hereafter may be, it is assumed that the welfare and happiness of the spirits of the dead depend to a very great extent upon the attentions of the living. People with traditional beliefs feel a strong obligation to their ancestors, and this obligation is fulfilled partly by the regular carrying out of the prescribed ritual duties of ancestor worship. These include the following:

1. Providing as elaborate and expensive a funeral and grave as the family can afford.

2. Observing prescribed rituals of mourning.

3. Visiting and cleaning the graves and performing ancestor rites before them, at least during the Tjing Bing festival in early April and sometimes also at the New Year or other times.

4. Maintaining a family altar and performing major ancestor rites before it, including the offering of incense, prostrate bowing, and elaborate food offerings, on at least four or five annual festival days and on the anniversary of the death of a deceased parent.

5. Performing less elaborate ancestor rites before the family altar on the first and fifteenth day of every month.

The traditional family altar is supposed to have ancestor tablets placed upon it, one for each deceased ancestor or married couple

[9] Lie Ping Lien, *Tentang Sembahjang Tuhan Allah (King Thi Kong)* (Semarang, 1950), pp. 10–12.

in the male line. About a foot high and three or four inches wide, these tablets are made of wood, with dragons or other figures finely carved upon them. In addition to the names and honorific titles of the deceased, a tablet usually bears the name of the reigning dynasty at the time of the death and the name of the person, usually the eldest son, who erects it. Each tablet is made of three pieces. Recorded in black ink on an inner surface are such details as the dates of birth and death of the deceased and the names of all the children. Actually, there are relatively few ancestor tablets in Semarang. There are no local craftsmen able to make them, and it is very expensive to order them from China. The tablets of the parents and ancestors of Totok families, and of some Peranakan families, are kept by relatives in China. Where there are no tablets, one or more pictures of important ancestors or a landscape painting are used instead.

In each family, it is the exclusive right and duty of the eldest living son to provide and maintain an altar, to care for the tablets, if any, and to see that the proper rites are observed, both at the altar and at the graves. His sons and his younger brothers and their sons are expected to participate in as many of the major rites as possible.

Almost half of the questionnaire respondents replied "yes" to the question: "Does your family have an ancestral altar?" It must be assumed that many of those who replied "yes" were referring to altars maintained in the homes of their paternal uncles, but visited by their own families on ceremonial days, or to altars maintained by relatives in China. On the other hand, it may be that many of the families of those who answered "no" also participate in ancestor rites outside their own homes. In spite of the unfortunate ambiguity of the question, however, the result may be taken to indicate that the maintenance of ancestor altars is still quite widespread in the Chinese community in Semarang. Families whose major altar is maintained in China or in the home of an elder relative often have subsidiary altars in their own houses.

Among the questionnaire respondents, just over half of the boys and about one-third of the girls reported that they themselves participate in family ancestor worship. But they indicated that about three-quarters of their fathers do. Although other factors are involved, the difference between generations may be accounted for partly by the fact that interest in carrying out ancestor rites is declining rather rapidly. Young people rarely care to make an issue out of it, however. Among both fathers and sons there are undoubtedly many participating in ancestor worship who intend to do so only so long as there are older members of the family who insist upon it. According to the questionnaire results, about one-quarter of the boys who do not believe in ancestor worship still participate in it. Chinese informants in Semarang were of the opinion that the proportion of young people who have no belief in ancestor worship but who participate out of deference to their elders is actually considerably higher than this. If so, many were reluctant to reveal the apparent inconsistency when replying to the questionnaire.

Table 5 shows the distribution of attitudes toward ancestor worship among male and female questionnaire respondents. Analysis of participation in ancestor worship by the parents of questionnaire respondents showed no significant difference between the relatively well-educated and the less well-educated groups. Nor is there any other evidence to suggest that Chinese young people in Semarang who are not in high school are significantly different from the questionnaire respondents in their attitudes toward ancestor worship. Thus the writer believes that Table 5 may be taken as a rough indication of the situation among all Chinese young people in Semarang.

Presumably the finding that more boys than girls believe in ancestor worship is partly due to the fact that it is primarily upon males that the responsibilities of carrying out ancestor rites fall. From an early age, boys are trained in the ritual and meaning of this religion, but girls receive very little instruction concerning it. By the same logic, elder brothers should show more belief in ancestor worship than do their younger brothers, because they are given more training and responsibility in ancestor rites. In the questionnaire data this was found to be the case, though the difference was not statistically significant.

Table 5. Belief in ancestor worship among Semarang high school students, by sex *

	Boys	Girls
Believe in ancestor worship	39%	25% †
Do not believe	45	56
No answer	16	19
	100%	100%
Number of cases	265	156

* Questionnaire respondents were asked to circle either "yes" or "no" after the question: "Do you believe in ancestor worship?"
† This figure is significantly different at the .01 level from the corresponding figure for boys.

The meaning of ancestor worship varies widely among those who participate in it. Probably the majority still believe quite literally that the spirits of their forebears come to the altar or grave on ceremonial occasions, observe their living descendants, hear their respectful prayers, and partake of the food offered them. Frequently ancestor rites are not begun until certain omens indicate that all the ancestors—who have been invited one by one in preliminary prayers—have actually arrived. On the other hand, the following view, written over fifty years ago by a Confucianist Peranakan, is an interpretation which would probably be accepted by many today—especially intellectuals and those familiar with the Chinese classics:

Of course, living people do not know whether or not the things which they offer are received and eaten. But such things are a sign that those who are worshiping still remember their ancestors or other relatives who are already in the spirit world.

If the spirits of the dead exist, it must be assumed that they can at least see the things which are offered them or that they can know that their family in this world still remembers them. This [assumption] is sufficient to satisfy those who are worshiping, who, because they do not cease to love, continue to want to serve.[10]

Rarely is there any magic involved in ancestor worship; that is, worshipers do not ask the spirits of their forebears for aid of a practical kind, since they do not believe that the spirits have supernatural powers in the material world. In rare cases, however, the ancestors are considered able to communicate directly with the living. A well-to-do professional man who had received his university training in Europe told the present writer:

I maintain our family altar because I am the oldest son: it is my duty. But it is more than that. When I am in difficulty or have a serious problem to solve, I go to the spirit of my father and ask his advice. On our altar are the ashes of my father, my grandfather, and my wife's father (since he had no sons). If my problem is especially serious, I go to my grandfather's spirit. They comfort and help me. You may believe it or not.

In most cases, however, the communication is believed to be one way only. Many families observe the traditional custom of giving regular reports about the conduct and welfare of the family, especially about such important events as births, marriages, and scholastic or commercial achievements. It is not uncommon for engaged couples to "introduce" each other to their ancestors before their respective family altars. These reports are an indication of the emphasis in ancestor worship on the behavior of the living.

[10] Quoted in Nio Joe Lan, *Riwajat 40 Taon dari Tiong Hoa Hwe Koan-Batavia (1900–1939)* (Batavia, 1940), p. 217.

Indeed, ancestor worship conceived as a religion cannot be separated from the kind of daily behavior which it prescribes for the living. In an excellent functional analysis of this religion, Marion Levy states: "Ancestor worship was in effect the canonization of the value of filial piety."[11] Designated by the Chinese word *hauw* (in Mandarin, *hsiao*), filial piety has very wide implications.

The basic idea of *hauw* is love, respect, and veneration for one's elders. Toward the living, it requires politeness, attentiveness, subservience, obedience, and care in old age. Toward the dead, it requires the observance of the rituals of ancestor worship as described above. Toward both living and dead, it prescribes these further obligations: to preserve one's body (for example, by avoiding danger) as a vehicle for the perpetuation of the family line; to defend and uphold the good name and reputation of the whole family; to maintain family habits and traditions; to increase the family fortunes as much as possible; and to provide a number of male heirs.

Hauw has even more general implications. The Confucianist Peranakan quoted above, after citing the Chinese saying that *hauw* is the basis of all moral behavior, explains it in this manner:

The child who sincerely loves and respects his parents will not do anything wrong or improper, for fear that his loving parents will be grieved or will get a bad name; he likes to do what is right, in order to give his parents a good name [literally, "fragrant name"], even if they are already in their graves.[12]

Thus ancestor worship is the ritual aspect of a religion of which the moral side comprises the traditional values and precepts of the Chinese family system. Ancestor worship not only supports and engenders the traditional values, but is also an expression of them: it is related to them as both cause and effect. Rituals, beliefs, and morals are mutually reinforcing. In view of the rapid growth

[11] Levy, *op. cit.,* p. 250.   [12] Quoted in Nio, *op. cit.,* p. 215.

of Christian religions, of rationalism, and of secular social and political ideologies in Semarang since World War I, it is perhaps surprising to find that about 40 per cent of Chinese high school boys there still believe in ancestor worship. Undoubtedly the main explanation for the persistence of these beliefs lies in the functional relationship between ancestor worship and the family system. Compared to most industrialized societies, at least, the traditions of family solidarity, family continuity, and filial piety are still very strong among the Chinese of Semarang. While they remain strong, ancestor worship receives support from them.

On the other hand, as will be shown in subsequent chapters, the family system is undergoing change away from the traditional patterns. Many Chinese express the opinion that the general decline in the observance of ancestor rites in the Chinese community is caused by the rising cost of ritual paraphernalia and special food offerings and by the increasing difficulty of coming together at family altars or graves, as families become more and more widely scattered geographically. These are no doubt significant factors. But in the view of the writer, the attraction of competing religions and ideologies and emergent family patterns incompatible with traditional filial piety are more important. There are continuing trends toward individualism, toward a narrowing of loyalties down to the immediate family, toward more equalitarian family attitudes and practices, and toward less strictness in child training. The new patterns fail to produce the feelings of strong obligation to and reverence for one's elders which are basic to ancestor worship. Indeed, ancestor worship is so closely tied to a family system which appears to be gradually passing away that it seems unlikely to survive, unless in greatly modified form, beyond two or three more generations.

Household Gods

The worship of household gods is not nearly so widespread in the Chinese community as is ancestor worship. According to informants, it is now relatively rare to keep a kitchen god and to observe the traditional New Year's ceremony of dispatching him to heaven to make his annual report on the behavior of the family. On the other hand, it is not uncommon to maintain a special altar for a particular god who has been traditionally worshiped in a given family. By far the most popular household gods in Semarang are Kwan Iem, the Buddhist Goddess of Mercy, and Kwan Kong, the legendary hero who has become the God of War. Kwan Iem is believed to be especially capable of answering prayers, particularly the prayers of women for children and for family welfare. Kwan Kong is believed to make men courageous and successful in their undertakings. Both these gods are also commonly found in public temples.

Like the ancestors, household gods are worshiped with prayers and food offerings on the first and fifteenth of each lunar month, on their supposed birthdays, and on other special days. They are also petitioned for special assistance whenever the family faces difficulties or uncertainties. Household gods, particularly images of Kwan Iem, sometimes get a reputation for especial potency throughout a neighborhood, and friends and neighbors often take their petitions to them instead of to a temple. Children may be ceremonially given in adoption to a household god, in the hope that they will receive special protection and assistance.

In the worship of household gods, there are varying mixtures of religion and magic. Like temple gods, they are expected to provide direct magical assistance. But they receive much more regular worship and veneration arising from nonutilitarian, religious motives than do temple gods. In the following example, the worship of a household god is linked to the religion of ancestor worship, with very little thought of deriving specific benefits from it.

In the home of Sie King Hwat, an intellectual of modest means, the writer was shown two altars. Over the ancestor altar were portraits of Mr. Sie's deceased parents; the family ancestor tablets were being maintained in China. Over the other altar was a large scroll painting of Kwan Kong and his two associates, with vertical inscriptions in large Chinese characters on either side. On the altar before this picture was an offering of three cups of wine and incense burning in a censer. Mr. Sie explained: "My father honored Kwan Kong. What my father honored, I dare not change. Everything is exactly as before."

In addition to gods for whom there are special altars, another god, the highest and most powerful of all, is worshiped in traditional Chinese households. By Peranakans this god is commonly called "Tuhan Allah"—a combination of a Malay and an Arabic word. In the Hokkian dialect used by most Totoks, the name commonly used is Thi Kong. More scholarly persons equate this god with the Thian and the Siang Tee of the Confucian classics, whereas narrators of folk legends use the name Giok Hong Siang Tee, which is probably of Taoist origin. At any rate, this god is regarded as the supreme ruler of heaven and earth, and is conceived to be omniscient and omnipotent.

On the ninth day of the first month of the Chinese lunar calendar, Tuhan Allah is honored in special ceremonies in all traditional Chinese homes. The worship of Tuhan Allah is also a formal part of all traditional wedding ceremonies. On these occasions no idol or other representation of the god is used, but a special high altar is set up for elaborate food offerings and the ceremonial offering of incense. On lesser occasions, such as the first and fifteenth of each lunar month, prayers to Tuhan Allah are addressed toward the sky, preferably from a doorway. In many homes, the main doorway is equipped with a small metal holder, where incense is placed after worship of Tuhan Allah. (Prayer with incense in the doorway is common also when the spirits of the ancestors are invited to major ceremonies, either directly or through the intermediary god, Toa Pek Kong.)

Although Tuhan Allah may be petitioned for aid, it is customary to go to lesser gods for particular types of assistance: their powers are more specific, if theoretically less potent. The major component in the worship of Tuhan Allah is thus, in most cases, religious: prayers to this god usually express veneration, gratitude, and praise, without any request for magical aid.

Temples and Temple Gods

There are thirteen temples in Semarang. With few exceptions, their architecture and decoration are patterned after temples in the emigrant areas of China. They are well cared for by neighborhood or community committees. Voluntary contributions, their major source of income, are sufficient to keep most of them in good repair. Some also derive revenue from landholdings.

The worship of temple gods is carried out individually, by the ceremonial offering of incense and sometimes by prostrate bowing as well. Most temples are not visited except on the first and fifteenth of each lunar month and on special feast days. But one may find worshipers in the major temples at almost any time. On important ceremonial days, there is a steady stream of people worshiping at the minor temples, and crowds pass through the major temples.

In addition to individual worship, there are regular public ceremonies and food offerings before temple gods. These are arranged and paid for by an officer called the *lotju* and his assistant. The two men are chosen annually from among applicants. This is done by means of a ritual drawing of lots, which is believed to express the will of the presiding god of each temple. As expenses usually exceed public contributions for ceremonial occasions, the *lotju* may suffer considerable financial loss. Thus the office is considered a religious duty or privilege, rather than a business proposition. The *lotju* is responsible for public ceremonies ranging from simple food offerings on the first and fifteenth of each lunar month to elaborate sacrificial feasts and rituals on major festival days and on the traditional birthdays of the presiding gods in each temple. On the most important of these ceremonial occasions, the *lotju* also provides public entertainment in front of the temple, sometimes for several days or even weeks: puppet performances of Chinese classical operas; Chinese, Javanese, or mixed orchestras, folk or modern; Javanese shadow-puppet (*wajang*) plays; performances by Javanese women dancers and singers; demonstrations of traditional Chinese "shadowboxing"; and performances by the lion and dragon teams of Chinese ceremonial societies.

Of the thirteen temples in Semarang, five are small neighborhood temples. The first of these was built about 1753, and the most recent in 1901.[13] In each case, the main god is Thouw Tee Kong, the earth god or neighborhood god, who is expected to maintain the prosperity of the people living in the locality and to protect them from calamity. This god is given the honorific title Hok Tik Tjing Sien (the True Spirit of Blessed Virtue), but is often merely called Toa Pek Kong (literally, Great Paternal Uncle), a name commonly used in Semarang for all intermediary spirits and minor gods.

In the first section of this chapter, there was mentioned a pilgrimage to Welahan on the occasion of the "birthday" of a temple god there. This god, Hian Thian Siang Tee (God of the Profound Heavens), has long been famous for miraculous healing powers. In 1905, a wealthy devotee established what might be called a "branch" temple in Semarang, where another idol of the same god was enshrined with great ceremony.[14] Every year since that time, as part of the birthday festivities, sacred ashes have been taken from the altar of the Welahan temple to "renew" the ashes in the incense urns before the idol in the Semarang temple. Although there are other temple gods in Semarang from whom cures may be sought and although some people still make the trip to Welahan for that purpose, the local temple of Hian Thian Siang Tee is visited by a relatively large number of people seeking supernatural medical aid or giving thanks for past cures. The beliefs

[13] Liem Thian Joe, *Riwajat Semarang* (Semarang, c. 1933), pp. 24, 172.
[14] *Ibid.*, p. 183.

and practices of temple healing will be discussed further in a later section of this chapter.

It is interesting to note that although Hian Thian Siang Tee is well known in China he is not known there for special healing powers.[15] On the other hand, very few of his worshipers in Indonesia are familiar with the traditional legends about this god, which originate primarily from the Chinese classic *Pak Joe*. When questioned about his origin, one Semarang informant stated that he was a heroic early settler, "perhaps a sailor of Sam Po." A newspaper "history" of Semarang relates that he was shipwrecked on the coast and was later deified by his followers, who settled down in Welahan.[16] Neither story is compatible with the original Chinese legends.

In four of the temples of Semarang, ancestor rites are carried out before the ancestor tablets of former residents of the city. The four temples are very different from one another. One of them, the largest temple in Semarang, was originally built in 1814 as a shrine for the ancestor tablets of a family by the name of Tan. For three generations this family was the wealthiest and most powerful Chinese family in all central Java. By the turn of the century, however, the fortunes of the descendants of the original founder had collapsed, and other families with the same name had achieved greater prominence. As a result, the temple was put into the hands of an association, the membership of which was open to everyone bearing the surname Tan. This association still attends to the finances and upkeep of the temple, and maintains regular ancestor rites there. At present, neither the chairman of this association nor the *lotju* is a descendant of the original founder of the temple, and only a portion of the 176 ancestor tablets which are regularly worshiped there represent members of

[15] See, for example, Rev. Justus Doolittle, *The Social Life of the Chinese* (London, 1868), p. 204.

[16] *De Locomotief*, Jubilee Number, May 5, 1951, pt. III, pp. 1–3. For another version of this story, see Liem, *op. cit.*, p. 7.

the original lineage. Two idols are also worshiped in this temple: Hok Tik Tjing Sien, the usual earth god or guardian spirit, and Khay Tjiang Sing Ong, the patron god of the Tan family. According to a stone tablet in the temple, the latter was the man, Tan Goan Kong, who "civilized" the people of Amoy in the Sung Dynasty.[17]

In Semarang, as in China, almost every surname is as common as is Smith in America, and some are very much more common. On the basis of several lists of names (including the Semarang telephone directory), the writer estimates that about one out of every eight Chinese in Semarang bears the surname Tan. Similarly, about one out of every eight is named Liem. Until recently, the Chinese generally assumed that all people bearing the same surname must be descendants of a common, though very remote, ancestor. Thus it was not unnatural for the Tan family temple to become a center for ancestor rites for all people of the same surname who cared to participate. The precedent had already been set by an association of Liems, who founded a common ancestral temple in 1881 close by the Tan temple. Such "surname temples" may be found in other parts of Southeast Asia, but not in China, where participation in ancestral temples was confined to paternal kin of known relationship.

A Semarang "surname temple" of a different type is that maintained by an association of persons bearing the name Kwee. This association established the temple about 1756, primarily for the worship of an early merchant-settler by the name of Kwee Lak Kwa, whose legendary supernatural powers led to his deification by the local Chinese community. An idol representing this personage was ordered from China and was given the honorific title Tek Hay Tjin Djin (The Immortal of the Shining Sea). This deity is also worshiped as a central figure in the main community temple in Pekalongan, a town on the north coast of Java near the site of Kwee Lak Kwa's legendary ascension into the heavens. Among

[17] Liem, *op. cit.*, p. 85.

the tablets worshiped in the Semarang Kwee family temple is that of Kwee Kiauw, the first Chinese captain of Semarang, who held that position from 1672 to 1684.

Another temple where ancestor tablets are worshiped is the Kong Tik Soe, a relatively large Chinese-style edifice adjacent to the main Buddhist-Taoist temple of the city, the Tay Kak Sie. The Kong Tik Soe was built in 1845 on the initiative of several community leaders, including Majors Tan Hong Yan and Be Ing Tjioe. The purpose of the temple, carved in Chinese on a stone tablet along with the names and donations of 123 contributors, was given as follows:

The central section of this edifice is for the worship of the ancestor tablets of those who give large contributions, and the side sections are for the tablets of persons who have no heirs. In addition, this building is intended to give shelter to travelers in distress, and to widowers, widows, and orphans that are to be pitied, and will serve also as a charity school to give education to children. All these are matters which must be attended to in this locality and cannot be neglected.[18]

The altars in the central hall of this temple are still devoted entirely to the ancestor tablets of wealthy persons, childless persons, and persons who do not expect their children to maintain the customary rituals. (A Dutch-educated Peranakan businessman informed the writer that he had already reserved a place in this temple for the tablet of his father, who is still living.) Ancestor rituals are regularly carried out in the main hall. In a side room, a Toa Pek Kong, or guardian spirit, is also worshiped. Other rooms in the building, once occupied by the Kongkoan, are now used by the Khong Kauw Hwee (Confucian Society) and its charity school, which will be described later.

The newest temple in Semarang is the "Women's Temple," established after World War II. Worshipers and supporters are all women, and the presiding deity is the goddess Kwan Iem.

The earliest temple in Semarang was also dedicated to Kwan

[18] Translated from a Malay version, as given in Liem, *op. cit.*, p. 106.

Iem. Ever since it was moved to its present site and rebuilt on a grander scale in 1771,[19] it has been the major center of traditional worship and ceremonial for the Semarang Chinese community. It is the Tay Kak Sie (Temple of Great Comprehension), which stands adjacent to the Kong Tik Soe temple. Since 1771, many changes and additions have been made. Although a small representation of Kwan Iem is now enshrined in the center of the main hall, the place of highest honor at the back of the hall is taken by three large gilded idols representing the Three Incarnations of Buddha.

Of the fourteen major idols worshiped in the shrines surrounding the three courtyards of the Tay Kak Sie temple, many are traditional Chinese deities of non-Buddhist origin. One of these, Poo Sing Tay Tee (Great Protector of Life), is considered especially potent in the healing of disease. Every year, on the anniversary of the arrival of this idol from China, it is carried through the streets of Semarang in a magnificent procession which includes temple banners and paraphernalia, Chinese and Indonesian orchestras, numerous floats depicting mythical and legendary scenes, costumed acrobats and clowns, and the impressive lions and dragons of the ceremonial societies.

Sam Po

The procession arranged for Poo Sing Tay Tee is, however, overshadowed each year by the even more magnificent parade in honor of Sam Po. For this reason the former god is popularly referred to as Sam Po Tjilik, or "Little Sam Po." This is but one indication of the fact that, of all the temple gods worshiped by traditional Chinese in Semarang, Sam Po is closest to their hearts and highest in their esteem. It is Sam Po who is considered most potent in protecting and prospering their community. It is said that in 1945, when authorities of the British occupation forces in Semarang advised the Chinese to evacuate the city, a delegation went to the Sam Po temple for guidance. Through the altar oracle

[19] Liem, *op. cit.*, pp. 48–49.

sticks, the god gave assurance that the Chinese of Semarang would not be harmed. There was no general evacuation at that time.[20]

Sam Po's position as the "patron saint" of the Semarang Chinese community seems to date from at least as early as the beginning of the eighteenth century. According to one source, the original cave which Sam Po was believed to have occupied during his supposed visit to Semarang in 1406 collapsed in 1704; soon afterward a new cave was dug, and idols of Sam Po and his four attendants, brought from China along with various ritual paraphernalia, were enshrined there.[21]

The earliest recorded worship of Sam Po in Semarang was in 1724, when the Chinese community held public ceremonies of thanksgiving at the site of the cave. To Sam Po was ascribed the growing prosperity of Chinese commerce in the area, as well as the freedom from disasters and disturbances. At this time a small pavilion was erected just outside the cave.[22] Since then, and especially since 1950, the Sam Po temple has grown into an impressive complex of shrines, pavilions, courts, gardens, and ornamental gateways and bridges. Most of this has been accomplished through the donations of wealthy merchants, some of whom had had their health restored after praying to Sam Po or to Kiai Djuru Mudi, whose tomb is near the cave.

Since Kiai Djuru Mudi is believed to have been either an Indonesian religious teacher or Sam Po's Islamic navigator, worship at his tomb is often done by burning spicewood or offering flowers according to Indonesian custom. Indeed, Indonesians may also be seen worshiping at his tomb, and on special days of the Chinese and Javanese calendars, many people of both ethnic groups come to worship and often to sleep in the temple grounds.

The annual parade in honor of Sam Po occurs on the last day of the sixth lunar month. This day is considered by some to be Sam

[20] De Locomotief, loc. cit.
[21] Tju Kie Hak Siep, Riwajat Sam Poo Tay Djien (Semarang, c. 1954), p. 20.
[22] Liem, op. cit., p. 20.

Po's birthday and by others to be the date of his original landing at the harbor of Semarang. With oriental pomp and grandeur, the idol of Sam Po is escorted by a lengthy procession to the Tay Kak Sie temple at the center of the Chinese quarter of Semarang and is returned the following day. Impressive ritual and ceremonial take place at both temples with the arrival and departure of the parade. Traditional Chinese annual festivals are also celebrated in grand style at the Sam Po temple.

The importance of Sam Po as a powerful and awe-inspiring deity is attested by the fact that in the most serious law suits Chinese witnesses may be required to take their oaths before the idol of Sam Po and sometimes also to "drink ashes" from the sacred urns on the altar. During the writer's stay in Semarang, this was done in two different cases. In one of these, which involved adultery and 200,000 rupiahs in blackmail, the Indonesian defense lawyer obtained permission from the judge to require nine Chinese witnesses to take their oaths and "drink ashes" at the Sam Po temple, while the single Indonesian witness took her oath before the dais of the central mosque of the city.

There is a more religious attitude toward Sam Po than toward the other temple gods of Semarang, in that more of the public and private worship of this deity reflects reverence, awe, and adulation, without utilitarian aims. There is no doubt, however, that the main function even of this deity is magical, since most of those who go to the Sam Po temple to worship are seeking direct supernatural assistance. Through the altar oracle sticks, worshipers receive guidance and help in such matters as choosing auspicious dates for important events, selecting or sanctioning marriage partners for children, promoting family prosperity or fertility, determining the sex of unborn children, and healing disease. The faith of the Semarang Chinese in the oracular powers of Sam Po may be judged from the following story, paraphrased from a history of Semarang by Liem Thian Joe, a present-day journalist and local historian:

In 1900, the Chinese of a certain street in Semarang began to build a neighborhood temple. Because of the objections of Arabs living close by, the municipal authorities ordered the construction to cease. Efforts to obtain permission to complete the temple were fruitless. Neither lawyers nor the Chinese Major were able to do anything. Finally, the officials of the proposed temple went to the cave shrine of Sam Po and received an oracle something like this:

> Construction may go on,
> For help is at hand,
> From a man you may meet,
> Whose home I'll point out.
>
> His residence is clear,
> Just Southwest of here.
> If you find the man,
> Your work won't be banned.

For several days the temple officials puzzled over this. It finally occurred to them that it might apply to a certain Dutch "surveyor" whose home was southwest of the proposed temple site. Through the aid of this man, a petition was sent directly to the Governor General of the Indies. The Governor General authorized the building of the temple, and it was completed the following year.[23]

In order to check the possible authenticity of this account, the present writer investigated a reproduction of the oracle book of the Sam Po temple. In the written explanation of the mystical verse corresponding to oracle stick number 25, the following words occur:

> For all troublesome matters, such as a grounded ship,
> Even if extreme difficulties have been encountered,
> To the Southwest there is a way.[24]

[23] *Ibid.*, pp. 170–172.
[24] Literal translation of the Chinese, which appears in Kam Seng Kioe, *Sam Po* (Semarang, c. 1955), p. 136.

Many legends attesting the supernatural powers of Sam Po have been passed from generation to generation in the Chinese community. The following is an example:

One day, about the year 1600, a Chinese went to worship in the cave where the Sam Po idol was enshrined. Several weeks later, as he had not returned home, his friends and relatives went to find him. But he had disappeared. They returned to the cave daily, but found not a trace.

Eight months later his relatives received a letter from him, sent from China. It told a miraculous story: He spent twenty days in worship and meditation in the cave of Sam Po. Then, in the night, it seemed that men came and lifted him up and placed him in a well in front of the altar to Sam Po. When he opened his eyes the next morning, he found himself on the banks of the river in his home village in China.[25]

The account that follows, written by a Chinese traveler who visited Semarang about 1783, shows the early importance of Sam Po in legend, ritual, and belief:

At Semarang there is a cave, called Sam-po's cave, at which it is commonly reported, that wonders are wrought; and every new and full moon, our Chinese ladies and gentlemen go in crowds to worship at the place.[26]

There are, of course, many Semarang Chinese who give no credence to the supposed supernatural powers of Sam Po. Nevertheless, he is regarded by virtually the whole Chinese community as a national or racial hero of special local importance. Therefore local newspapers, magazines, and books year after year tell and retell the legends and historical accounts of Sam Po's voyages. They also emphasize the interest, beauty, and popularity of the Sam Po temple as a place of pilgrimage.

[25] *Ibid.*, p. 14.

[26] Ong Tai Hae, *The Chinaman Abroad; or, A Desultory Account of the Malayan Archipelago, Particularly of Java* (English trans., Shanghai, 1849), p. 21.

Annual Festivals

Most of the annual festivals and holidays traditional in China are also celebrated by the Chinese in Indonesia. In different cities different festivals may assume major importance. Tjap Go Meh (the Spring Festival) in Djakarta and Pehtjun (the Dragon Boat Festival) in Djuana are celebrated with considerably greater public festivities than in Semarang. In addition to the days celebrated in honor of Sam Po and Poo Sing Tay Tee, the most important festivals in the Semarang community are the following:

The New Year. This is primarily a family festival, a period of at least a week during which adults and children alike devote themselves to feasting, entertaining and visiting relatives, dressing in fine new clothes, giving presents, and indulging in various kinds of amusement. In traditional families, worship and ceremonial food offerings before the ancestral altar are an important part of the festivities, as well as temple and home worship of certain gods.

Tjing Bing. Sometimes referred to as the Feast of the Tombs, this is also primarily a family celebration. During the first days of April, crowds of Chinese may be seen going and coming along the roads to the graveyards in the hills in the outskirts of Semarang. The tombs are cleaned, swept, and repaired, and elaborate offerings of food and ritual worship are carried out before the tombstones of deceased parents and grandparents. The graves of remoter relatives are also visited, and ancestor rites are performed at the home altar as well. Many Christians and persons of no religion also visit family graves, and pay their respects in their own way.

King Hoo Ping. Known among Peranakans as Sembahjang Rebutan (which might be translated "Snatch Away Festival"), this is a period at the end of the seventh lunar month, during which public ceremonies honor the wandering spirits of those who have no descendants to pay homage to them. On successive days, the rites are carried out in four or five different parts of Semarang, including at least two temple courtyards. In each place, an elaborate altar and a large platform are constructed. The platform, from four to twelve feet high, is covered with a lavish display of offerings, including fruit, cooked delicacies, pastries and steamed breads, bags of rice, yardgoods, and fancy paper flags and decorations. A monk and two local officiants (the *lotju* and his assistant) perform a complicated ritual, and a large number of men, women, and children pay their respects to the wandering spirits by incense offering and prostrate bowing. Suddenly many of the bystanders, mostly Indonesians, clamber onto the platform and scramble for as much of the food and other offerings as they can gather. The officiants and their assistants offer token resistance, but the platform is completely looted within a few minutes, amid general hilarity. Hence the name "Snatch Away Festival."

Tiong Tjhioe. This, the Mid-Autumn Festival or Moon Festival, is celebrated on the fifteenth of the eighth lunar month. Special "moon cakes" are enjoyed by all and are included in ceremonial food offerings to the ancestors. As on other festival days, public worship is performed at various temples, and entertainment provided in temple courtyards includes Chinese, Indonesian, or modern orchestras and Chinese or Indonesian puppet shows.

As has been suggested above, these and some of the other festivals are celebrated not only by adherents of traditional Chinese religion. The majority of Christians and agnostics observe some of them too, by maintaining at least their secular traditions. Like Valentine's Day in the West, what were once primarily religious festivals have survived among people who have lost or changed their religious faith. They have survived by secularization. Writing of the Spring Festival in a contemporary popular magazine, a Peranakan author said:

Those of us who are "modernists" need not regard the Tjap-Go Meh festival from a religious point of view; instead, we should regard it as a cultural institution which we have a responsibility to maintain as best we can.[27]

The continued celebration of the New Year according to the old lunar calendar is an indication of the "survival power" of traditional festival holidays. The Western calendar has long been used in Semarang for all practical purposes. Logic and sometimes even nationalism have made January 1 a rival date for New Year's festivities. After the 1911 revolution in China, successive Chinese governments usually discouraged the celebration of the traditional New Year. The feeling grew, at least in the middle class, that this was a peasant festival inappropriate to modern life. Only the Western calendar was officially recognized, and the printing and the sale of traditional lunar calendars were even prohibited in some parts of China under the Kuomintang.

At the end of 1912, the new republican government of China informed the Semarang Sianghwee that New Year celebrations were being transferred by law from the first of the traditional lunar year to January 1 and suggested that the overseas Chinese should follow suit. At the next meeting of the Sianghwee, this proposition was discussed. It was agreed that since the lunar date had been celebrated for thousands of years, it was a tradition difficult to change. The Sianghwee finally took the position that it was a matter for each individual to decide for himself.[28] The Semarang Chinese have continued to celebrate the traditional date ever since, with both family and community festivities. Among the fifty families covered in the interview survey, every one celebrates the traditional New Year's holidays; only three Christian and three non-Christian families have some kind of festivities on January 1, and these are in addition to celebrations at the traditional time.

[27] *Star Weekly*, no. 475 (Feb. 5, 1955), p. 30.
[28] *Boekoe Peringetan, 1907–1937, Tiong Hwa Siang Hwee, Semarang* (Semarang, 1937), p. 16.

Magical Beliefs and Practices

The concept of magic used here is a very broad one. It includes every prescription as to what one should do in order to gain the assistance of supernatural forces for concrete ends, as well as prescriptions and proscriptions as to how to avoid the misfortunes which supernatural or mystical forces might otherwise bring about. For example, the simple conviction that to break any household article on New Year's Day will bring bad luck is a traditional magical belief of the Semarang Chinese. The use of paper charms over doorways is a magical practice still widespread in the Chinese community. A comprehensive catalogue of such beliefs and practices could not possibly be included here. Instead, a few of the most important will be discussed.

The belief that certain days are propitious and others inauspicious is still widespread in the Chinese community. Some use the traditional Chinese calendar to determine such days. However, among Peranakans at least, it is more common to use the Javanese calendar, or *nogo dino*. In selecting a date for travel or for a wedding or a funeral, many consult both calendars. In case of conflict, the Javanese calculation is often given more credence, because it is considered to be adjusted to the environment. Recently, a wedding was set for a certain date, on the basis of the *nogo dino*. After the invitations were sent out, it was discovered that according to traditional Chinese calculations the date chosen was an extremely unlucky one. The families concerned became alarmed and consulted various authorities as to what they should do. They finally decided not to change the date, after one local sage explained that the Chinese calculations were not applicable in Java because of the differences in natural environment.

There is considerable interest in various kinds of astrology among the Semarang Chinese. The newspapers devote regular columns to it, and other periodicals have fairly frequent articles on horoscopy and traditional magic.[29] Pai Ching Tze, a Semarang astrologer who advertises 25-rupiah consultations, recently published a book on the "secrets" of his art.

The Chinese community has always had its diviners and practitioners of astrology and horoscopy, both professional and amateur. Originally these were men well versed in Chinese magical lore, with an impressive knowledge of religious and mystical classics in the Chinese language. In recent years, however, Western and other Eastern astrological and magical traditions have been added to, or have even supplanted, the ancient Chinese techniques, at least among some Peranakan practitioners whose knowledge of the Chinese written language is weak.

The aid of astrologers and diviners is sought in such matters as forecasting future events, choosing auspicious dates for public or private events, selecting marriage partners, or giving propitious names to children. They may also be consulted in matters of *hong soei* (in Mandarin, *feng-shui*). This is the Chinese system of geomancy by which sites for graves, houses, or other buildings are chosen. The degree of good fortune or ill fortune which may be expected from the use of a given site is determined by such circumstances as the nature of the soil and the relative direction of hills, streams, lakes, or temples. The following account will illustrate the traditional importance of geomantic beliefs in the Chinese community.

In 1924, the Semarang municipal government decided to fill in a stagnant pond in the Chinese quarter, because it was considered a dangerous source of malarial mosquitoes. Once before, the Chinese had raised objections to filling this pond, because it was believed to mark the center of the city and to be necessary to the continuing good fortune of the community. A public meeting [Kok Sia Thoan] was now called to discuss the question. At least thirteen Chinese organizations sent representatives, and the Chinese officers, from ward

[29] See, for instance, "Horoscoop Bung Karno," *Liberal,* III, no. 72 (Jan. 22, 1955), 2–3.

heads to the Major for Semarang, were present. The Dutch assistant commissioner, who had been invited to be chairman of the meeting, explained the decision of the municipal council and added that it was thought that by this time the superstitions with regard to the pond might have diminished greatly. Apparently such was not the case, however, for the assembly passed a resolution requesting the municipal government not only to leave the pond, but to repair it and to clean it periodically. It also sent a petition to the Governor General in Batavia, requesting that the beliefs of the Chinese community with regard to the pond should not be violated.

Two years later, the Chinese were informed that the Governor General had acceded to their desires and that the Health Department would clear the pool of mosquito larvae every month. In 1930, the municipal government built conduits to and from the pond, so that the water could be kept running and the periodic cleaning could be dispensed with.[30]

Belief in geomancy, as in other forms of magic, is gradually declining in the Chinese community. But the fact that it is still important to many people may be seen from the sequel to the above story:

A few years ago, a turning truck knocked down part of the wall which separates the pond from the narrow street. Public contributions were collected not only to repair the wall, but also to put up iron posts to protect it. And every year, on the twenty-ninth day of the twelfth lunar month, public worship ceremonies are held at the site of the pond.

Probably the most prevalent form of "magic" in the Chinese community today is the seeking of direct supernatural aid from temple gods. General health, wealth, or well-being may be asked for, or specific desires, such as the birth of a male child. Such requests may be made in simple, direct prayers or through the ritual use of oracle sticks, which are believed to reveal whether the worshiper's prayers will be answered. On the altar before certain gods, there is a large bamboo container in which are placed twenty-eight

[30] Liem, *op. cit.*, pp. 262–263, 270–271.

oracle sticks, each bearing a number. After respectful worship and some magical ritual, the petitioner shakes the container until one stick falls out. The temple attendant then interprets the god's reply by reference to a book which contains a picture from a legend, a portrait of a mythical figure, a mystical verse, and an "explanation" for each numbered stick. In many cases, petitioners make a vow promising to fulfill some service to the god if their prayers are answered—for example, a large contribution, a new altar, or bimonthly worship over a period of years.

As already noted, certain gods are considered to have special healing powers—especially, in Semarang, Hian Thian Siang Tee, Sam Po, and Poo Sing Tay Tee. In the case of such gods, another container of sticks is provided on the altar in addition to or instead of oracle sticks. The petitioner is not healed on the spot, but receives from the temple attendant a prescription for a herbal remedy the ingredients of which may be obtained at a traditional Chinese medicine shop. In the case of the Sam Po temple, there are ninety-nine such prescriptions, corresponding to the numbers on the altar sticks.

There are several traditional Chinese medical practitioners in Semarang and about fifty Western-trained doctors, half of them Chinese. They are all well patronized by the Chinese community. Occasionally, too, Chinese go to Indonesian practitioners, or *dukun*. In addition, there is a very large commerce in patent medicines, which are advertised as home cures for everything from common colds to old age and impotence. Nevertheless, many Semarang Chinese go to the temple gods for medical aid or at least patronize them when other methods have failed. The following are three of the many stories of temple cures which were told to the writer by persons involved.

An import-export businessman, with a modern Chinese high school education, had kidney trouble. Western-trained doctors were unable to help him. He took the advice of friends and went to the temple of Hian Thian Siang Tee. Since he was ignorant of temple worship, the temple assistant helped him through the ritual. He received a prescription which required him to drink the soup formed by boiling certain herbs inside a whole duck for two hours. His ailment was completely cured, and he now returns to the temple more or less regularly to offer thanks.

The daughter of a bank cashier and a midwife (both Dutch educated) became seriously ill. The parents "wasted" 800 rupiahs on doctors, but Western medicine could not help the child. So they went to a temple god and got a prescription which directed them to boil certain herbal leaves in water and then administer the water as medicine. This cost them only 10 rupiahs, but it cured the child. When the child was well, they took her to the temple to express their gratitude. Since that time they have continued to worship at the temple on the fifteenth of every month and have sought cures for other ailments there.

A Western-educated Peranakan doctor told of one of his patients who had cancer in the arm. After checking his diagnosis by X-ray and consultation with three other doctors, two of them Dutch, he recommended amputation. The patient refused, and obtained a "cure" from a temple god instead. Some time later the doctor examined the patient's arm and could find no sign of the former ailment.

A further indication of the amount of faith put in temple medical aid may be obtained from the questionnaire results. The following question was asked:

Mr. and Mrs. K remained childless after being married for many years. Friends advised them to pray for children at some well-known holy place. What is your opinion of the advice given by their friends?

The following are some of the replies given by Chinese high school students:

Such things are possible, but it is better to be examined by a doctor.

I consider the advice correct, because from my own experience in several situations I know that it is a fact that really genuine prayers may be answered.

My opinion is that the friends' advice was pure superstition, and I never approve behavior that is not logical.

Their prayers might be answered if they have faith.

Concerning such holy places, I don't really know. But sometimes prayers at such places are answered. So if the K's have faith in them, they should try it out.

They may follow their friends' advice—it's no trouble to try!

Better to adopt a child of good parentage, if they want to have a child who will someday repay their troubles.

In a statistical analysis of the replies to this question, no significant difference between Chinese Protestants, Catholics, and persons of no religion was found, except that a number of the Catholics suggested "praying to God" instead. In all three groups, about 13 per cent approved of the "magical" advice given, and about 6 per cent thought it would be all right to try prayers at some holy place, at least if the persons concerned had faith in them. Of the respondents who adhere to traditional Chinese religion, 19 per cent gave unqualified approval to such prayers, and a further 32 per cent considered them worth trying.

Interpretation of these results must be cautious, because of the ambiguity of the question. The wording was intentionally vague, so that the question would be equally applicable to Chinese temples and to Indonesian tombs and holy places. It may be, however, that some of the Christians had Christian shrines in mind when they indicated approval. If the Christians are omitted, it is safe to say that at least a tenth of the Chinese students in Semarang have faith in temple "magic," and another tenth might at least be willing tc try it. Since high school students are one of the least traditional groups in the community, it may be concluded that a substantial proportion of the Chinese in Semarang believe in the efficacy of temple prayer. And many who usually consult doctors may go to a temple as a last resort.

The Persistence of Traditional Religion and Magic

Ordinarily, the persistence of tradition needs no special explanation: it passes with apparent ease from one generation to the next by teaching and example. It is primarily deviation, innovation, and cultural change which call for explanation.

In the case of the Chinese community in Semarang, however, as brought out in Chapter II, there have been unusually strong historical influences against maintaining traditional beliefs and customs—that is, the effects of living among and intermarrying with the Indonesian people, the education and example given by the powerful and respected Dutch colonials, and the attraction of a modernist ideology associated with a strong Chinese nationalist movement which was inspired and to some extent led from China. In view of these pressures for change, it may be well to review here some of the factors which help to perpetuate traditional religion and magic in the Semarang community.

In the first place, it must be recognized that the magical beliefs and practices associated with traditional Chinese religion offer direct and concrete rewards. Almost every member of the community has relatives, friends, or acquaintances who are convinced that temple gods have answered their prayers for such things as the birth of a male child, recoupment of business losses, or recovery from a serious illness.

Secondly, in all societies the family is one of the major mediators of tradition. Where the family unit is relatively strong and where parents and grandparents command a relatively high degree of loyalty and respect, as in most sections of the Semarang Chinese community, the family system may be regarded as an especially important force on the side of tradition. For instance, as mentioned in an earlier section of this chapter, the explanation which a Totok intellectual gave for maintaining the worship of a household god was: "What my father honored, I dare not change." Another example of the important role of the family in maintaining traditional religious practices may be found in the words of a medical student, who explained his conscientious practice of ancestor worship in this way:

When I was five, Father sent me to a Dutch Catholic school. One day, when I was about ten years old, my father found me praying in the Catholic way. I was so young that I naturally respected the religion of my teachers. But Father was alarmed. From that time on, I was given the task of caring for the family ancestral altar, even though I was not the eldest son. And Father carefully taught me all he knew about Chinese family traditions, ceremonies, festivals, and so forth. I had to clean the family altar—no servant was allowed to touch it—and take major responsibility for regular ancestor rites until I left home for college.

Finally, it seems apparent that nationalism plays an important role in the maintenance of Chinese traditions. Elsewhere [31] the writer has dealt at some length with the nationalist feelings of different Chinese groups in Indonesia and has elaborated a distinction between three kinds of "nationalism": political, cultural, and racial.[32] At this point it is important only to note that, in spite of the strong nationalist movement which thrived among the Chinese of Indonesia in the first half of the present century, a major proportion of the Chinese community today has no political loyalty either to the Peking or to the Taiwan government; but the nationalist movement did succeed in reviving cultural nationalism among the great majority of Chinese in Indonesia, and in strengthening the racial nationalism which few had ever lost. An example of cultural nationalism, as distinct from political nationalism, is given in the following statement of a Dutch-educated government employee in an interview with the writer:

If you ask me what Chinese culture is, I cannot say. We cannot define it exactly, but we know that we like it and want to keep it. Partly it is the language. We believe that our children in this country should go to national [Indonesian] schools, but we also want them to learn

[31] Donald E. Willmott, *The National Status of the Chinese in Indonesia* (Cornell Modern Indonesian Project, Ithaca, N.Y., 1956), pp. 65–73.

[32] The writer does not recognize the Chinese as a "race." Rather, they are a distinct national and ethnic group within the Mongoloid race. The term "racial nationalism" is used in order to draw attention to the *belief* in racial identity, which is a major component of the concept. The term "ethnic nationalism" was unsuitable because of the possibility of confusion with "cultural nationalism."

Chinese. We want them to be loyal to Indonesia as their country, but we hope that they will not forget Chinese culture.

In the writer's opinion, the fairly widespread feelings of cultural nationalism in the Semarang community tend to strengthen allegiance to traditional religious and magical beliefs and practices. The acceptance of Christianity would violate the cultural loyalty of many Chinese. Even racial nationalism, insofar as it promotes the desire to associate with and be identified with other Chinese, may be a factor in maintaining tradition. Participation in the ceremonial societies and in religious processions may be motivated partly in this way.

The relationship between religious traditionalism and racial and cultural nationalism must remain an unsubstantiated hypothesis, because the connection, if it exists, is primarily an unconscious one. Aside from the writer's own impressions, the only additional evidence which can be offered here is the following interpretation of the significance of Chinese New Year's celebrations. It appeared in an anonymous article in an Indonesian-language magazine intended primarily for Peranakans.

In recent years the Chinese people have celebrated the New Year in Indonesia because it is a tradition, because it is linked to their beliefs, but also, intuitively, because it strengthens the bonds among them, in maintaining themselves in a foreign land.

It is a sign that they are still among their own, in both physical and spiritual life.

The celebration of the New Year also breaks down the feeling of isolation in a foreign land; it makes the Chinese feel sociable, among their own, and thus strengthens their group feeling.[33]

Thus a relatively strong family system, the concrete rewards believed to be obtainable through ritual worship, and racial and cultural nationalism are three of the factors which help to main-

[33] From an anonymous article, "Imlik didalam Perantauan Tionghoa," in *Liberal*, III, no. 72 (Jan. 22, 1955), 80.

tain traditional magic and religion among the Semarang Chinese. In the discussion of the Semarang churches which follows, some of the attractions of Christianity will be suggested. Finally, two Chinese religious societies which seem to combine the strengths of both traditional religion and the churches will be described.

Christian Churches

It is reported that in 1926 there were less than three thousand Chinese Protestants and only about three hundred Chinese Catholics in all of Java.[34] Of these, not more than a few hundred Protestants and a handful of Catholics could have been in Semarang. By 1955 there were probably about five thousand Protestants and about two thousand Catholics in the Chinese community of this city. More than a tenth of the total Chinese population is Christian, and the proportion is steadily increasing.

Beginning in 1905, half a dozen Chinese graduates of St. Joseph's School in Singapore held weekly meetings of study and worship in Semarang, under the guidance of a Dutch Catholic priest. It was not until 1923, however, when Father Beekman established an orphanage for Chinese children, that Catholic work among the Chinese of the city really got its start. In 1936 one of the grand old family mansions in the Chinese quarter, the Kebun Dalam (Inner Garden), was bought by the Catholic church. The orphanage was moved there, and a school was established. Today there is also a church at Kebun Dalam, with regular services and a largely Chinese congregation. The two other Catholic churches of Semarang are attended by many Chinese too, as well as by Dutch and Indonesians.

The Catholic church operates a number of kindergartens and elementary schools, half a dozen secondary schools, and a normal school. The majority of these are quite new, and the quality of teaching is high. Indonesian is the language of instruction. Most

[34] J. Moerman, *In en om de Chineesche Kamp* (Amsterdam, 1932), pp. 94–95.

of the schools have both Chinese and Indonesian pupils. The Kebun Dalam school, however, is almost entirely Chinese, because of its location in the Chinese quarter. At the end of 1954, a new school was established—the Yu Te Shueh Hsiao—in which the language of instruction is Chinese. Two recently immigrated Chinese priests head its staff. In addition, there is an excellent Catholic hospital in Semarang, served by Dutch, Chinese, and Indonesian doctors, nurses, and sisters.

As mentioned earlier, the lay organizations of the Catholic church in Semarang are separated along ethnic group lines. In 1940, Father Beekman founded the Bond Katoliek Tionghwa, or the Chinese Catholic Association. In 1948 it was renamed the "Chung Chin Hui," and in 1949 it joined a federation of Chinese Catholic associations of different cities of Java. The Semarang Chung Chin Hui has separate sections for sports, art, propaganda, social welfare, library, and women's activities. It also publishes two periodicals, the *Madjalah Chung Ching Hui* and the *Sin Sheh Hui*. These include articles in Indonesian and Dutch on religious topics and on such problems as the position of women, the social relations of adolescents, and even politics. They also include lists of "objectionable" and "condemned" movies and of contributors to the church (along with the amount given by each person).

Another Chinese Catholic organization is the Maria Kongrasi. This group of about sixty selected laymen meets once a month for worship and for the assignment of special tasks such as visiting the sick, collecting money for the church, praying for certain people who are in trouble, finding jobs for unemployed Catholics, providing relief for the destitute, distributing Chinese New Year's gifts to the needy, and encouraging church attendance.

In contrast to the Catholic churches, the major Chinese Protestant churches in Semarang now have no official international affiliation. But they have close ties with missions and mission churches. Until 1935, Chinese Protestant converts joined the Geredja Kristen Djawa (Christian Church of Java), a church established by a Dutch Protestant mission. Most of the members of this church were Javanese. During the twenties, Chinese members from various cities held successive conferences in efforts to establish a church of their own, but failed. Beginning in 1932, Dutch and Chinese missionaries of the Dutch Reformed Church came regularly from a nearby town, Salatiga, to hold evangelistic services in the Chinese quarter of Semarang. As a result of this work, a new church organization, the Tiong Hoa Kie Tok Kauw Hwee (Chinese Christian Church), was established in 1935. Its first minister, Rev. Liem Siok Hie, is one of the two ministers serving this church in Semarang today. For many years, worship services of the Chinese Christian Church were held in the building of the Christian Church of Java and in the home of Rev. Liem Siok Hie in the Chinese quarter. In 1953, however, a large new building was completed. In addition to the services which are held in the new church, the Chinese Christian Church also holds weekly services in the building of the Dutch Reformed Church, which is located in another part of the city. The combined congregations now number over thirteen hundred persons, about two-fifths of them baptized. Since 1951, the Chinese Christian Church in Semarang has had the assistance of two Dutch missionaries, but all services and meetings are conducted in the Indonesian language.[35]

The Chinese Christian Church of Semarang joins with the Dutch Reformed Church in operating a club and recreational center in a downtown area. It co-operates also with other Chinese and Indonesian Protestant churches in running elementary and secondary schools in Semarang and a theological school in Jogjakarta. It has branches in Pekalongan, Tegal, and Purwodadi and is a member of the Central Java Synod, a federation of Chinese Protestant churches throughout the province. In 1955 this

[35] Material on the history of the Chinese Christian Church was obtained largely from an article in the Sin Min of April 6, 1955. The information was later checked by an active member of the church.

synod held a conference with the corresponding synods of East and West Java, with a view to developing an integrated organization and conformity of hymnbooks, liturgy, and catechism.

The Chinese Christian Church of Semarang has active youth and women's organizations. The youth group, the Chi Tu Chiao Tsing Nien Hui (Christian Youth Association), has three hundred members participating in the following sections: sports, scouts, recreation, worship, library, singing, and girls' activities. It also publishes a magazine, and in 1955, it produced an amateur play which earned 25,000 rupiahs (about $2,200 in U.S. currency) toward a fund for building a new parsonage.

Parallel to the Tiong Hoa Kie Tok Kauw Hwee (Chinese Christian Church) is the Hwa Kiauw Kie Tok Kauw Hwee (Overseas Chinese Christian Church), the difference being in the language used. Since the latter holds services in Chinese, its congregation is entirely Totok. It too originated from Dutch mission work, and although it has a new church building, it holds regular services in one of the Dutch churches as well.

An even faster-growing Protestant group than either of these is the Sing Ling Kauw Hwee (Church of the Holy Spirit), a Chinese fundamentalist church. It began in 1946 with a congregation of seventy members. Weekly worship services were held in a local theater. Within a year and a half the congregation had grown to three hundred. In 1950 a large new church building was completed. And by 1955 it had a congregation of about 900 adults and 850 children and young people.

In addition to co-operating with the Tiong Hoa Kie Tok Kauw Hwee in running two elementary schools, a junior high school, and a normal school, the Sing Ling Kauw Hwee has an active social service program. Its youth section, Pemuda Buat Kristus (Youth for Christ), conducts an "illiteracy school" for underprivileged children and a program of visiting the sick. Its women's auxiliary also engages in charitable activities, such as assisting the local orphanage for Chinese girls.

In its theological position, the Sing Ling Kauw Hwee is a Pentecostal church, and, indeed, it has close ties with the local United Pentecostal Church, which is run by American missionaries. The two churches jointly publish a monthly magazine, the *Kabar Selamat* (Glad Tidings). But the Sing Ling Kauw Hwee, according to its minister, Rev. Tan Hok Tjoan, is completely independent and self-supporting, "so that the growth of the church will always be free from undesirable influences." [36]

The United Pentecostal Church also has many Chinese among its followers, but the Sing Ling Kauw Hwee is more attuned to Chinese traditions. For one thing, the minister of the latter, Rev. Tan Hok Tjoan, is said to have a more intellectual and less emotional approach to religion. The services which he conducts are not characterized by the shouting and the emotional pitch of the mission church. Then, too, the Sing Ling Kauw Hwee is more broad-minded and less exclusive in its relations with outsiders. It participates in the joint services of the combined Protestant churches of Semarang at Christmas and Easter. It is the head of a federation of eight Sing Ling Kauw Hwee churches of other towns and maintains a vigorous evangelistic program. But according to Rev. Tan Hok Tjoan, his church does not like to open branches in localities already served by other Protestant churches. "We don't want the outside world to get the impression that competition has grown up among the Christian churches," he explained.[37]

There are four other missions in Semarang which are winning an increasing number of followers among Chinese as well as Indonesians: the Baptists, the Seventh-Day Adventists, Jehovah's Witnesses, and the Salvation Army. In addition to evangelical work, the Baptists have opened a theological seminary, the Seventh-Day Adventists run a school, and the Salvation Army operates an eye hospital and a home for the sick and destitute.

[36] *Sin Min,* May 18, 1955.   [37] *Ibid.*

Social and Cultural Influences of Christianity

In some parts of the Far East, Christian missions have been the primary source of Western cultural influences. In Semarang, however, the missions have been active only in the past two or three decades, whereas Western business and government institutions have been in direct contact with the Chinese community for at least two centuries. Most of the mission schools of Semarang were established after World War II, but some of the modernist Chinese schools and government schools date from the time of World War I or earlier. Among the Semarang Chinese, therefore, Christians are not generally more Westernized than non-Christians of comparable education and social position, but are different from them primarily in ways specifically related to religion.

In the first section of this chapter general religious attitudes of the Chinese were discussed, and it was seen that these attitudes are to be found even among Christians, at least to some extent. This section is concerned with the other side of the phenomenon —the extent to which traditional patterns have been changed by Christianity. Religious tolerance will be considered first. It has been pointed out that very few non-Christians regard religious faith as an important consideration in the choice of a marriage partner, whereas the majority of Christians do. About 70 per cent of the Catholic and 40 per cent of the Protestant questionnaire respondents included religion among the three most important considerations in the choice of a spouse. Only a minority of the Christian parents were married to non-Christians. One of the Catholic women interviewed in the survey said, when asked about "intermarriage," that she saw no objection to marriage between persons of different races, but was strongly opposed to marriage between persons of different religions.

The churches in Semarang strongly oppose marriage between Christians and non-Christians. This question was recently discussed in the first issue of the Chinese Protestant magazine *Ma-*

djalah Kita. There, in a column of advice on love and marriage which became a regular feature of the magazine, "Uncle Romeo and Aunt Juliet" wrote: "Marriage between a believer and a non-believer is forbidden according to the Bible." In reply to a question as to why many Christian men marry non-Christians, the same writers said that there may be a shortage of Christian girls in some congregations or that certain non-Christian girls may be more beautiful (or can make themselves so) or more friendly, cheerful, or clever at enjoying themselves. "But all these reasons should not divert our young men from God's commandment," concluded "Uncle Romeo and Aunt Juliet." [38]

Like religious tolerance, traditional Chinese eclecticism is also considerably reduced among Chinese converts to Christianity. Many Chinese are devoted to two or more of the traditional Chinese religions: Confucianism, Taoism, and Buddhism. In Semarang, Theosophy is often added to this list. Unlike these religions, however, Christianity is exclusive. Chinese Christians in Semarang have given up any adherence to other religions. Nevertheless, as noted, ancestor worship is not considered a "religion," and a certain number of Christians still participate in it in one way or another; there was even the case of a Catholic participating in temple worship.

Praying to temple gods is forbidden to Christians. But different churches have compromised to different degrees in the case of ancestor worship. The more conservative Protestant churches require converts to bury their ancestor tablets. No Protestant church allows the carrying out of the traditional ritual of bowing and offering food and incense before an ancestral altar. But many Protestants visit family graves at the time of the traditional festival of Tjing Bing.

How to show respect toward the dead was a subject of controversy at a classis of the Chinese Christian Churches of Central Java in 1938. Some thought that the traditional Chinese ritual

[38] *Madjalah Kita,* I, no. 1 (Oct.–Nov., 1954), 20–21.

gestures of clasping the hands (as in prayer) and bowing a number of times or even of burning incense were acceptable, provided that the intention was "correct." Others insisted that any such actions would be a violation of the Second Commandment. On the basis of Corinthians 8:1–13, the classis finally agreed that although certain acts were not wrong in themselves they might mislead others who did not understand the Christian view of them. Their conclusion was as follows: "It is not wrong to render honor by bowing the head, but rendering honor according to general Chinese custom is not right for Christians." [39]

Catholics are generally allowed to maintain traditional rituals, provided that the meaning attached to them is adjusted to Catholic dogma. Among six Catholic families interviewed in the survey, two take no part in ancestor worship under any circumstances; two participate when friends or relatives expect them to, but maintain no altar or ritual in their own home; and two maintain both altar and ritual. One of the last two families carries out the unusual responsibility of maintaining the ancestral altars for both sides of the family. In this family, however, the deceased mother, who was a Catholic, "is remembered more in the Catholic way" and is not included among the ancestors who receive attention at the altar.

Among the Chinese questionnaire respondents, one-quarter of the Catholics and one-eighth of the Protestants replied "yes" to the question: "Do you believe in ancestor worship?" Seven-eighths of the adherents of traditional Chinese religions answered this in the affirmative. Doubtless the meaning of "ancestor worship" was interpreted differently by Christians and non-Christians; but it has a wide variety of meanings even among the latter.

Thus in matters relating to religion, considerable differences were found between Christians and non-Christians, although Christians have by no means completely rejected Chinese traditions.

Christians also differ with regard to nonreligious matters in

[39] *Ibid.*, I, no. 3 (Feb.–March, 1955), 17.

which direct teachings of the church are involved. In the case of divorce, Catholic Chinese have usually (though not always) accepted the position of the church. Among the questionnaire respondents, about 26 per cent of the Catholic students were of the opinion that divorce may be advisable under certain circumstances. In all other groups, including Protestants, the percentage expressing this opinion ranged from 50 to 60 per cent. The difference between Catholics and non-Catholics is significant at the .01 level.

With regard to Western-style social dancing, too, the Catholic church has taken a more conservative stand than the Protestant church. As a result, it was found that 40 per cent of the Catholic respondents, but only 13 per cent of the Protestant respondents never participate in dancing. This difference is significant at the .01 level. Among non-Christian respondents, the proportion who do not dance is 48 per cent for persons of traditional Chinese religions and 28 per cent for persons of no religion. Neither of these percentages differs significantly from that for Catholics, which falls between the two.

With regard to political orientation, the churches are quite specific in their teaching. Catholics are urged to vote for the Partai Katolik (Catholic Party), and Protestants are advised to vote for the Partai Kristen Indonesia (Indonesian Christian Party, usually abbreviated to "Parkindo"). An article in the first issue of the Protestant magazine *Madjalah Kita* declared that the only way for a Christian to do his duty toward God, himself, his country, and his fellow man was to vote for Parkindo candidates; he should not vote for Christian candidates of other parties, as they would have to compromise too much, according to the article.[40] Thus, insofar as the churches are able to overcome the local Chinese indifference to politics, their effect is to orient Christians toward participation in Indonesian politics as Protestant and Catholic minorities.

The teachings and cultural orientations of the churches con-

---

[40] *Ibid.*, I, no. 1 (Oct.–Nov., 1954), 15.

stitute a strong influence against allegiance to either the Taiwan or the Peking governments. Not only are the churches strongly anti-Communist, but they often promote allegiance to the Indonesian state. The great majority of Chinese Christians are Indonesian citizens, and they are less attracted to China than is any other group in the community.

As mentioned in Chapter I, Chinese born in Indonesia automatically became Indonesian citizens unless they specifically rejected Indonesian citizenship during the period from December 27, 1949, to December 27, 1951. In the case of persons under the age of eighteen, such rejections, if desired, were made by their parents or legal guardians. As was to be expected, a disproportionately large percentage of those who chose Chinese citizenship in this manner were students and young people. Among the questionnaire respondents who were born in Indonesia, only 6 per cent of the Catholics and 14 per cent of the Protestants had lost their Indonesian citizenship through rejections. The corresponding percentage for those of traditional Chinese religions was 42 per cent, and for those of no religion, 41 per cent. Although the difference between Catholics and Protestants was not significant, the differences between these two and both of the others were significant at the .01 level. In Chapter I it was estimated that among the total Indonesia-born Chinese population of Semarang only about 11 per cent became Chinese citizens by option. From a comparison of this with the above figures for student youth, it can be concluded that the proportion of older Christians who gave up their Indonesian citizenship must have been extremely small.

In their cultural orientations too, Chinese Christians differ from non-Christians. (Here "culture" is being used in its more popular and restricted sense of intellectual and esthetic pursuits.) The fact that Christians feel almost no bond to modern China has lessened their interest in Chinese culture and made them more susceptible to Western and Indonesian influences. Education in Christian schools and direct and indirect contacts with missionaries from Europe and America have increased their interest in Western ideas and values. These factors are especially important for those who have been raised in Christian families. In the case of most converts, as will be shown in the next section, a Western outlook is probably as much a cause as a result of conversion to Christianity. Whatever the explanation, the differences between the intellectual and esthetic orientations of Christian and non-Christian Chinese is very marked.

Table 6. National origins of the favorite authors listed by Chinese respondents of Christian and non-Christian groups *

National origins of favorite authors	Students of Christian religion	Students of Chinese religion	Students of no religion
Chinese	17%	44% †	74% †
Indonesian	34	22	15 †
Western	74	57	41 †
Number of replies	(53)	(72)	(148)

* Based on replies to the question: "Who are your favorite authors?" Since respondents sometimes listed several authors of different national origins, columns add up to more than 100 per cent.

† These figures differ significantly at the .01 level from the corresponding figures in the first column.

The questionnaire results shown in Table 6 confirm this conclusion. Respondents were asked: "Who are your favorite authors?" The national origins of the authors listed by respondents of different groups may be taken as a rough indication of the cultural orientations of these groups. Different language abilities are not in themselves an important factor in determining the choice of favorite authors, since translations of works of the most popular Chinese and Western authors are available in Semarang. Thus the mention of Lu Hsün or Lin Yu-tang, even when listed as favorite authors by students who read their works only in Indonesian or Dutch, is taken as an indication of a Chinese cultural orientation.

Table 6 shows that the Christian students, as a group, are much more attracted to Western culture (at least in intellectual and esthetic matters) and much less interested in Chinese culture than are the non-Christian students. And Christian students appreciate Indonesian authors considerably more than they do Chinese authors. The reverse is true among non-Christians.

Certain differences have been found between Christians and non-Christians. But there are many areas in which they differ little or not at all. For example, the interview and questionnaire surveys failed to show any significant differences in family structure. The average number of children in Christian families was 5.4, and in non-Christian families, 6.3. This difference might have reached statistical significance had the number of replies been great enough. But it is probably due mostly to the somewhat higher level of education among Christians, rather than to religious differences as such. (Catholics could not be reliably compared with Protestants for family size, again because of the low number of replies.)

The questionnaire respondents were asked how many children they would like to have, if married. The average number of children desired by the Christian students was 4.5, and by non-Christian students, 4.4. Similarly, there was no significant difference in the numbers who reported having friends of the opposite sex or who wanted to have their parents choose a marriage partner for them. A slightly higher proportion of Christians than of non-Christians reported that their parents had made their own decision to get married, but the difference was not significant. About as many Christian as non-Christian parents were said to be willing to allow their children to choose their own marriage partners.

It may be concluded that in the Semarang Chinese community Christians differ from non-Christians chiefly in areas closely related to religion—that is, in religious beliefs and practices, in certain moral teachings, and in political orientations. They differ also in intellectual and esthetic interests. With regard to other aspects of culture, such as marriage and family patterns, non-Christians have apparently been affected as much by nontraditional influences as have Christians. In some parts of the Far East, missions have been the major or even the exclusive source of Western influences. In Semarang, however, they have had a significant effect only in the last few decades. Of much longer duration and of greater importance have been contacts with European government and business institutions, education in government and Chinese "modernist" schools, and exposure to Western books, periodicals, and motion pictures. Apparently, these have affected Christians and non-Christians about equally.

The Attraction of the Churches

The various Christian churches of Semarang have been gaining followers at a rather rapid rate in the Chinese community. They have done this in spite of certain obstacles. For one thing, traditional Chinese religious beliefs and practices have shown greater resistance to change in the Semarang community than in China itself. Further, for Chinese to adopt Christianity means giving up, to a certain extent at least, ingrained habits of religious tolerance, eclecticism, and this-worldliness.

It therefore becomes a problem to explain the peculiar attractions of Christianity which enable it to overcome these obstacles. Only the cultural, social, and psychological aspects of the problem will be considered, and not the religious and philosophical merits of different religions. Even the ardent evangelist realizes that most converts are attracted, at least initially, by other than purely religious considerations. Interpretations in such a field must be tentative and impressionistic at best, and only suggestions can be made of what some of the nonreligious considerations may be.

In the first place, Western culture in general enjoys a position of high prestige and respect in the eyes of many Chinese. The roots of this prestige lie in the historic military, economic, political, technological, and social superiority or dominance of the white man over the peoples of Asia. In Chapter II these factors were shown at work in Semarang itself. Today, Western-type education, moving pictures, and books and magazines, among other things, help to perpetuate the prestige of Western culture. From classical music to the latest style of bathing suit, things from the West are often valued merely because they are Western. Christianity, being the religion associated with the West, shares in the general prestige, at least for some people.

In addition, the missionaries who have urged Christianity upon the Chinese have often been people of high personal prestige. They have shared in the aura of superiority surrounding Westerners in general. They have also been respected for their comparatively advanced education and general knowledge. In many cases, personal qualities such as friendliness, devotion to duty, or willingness to make sacrifices in the service of others have won high admiration, esteem, and affection. For example, both Catholic and non-Catholic Chinese have told the writer, in terms of highest praise, how indefatigably the Jesuit and Franciscan teachers in Semarang Catholic schools devote themselves to the welfare of their students—in the classroom, in extracurricular activities, in individual attention and assistance, and in home visiting. This type of relationship creates a psychological identification with individual missionaries which facilitates the adoption of their beliefs.

In a previous section, the many educational, medical, and charitable activities of various missions were described. These services create feelings of gratitude, indebtedness, or obligation among those who receive their benefits, and this in turn creates a greater willingness to comply with the wishes of those who provide them.

In some cases, a desire to gain certain concrete benefits may form a considerable part of a person's motivation in becoming a Christian. Educational opportunities, scholarships abroad, business contacts, even just the chance to associate with foreigners and to gain fluency in the English or Dutch language, are among the advantages which may be visualized by prospective converts, no matter how sincere their interest in Christianity as a religion.

Christianity may also serve intellectual and emotional needs. The modernist movement, which began at about the turn of the century, placed great emphasis on science and technology; it undermined faith in the traditional Chinese religion and magic of temple gods and ancestor worship. But many who learned to reject "superstition" were not prepared to give up religion. Christianity was the predominant religion in the nations where science and technology were most advanced. Thus Christianity was probably more satisfying than traditional Chinese religions for many who had accepted the new currents of thought.

There is no doubt, also, that the Christian churches represent a type of organization highly compatible with the traditions and needs of the Chinese community. They are local organizations serving many different functions and emphasizing group solidarity and close personal relations. In contrast, participation in traditional Chinese religion is usually on an individualistic or familistic basis. Prayer to a temple god or worship during a public festival does not provide the emotional support from the group which is felt in a church congregation, both in worship services and in social get-togethers. It seems likely that a need for belonging to a group is relatively strongly felt among people of a minority group in an alien society and that the Christian churches may to some extent serve to satisfy this need among Semarang converts.

Finally, Christianity offers certain psychological satisfactions not provided by the traditional Chinese religions. These are too varied and intangible to be discussed in detail here, but a few suggestive examples may be given. A non-Christian Chinese pointed out to the writer that the concepts of personal salvation and of a heavenly paradise presented by the Christian churches provide much greater consolation than the shadowy spirit world and dutiful respect of descendants offered by the religion of ancestor worship. The role of the Christian minister or priest as leader, protector, adviser, confidant, and "father" is of great psychological value for some, and the group praying, singing, and shouting of the Pentecostals is an emotional release for others.

These, then, are some of the factors which have enabled Christian churches to expand so rapidly in the Chinese community of Semarang.

Probably it is in the Christian schools that these various factors impinge most directly upon non-Christians. Evidence of the importance of these schools in gaining converts is to be found in the questionnaire results presented in Table 7, which compares the distribution of religious preferences of pupils in Christian and non-Christian senior high schools with that of their parents.

Table 7. Religious preferences of Chinese pupils—and their parents—in Christian and non-Christian high schools

Religious preferences	Pupils in non-Christian schools	Parents	Pupils in Catholic schools	Parents	Pupils in Protestant schools	Parents
Catholic	5%	1%	51%	12%	7%	4% *
Protestant	13	6	9	10 *	40	19
Chinese religions	23	45	5	24	7	28
No religion	59	48	35	54	46	49 *
	100%	100%	100%	100%	100%	100%
Number of cases	298	637	151	227	75	144

* These figures do not differ significantly from the corresponding figures in adjacent columns to the left. All other figures differ significantly at the .01 level from the figures in corresponding adjacent columns.

First of all, even in the case of non-Christian schools there is a higher proportion of Christians among the students than among their parents. This is an indication that the Christian churches contact and attract a certain number of young people through channels other than schools. But the difference between students and parents in the proportion who are Christian is much more striking in the case of Christian schools. In the two Catholic schools represented in the sample, about one-half of the students adhere to Catholicism, although only one-sixth have Catholic parents. Thus about one-third of the pupils of the Catholic schools may be regarded as converts. In the one Protestant school the proportion of converts is somewhat lower, but still substantial. A few children of Catholic parentage attend the Protestant school, and vice versa, but in these cases conversion rarely occurs. Both Catholics and Protestants draw most of their converts from among students whose parents adhere to traditional Chinese religions. The Catholic schools are also successful with students whose parents profess no religion. The greater influence of the Catholic schools may be partly due to the fact that many of their teachers are priests and nuns, whereas none of the teachers in the Protestant school are so directly concerned with religion.

Columns under the heading "Parents" in Table 7 represent a total of the figures for fathers and mothers. Since there were more Christians among the mothers than among the fathers, the influence of the Christian schools would appear greater if the religious preferences of students were compared with those of their fathers only, and less if compared to those of their mothers only. Even in the latter case, however, the converting influence of the Christian schools is still marked; and the number of Christian students exceeds that of Christian mothers even in non-Christian schools.

There is no doubt that the Catholic and Protestant school systems are in large measure responsible for the rapid growth of churches in Semarang in the past decade or two.

This outline of the factors contributing to the growth of the churches in Semarang suggests that the appeal of Christianity is primarily religious, rather than magical. That is, those who turn to Christianity are usually seeking a new personal orientation and an identification with new groups and persons. Most of them are not seeking new ritual techniques for gaining immediate ends through supernatural intervention. The most notable exception to this is a relatively small number of converts who are brought into the church by fundamentalist faith healers.

Theosophy and Islam

Before contrasting two Chinese religious societies with the churches, brief mention should be made of two other religions: Theosophy and Islam.

There is an impressive Theosophical lodge in Semarang, called the "Lodji Açoka." It has a fairly large membership of both Chinese and Indonesians. Officers and lecturers are from both ethnic groups, and the active youth branch is also mixed. Indeed, it is probably the best example in Semarang of co-operation between the two ethnic groups in a religious organization.

Theosophy does not have a popular appeal among the Chinese, because of its emphasis on the mystical and the occult. Primarily it attracts students and intellectuals who are not satisfied with traditional religious beliefs and practices, but who are convinced that Western science and rationalism cannot provide a satisfying way of life. Theosophy is not an exclusive religion, and many of its followers in Semarang also participate in the Sam Kauw Hwee (Three Religions Society), which will be described in the next section.

There is no record of Moslem Chinese coming to Indonesia since the time of Sam Po. A certain number of Chinese have been converted to Islam since that time, but mostly in Sumatra, Borneo, and the Celebes. In Java there are perhaps several hundred Chinese Moslems, some of them in positions of some prominence. But in Semarang there is not a single well-known Chinese of the Islamic faith. Among about five hundred Chinese questionnaire respondents, only two had Moslem parents; and in these two cases, the children did not follow the religion of their parents. In 1938, Semarang was visited by Chinese Moslem evangelists of the Persatuan Islam Tionghoa (Chinese Moslem Association). They preached at meetings held at the Hwa Joe Hwee Kwan, but with little success. There are probably only fifty to one hundred Moslem Chinese in Semarang today.

In view of the fact that many of their female ancestors were Indonesians of Moslem religion, it may appear strange that so few present-day Chinese adhere to this faith. Some of the reasons are readily apparent, however. Firstly, the strongly patriarchal character of the Chinese family system made it unlikely that Chinese husbands would accept the religion of their Indonesian wives or permit it to be taught to their children. Secondly, in contrast to the situation with regard to Christianity, the Chinese had no general respect or admiration for the civilization associated with Mohammedanism, either in Arabia or in Indonesia. On the contrary, Arab traders were in direct competition with the Chinese, and the hostility between the two groups sometimes erupted into violence.[41] Thirdly, as noted in Chapter IV, the economic, social, and political situation under the colonial regime was such as to create prejudice and hostility between the Chinese and the Indonesian people. And finally, Indonesian Moslems have made no attempt to convert the Chinese in Semarang except on rare occasions, and they have not been in any position to offer services comparable with Christian schools, hospitals, and charitable institutions. The Chinese therefore have very little knowledge of the Mohammedan religion and little reason to be attracted to it under present circumstances.

The Confucian Society and the Three Religions Society

A description and discussion of the Confucian Society and the Three Religions Society have been reserved for the end of the present chapter because the writer believes that their existence

[41] *Boekoe Peringetan,* pp. 14, 16.

can best be understood in the light of the challenge which the churches on the one hand and the secular "modernist" outlook on the other have given to traditional Chinese religion and magic. These societies represent what may be called "neotraditionalism" —that is, the attempt to revive and propagate the teachings of the founders of traditional Chinese religions in a form compatible with the modern age.

The Semarang Khong Kauw Hwee (Confucian Society) holds weekly or biweekly religious meetings, issues booklets an Confucianism, and runs a charity school. The society has several hundred members and supporters, mostly Peranakans, and its affairs are managed by elected officers, as in other Chinese organizations.

The regular meetings of the Confucian Society are held in the central ancestral hall of the Kong Tik Soe temple. A picture of Confucius is placed on the main altar, and some members offer ceremonial homage before it, either before or after the meeting. The program usually consists of a lecture on the teachings of Confucius and a period in which questions from the audience are discussed by the lecturer. The language used is Indonesian, although special terms may be given in Chinese as well, and even written on a blackboard in Chinese. Recent lecture topics have included the following: "Living in peace in the midst of society," "Rational and mystical feelings," "The nature of religion," and "Can we carry out correct traditional behavior in modern society?" At a meeting which the writer attended, some fifty persons were present, mostly middle-aged men. At a Spring Festival ceremony held by the Confucian Society, some 250 persons were reported to have attended.

The school run by the Confucian Society is unusual in several respects. The 170-odd pupils come from families who cannot afford to send their children to other Chinese schools. There is no tuition, and many of the children are given their school supplies as well. The pupils receive a four-year course in arithmetic, reading and writing in Chinese and Indonesian, and a few other subjects; they also receive religious instruction. In addition, handwork and crafts form a major part of the program—for instance, sewing, shoe-making, and the manufacture of toys, puppets, and other knick-knacks. The purpose of the craftwork is to teach skills which can be used vocationally after leaving school, as well as to raise money for the school through the sale of the objects made. Most of the expenses of the school are covered by voluntary contributions, however. The eight teachers receive only token salaries.

The Society teaches Confucianism not only to the pupils in its school, but also to children of its members. Before the regular adult meetings of the Society, religious instruction is given to the children. The children also learn songs of religious and moral significance.

Most of the lecturing, writing, and day-to-day work of the Confucian Society is done by Lie Ping Lien, whose position as "general officer" is similar to that of the general secretary of a Y.M.C.A. A Peranakan of about sixty years of age, Mr. Lie is gentle, kindly, polite, devoted to the welfare of others, and well versed in the ancient classics—in fact, a model Confucian gentleman and scholar. His character and his impressive, self-taught knowledge of the Chinese classics have won him high esteem among members of the Society, as well as widespread respect in the community at large.

The religion propagated by the Confucian Society is virtually devoid of magic. It calls for an "upright" way of life, which is a matter primarily of personal righteousness and public service, and secondarily of ceremonial devotion to the ancestors and to the Supreme God, Tuhan Allah. In this view, the purpose of tradi-tional home and temple worship is not to ask for special favors, but to purify oneself and to offer honor and praise. Indeed, many of the magical beliefs and practices of temple worship are re-garded as superstitions appropriate only for the spiritually illit-erate.

Confucian societies have been organized in various parts of

Indonesia over the past forty years or more. In 1955, a federation of the Confucian societies of the following localities was organized: Surakarta, Surabaja, Bandung, Malang, Tjirebon, Bogor, and Tjiampea. Although the Semarang Society sent an observer to the conference, it did not join the federation.

The Sam Kauw Hwee (Three Religions Society) is a branch of the Gabungan Sam Kauw Indonesia (Three Religions Federation of Indonesia), which held its third annual congress in May, 1955. Most of the thirty-odd branches of this federation, like the Semarang branch, have been established only a few years. The purpose of the organization is to unify, propagate, and practice the three religions: Confucianism, Buddhism, and Taoism.

Some of the affiliated branches of the Three Religions Federation are local Confucian societies. In Semarang, the two organizations have no direct connection, but many of the participants in the Confucian Society take part also in the activities of the Three Religions Society. The membership of the latter is, again, mostly Peranakan Chinese, but it also includes a few native Indonesians. Many of the Indonesian and Chinese participants are also active in the Theosophical Society of Semarang.

The Semarang Three Religions Society holds regular meetings similar to those of the Confucian Society. In addition to lectures, however, prayers and Buddhist chants form part of the program. The following are examples of recent lecture topics: "Karma and reincarnation," "Democracy in the teachings of Mencius," "Main outlines of the teachings of Buddha," and "Atman and Atma." The language used is Indonesian.

The main publication of the Sam Kauw movement is *Tri Budaja*, a magazine issued monthly by the Djakarta headquarters of the Federation. This includes articles on the teachings of the founders of the three religions, news of various Federation branches, poems and short stories, a children's page and a women's page (giving vegetarian recipes, for instance), and articles on topics of current or religious interest. In addition, some publications are issued in Semarang. For example, a translation of one of the Confucian classics, *Tiong Yong* (The Doctrine of the Mean), was recently undertaken.

The Semarang Three Religions Society has established a consultation bureau for its members: those with personal or domestic problems may obtain advice from doctors, lawyers, and engineers who have agreed to serve as counselors. In addition, there are plans for establishing a place of seclusion in the country, where members may go for meditation, and possibly also a home for the aged.

The Three Religions Federation has an outstanding religious leader in the person of Bhikkhu Ashin Jinarakkhita. He is a Peranakan of Indonesian citizenship. Originally his name was The Bwan An. Soon after his return from Holland with a degree in engineering, he became the head of the central committee of the Three Religions Federation. Then he spent some time in Burma and became a Buddhist monk there, receiving the title "Bhikkhu" and the new name. After attending the international conference of the World Fellowship of Buddhists which was held in Rangoon in December, 1954, he returned to Indonesia and became a traveling evangelist for the Three Religions Federation.

Bhikkhu Jinarakkhita came to Semarang several times in the spring of 1955. He gave a number of lectures in the Kong Tik Soe temple, in the hall of the Hwa Joe Hwee Koan, and in the meetinghouse of the Theosophical Society. He also led public-worship ceremonies in the Tay Kak Sie temple and gave instruction in meditation. It was said that, as a result of his visits, the Three Religions Society gained many new members. In addition, according to the chairman of the Semarang Society, six young Indonesians and eleven Chinese (including two girls) asked to become disciples of the Bhikkhu.

There is no doubt about the Bhikkhu's ability to inspire those who hear him. He is young, soft-spoken, and modest, but speaks with great conviction and clarity. He appears to be especially calm and untroubled inwardly. His hearers are also greatly impressed by the fact that he renounced wealth and professional success for a life of simplicity and poverty.

The religious teachings propounded by the various lecturers of the Three Religions Society cannot be said to form a single religious faith or outlook. For instance, the doctrine of reincarnation has not been reconciled with ancestor worship, and the somewhat different ways of life implied in the Rectitude of Confucianism, the Renunciation of Buddhism, and the Passivity of Taoism are advocated separately or together. Many members and lecturers are adherents primarily of one of the three religions, while borrowing congenial ideas from the other two. Bhikkhu Jinarakkhita is primarily a Buddhist.

This eclecticism has at times caused difficulties within the Three Religions movement. For example, there have been serious suggestions that the three religions should be ranked in order of importance. The great majority oppose this view. Various lecturers, including the Bhikkhu, insist that the three religions have no dogmas and that it is the responsibility of each person to work out his own beliefs according to personal preference. Therefore the Three Religions Society is an association of people who are seeking in one or all of the three religions a personal orientation, a satisfying way of life, and convincing beliefs about the mystic or supernatural. As there is no creed, no prescribed or regularized ritual, and no religious hierarchy, it can scarcely be regarded as a church or "organized religion."

Nevertheless, remarkable parallels can be drawn between the Christian churches and both of the neotraditional societies. This is not to imply that the Confucian Society and the Three Religions Society have mimicked the churches. Rather, faced by the challenge not only of the churches, but also of the secular "modernist" outlook, the organizers of these two societies have adopted realistic innovations intended to give to the traditional Chinese religions a form and an organization consistent with the attitudes and the needs of the present generation.

Traditional Chinese religion was not organized or practiced in such a way as to provide for solidarity, emotional support, a variety of activities, and close personal relations among a body of believers. Like church congregations, the Confucian Society and the Three Religions Society have a regular membership, frequent meetings (usually on Sunday), and various group activities.

Traditionally there were no regular religious leaders to teach, inspire, and counsel followers. The lectures which members of the two societies now hear might very well be called "sermons." The leaders also perform individual counseling functions, and in the Three Religions Society this practice has been regularized in the consultation bureau. Finally, in such leaders as Lie Ping Lien and especially Bhikkhu Jinarakkhita is found the ability to inspire respect, confidence, and loyalty. Their influence is based upon learning, self-sacrifice, and personal qualities. In these respects, they rival the most effective Christian missionaries.

In traditional Chinese religion, religious instruction was left to the home. Like the churches, both the Confucian Society and the Three Religions movement have recognized the importance of special religious training for young people. This is seen in the school and the "Sunday school" of the Confucian Society. The Three Religions Federation has organized an affiliated youth association, the Persatuan Pemuda Pemudi Sam Kauw Indonesia (Indonesian Union of the Boys and Girls of the Three Religions), with branches in many localities. In addition, the Federation's 1955 congress decided that one of the days of the New Year holiday should be institutionalized as a special Children's Day by selecting a traditional god or goddess to give out presents to children in Santa Claus fashion. The idea was avowedly patterned after the Western Christmas.

Like the churches, too, the neotraditional societies have felt a responsibility to engage in public service of various kinds. The school of the Confucian Society and the proposed old people's home of the Three Religions Society are examples.

It has been pointed out that many important magical beliefs and practices are associated with traditional Chinese religion. In both the churches and the neotraditional societies, however, the appeal is primarily religious and not magical; that is, the function is to provide personal orientation, a meaningful way of life supported by a group, new loyalties, and satisfying beliefs about the mystical and the supernatural.

Unlike Christian converts, however, many neotraditionalists maintain the magical beliefs and practices of home and temple. Indeed, neotraditionalism combines the strengths of traditional religion with the benefits of church-type organization and outlook which have been mentioned above. Not only does it allow the practice of temple magic. It also is consistent with Chinese family tradition and is extremely congenial to cultural and racial nationalism.

The following quotation from a book (written in Indonesian) on Chinese marriage and funeral customs will serve to illustrate the way in which neotraditionalism receives support from cultural nationalism:

If the Chinese cannot hold firmly to their National spirit, it will mean the gradual collapse of the Chinese nation. . . . Most people do not well understand the full meaning of Nationalism, which may be said to involve three important aims which comprise the foundation of national spirit, that is: (1) *language*—as the saying goes, "to know your language is to love your country," (2) *Religion,* Correct manners and customs, (3) *education.* . . . We cannot discuss all of these here; we shall elaborate only the two points concerning Religion and Correct manners and customs, which are the basis of personal righteousness, in order that we may strengthen the spirit of nationalism insofar as possible according to the teachings of our Great Prophet and Teacher, Confucius.[42]

The prestige of the West may have a strong influence even upon those who are ideologically Chinese cultural nationalists. This is

[42] L. T. Y., *op. cit.,* pp. 4–5.

a paradox for which neotraditionalism offers a better solution than does unmodified traditional religion on the one hand or Christianity on the other. The writer has heard Three Religions Society leaders, including Bhikkhu Jinarakkhita, appeal both to cultural nationalism and to the feeling of respect for the West, with statements like this:

The West, with all its technological achievements, its learning, and its avowed Christianity, is spiritually bankrupt. The people of Western nations are becoming dissatisfied with their way of life. Many of them have discovered the spiritual superiority of our Eastern religions. If *they* have recognized the greatness of our religious teachings, we should be ashamed not to have done so ourselves!

The following excerpt from a letter sent to the present writer two years after his departure from Indonesia will serve as a concrete example, as well as a summary, of the various strengths of neotraditionalism. It was written by a Peranakan professional, who is an enthusiastic participant in the Three Religions movement.

The Sam Kauw Hui is becoming a world commonwealth of Buddhistic-Taoistic-Confucianistic followers, I think. Especially among the Overseas Chinese here it is becoming very popular after the arrival of so many prominent priests (bhikkhus) of American, English, Australian, and German descent in Indonesia. The ambassadors of Ceylon, India, Burma, Siam, Cambodia, and Japan are supporting them fully, and many prominent Balinese, Javanese and even Sundanese (from Bandung) are now followers in Indonesia, and this figure is increasing daily.

My wife and I both want to join the "weisak" (general annual meditation) at the ancient Borobudur temple this year in June. . . . Every human being needs an internal faith in times of failure in life. The seed within us may become apathetic, but it is still healthy and recipient to a real religion. Bhikkhu Jinarakkhita can give us satisfaction, and can fulfill these wishes, because he is simple and self-sacrificing. There is another important factor, which has sped our conversion to the Sam Kauw Hui, i.e. the former Dutch colonial policy of government financial support of missions. The missions became pressure groups, handling their religion sometimes selfishly in the eyes of the people. . . . In this situation, people are now looking for a new faith and have found internal satisfaction in the old religion. [Parentheses are in the original letter.]

In view of the analysis of the strengths of neotraditionalism which has been presented above, one might conclude that the total membership of the Confucian Society and the Three Religions Society may someday rival that of the Christian churches. However, the future of the various religious groups in Semarang depends upon many factors which cannot be predicted—such as changes in the relative importance of Chinese cultural nationalism and respect for Western culture. Therefore predictions are unwise. But some of the weaknesses and limitations of neotraditionalism should be noted.

The Confucian Society and the Three Religions Society are very loosely organized associations. They have no ritual initiation to membership, no obligation or rationale for regular attendance at meetings, no institutionalized provisions to assure or encourage continuing participation and permanent involvement. Meetings seem designed primarily for those who are questing for a satisfying religion, who want answers to religious questions. There is little to attract or hold those who are satisfied with their religion. If this is true, the membership of the neotraditional societies seems likely to be characterized as much by continuous turnover as by cumulative increase. The number of nonparticipating sympathizers may continue to increase without substantially strengthening these organizations. By contrast, the churches have many institutionalized procedures which help them not only to keep converts participating in the life of the church, but also to win the children of converts more or less automatically.

A second weakness of the neotraditional societies is that many of their basic teachings do not accord with the predominant values of the majority of the Chinese community in Semarang. For instance, passivity, meditation, and renunciation are scarcely compatible with individualistic striving for commercial or professional success. On the other hand, in the opinion of the writer, Christianity has gradually adjusted itself to the values of capitalistic individualism. This may be one of the major reasons why the churches in Semarang have been especially successful with young people, whereas the neotraditional societies have thus far attracted primarily older people. The latter are more attached to tradition by sentiment, in any case; but also, having joined in the struggle for personal success, some of them have found that it has not brought satisfaction.

Finally, it must be remembered that the churches have been able to depend upon considerable outside help, both for leadership and for financial resources, at least during their early years of growth. The neotraditional societies not only lack such outside support, but have so far received little aid from the wealthiest group in the Chinese community.

In view of these weaknesses along with the strengths of the neotraditional societies, the writer does not anticipate any major change in the relative popularity of Christianity and neotraditionalism, unless considerable changes in the cultural orientations of the Chinese community occur. It seems more likely that both religious positions will face increasing difficulty in countering the influence of the secular "modernist" outlook.

Summary

The Chinese in Semarang, like their compatriots in China, have a traditional tendency to be tolerant, eclectic, this-worldly, and agnostic in their outlook on religion. Traditional religious and magical beliefs, such as ancestor worship and temple ritual, are declining in prevalence, but not so rapidly as in China. The secular ideologies which have gained popularity in China since the 1911 revolution have had much less appeal in Semarang. There is a substantial proportion of the community which adheres to no religion and increasingly takes a secular, "modernist" outlook. On the other hand, both Christian churches and Chinese neotraditional societies have become increasingly important in the Chinese community.

CHAPTER X

Family and Kinship

The Chinese immigrants who settled in Southeast Asia came from parts of China in which the tradition of the patriarchal extended family was especially strong. In the Semarang Chinese community today, certain aspects of that tradition have been abandoned, others have been seriously challenged, and still others remain substantially intact. Among some groups in the community, change has proceeded much farther than among others. In the discussion of the family and kinship system of this community, those aspects which are most relevant to the problem of change will be emphasized. The description applies primarily to the Peranakan group, because of insufficient data about Totok family relations.

Family Types and Family Composition

Sociologists who have studied the family system in China distinguish two types of extended family: the stem family and the joint family.[1] In the typical stem family, *one* of the sons after marriage continues to live with his parents and unmarried sib-

[1] Olga Lang, *Chinese Family and Society* (New Haven, 1946), pp. 14–15; Marion J. Levy, Jr., *The Family Revolution in Modern China* (Cambridge, Mass., 1949), pp. 55–56.

lings, and his wife and children become part of the family. A stem family may also consist of parents and the family of a married daughter. All families may be "broken" by death, divorce, or separation, and therefore a broken stem family could consist of as few as two people: a parent and a son- or daughter-in-law. The joint family differs from the stem family in that *more than one* married son or daughter remains with the parents and their unmarried children. A broken joint family could consist of a minimum of two people: for instance, the wives of two brothers. Although stem and joint families may include three or more generations, the conjugal family is limited to two: parents and unmarried children. Its minimum form is a childless couple or a parent and one child.

Students of the Chinese family agree that the traditional ideal in all classes of Chinese society has been the joint family, at least until quite recent times.[2] Even among the peasantry, where external circumstances usually made it impossible, parents longed to keep their married sons at home and to live long enough to see their grandchildren, and perhaps their great-grandchildren, playing in their courtyards.

The joint family is still considered ideal by a small minority of the Chinese in Semarang. But the great majority have adopted a new ideal—the conjugal family. Among the fifty housewives interviewed in the survey, all but three favored the conjugal family. One stated that she would prefer to have her sons remain in the home after they are married. Two others preferred stem or joint families, provided that "co-operation is possible" or that "no quarrels arise." But most informants agreed that one could not expect harmony in the extended family. One said: "In Chinese families there are too many quarrels if the family sticks together. Quarrels and hard feelings are common between mothers-in-law and daughters-in-law and between sisters-in-law. So they separate if they can."

[2] Lang, *op. cit.*, p. 16; Levy, *op. cit.*, p. 59.

In the questionnaire survey, high school students were asked the following question:

Young man E was the only child of Mr. and Mrs. G. When E got married, Mr. and Mrs. G wanted the young couple to live with them. However, E's employer offered to give E a house of his own. What should the young couple do? Why do you think so?

In spite of the fact that this question puts the weight of filial piety and humanitarianism on the side of the stem family, 54 per cent of the respondents favored the separate conjugal family and another 10 per cent suggested compromise solutions. The most common reasons given were the desirability of avoiding quarreling and unpleasantness, which were considered likely or even inevitable in the stem family, and the desire of young people for freedom and independence.

Among the 34 per cent who were of the opinion that the young couple should live with the parents, the majority gave as their reason the love, obedience, or responsibility of children toward their parents. For instance: "If he really loves his parents, he must obey them." Only a few of the replies suggested real preference for the stem or joint family. For example, "I should like to live with my parents, because by so doing I would be able to repay their goodness to me."

The sample of housewives is small, and it includes too high a proportion of Christians and Peranakans to be representative of the whole community. Similarly, the questionnaire respondents do not include enough young people from the lowest socioeconomic group. Therefore there is a possibility that preference for the conjugal family is not quite as widespread as these data suggest. Nevertheless, it is obvious that very considerable changes have taken place in the ideal patterns of family composition.

This writer believes that the increasing preference for the conjugal family is due not only to the reported difficulties of joint family life, but also to the declining importance of economic co-operation in large family units. Rapid growth in the numbers of professionals and wage and salary earners (mostly white-collar employees) has meant that fewer and fewer young couples are economically dependent upon their parents. In addition to these factors, it seems likely that emulation of the West has played a part in the increasing preference for the conjugal family.

On the question whether practices have changed in accordance with the new ideal, the situation is not nearly so clear. In the first place, it is impossible to ascertain exactly what the "traditional" practices were in the emigrant communities of South China. Taking the existing evidence for China as a whole, Levy concludes that "the type of family in which the average Chinese lived during the 'traditional' period must in fact have been the *famille souche* or 'stem family.' "[3] It is generally agreed that the joint family was common only among the gentry. The conjugal family was found in all classes, but was most common among the rural and urban laboring classes.

Surveys reported by Olga Lang show that during the 1930's the number of conjugal families varied from 54 per cent among farm laborers to 12 per cent among landlords in North China villages and from 58 per cent among wage earners to 50 per cent in the middle class in nonindustrial cities of North China. A survey in Central China, which did not divide respondents by class, showed that 66 per cent of urban families and 45 per cent of rural families were conjugal in form. A very much smaller sample surveyed in Fukien province, the homeland of many Semarang immigrants, showed similar results.[4]

These data may now be compared with the results of the interview survey in Semarang. Among the fifty families covered, 50 per cent were conjugal, 40 per cent were stem, and 10 per cent were joint. Comparable figures for the middle class in nonindustrial cities of North China twenty years earlier are 50 per cent, 34 per cent, and 16 per cent, respectively.[5] It must again be

[3] Levy, *op. cit.*, p. 55.   [4] Lang, *op. cit.*, pp. 136–138, 350.   [5] *Ibid.*, p. 136.

pointed out that the Semarang sample was small and somewhat un-representative. But the similarity of results suggests that, with regard to family types, the Semarang Chinese today are little different from comparable groups in China two decades ago. Furthermore, from these figures it appears likely that in both cases the proportion of conjugal families is only slightly higher than the proportion which existed in cities of China before the influence of Western culture was felt, and only about 10 per cent higher than in the rural areas from which some of the immigrants came.

If this analysis is correct, the ideal for family composition has changed much more than has the practice. Undoubtedly one reason for this is the acute housing shortage in Semarang, which makes it extremely difficult for a newly married couple to establish a new home. Another reason, deference to the wishes of parents, has been suggested in the results of the student questionnaire survey and will be discussed further in a section on filial piety.

In spite of the apparent similarity in the proportions of different types of family in Semarang and China, it appears that there have been certain changes in patterns of family composition in Semarang. For one thing, the majority of traditional stem families were formed by the addition of a daughter-in-law to a conjugal family. Among the nineteen stem families in the sample, eight were composed of a husband and wife, their children, and the mother of one (or, in one case, of both) of them. This may indicate a trend toward what may be considered a more Western type of stem family—that is, one that is formed by the addition of a dependent mother-in-law to a conjugal family. The lack of additional data on this is unfortunate, because the social and psychological differences between the two stem families, depending on who comes as the outsider to the original unit, are very great indeed.

An even more striking change is suggested by the finding that among the nineteen stem families fourteen of the married couples

are living with one or both of the *wife's* parents. Similarly, in five
of the eight conjugal families which have relatives in the household, the relatives are the wife's. Although the sample is small,
evidence from this and other sources leads to the conclusion that
in most sections of the Chinese community there has been a change
from the traditional patrilineal, patrilocal family system to a
bilateral, bilocal or neolocal pattern—that is, to a system in which
the wife's kin are as important to the family as the husband's kin
and in which married couples may live with either the husband's
or the wife's family or with neither.

The writer believes that the rising status of women was the
major reason for this change. Long before the "emancipation"
movement after World War I, the local wives of Chinese immigrants had a higher status than had married women in China. The
position of women vis-à-vis men was strengthened by the fact that
there was a shortage of potential wives for the Chinese immigrants.
In addition, the Javanese wives of most of the immigrants played
an almost indispensable role as business partners. Thus the "bar-
gaining power" of women was considerable, and their desires with
regard to place of residence and family relations had to be considered. This has become more and more true with further gains
in the status of women in recent decades. The trend will be discussed in detail in a later section.

Javanese culture was also an important factor in undermining
the traditional Chinese pattern. The Javanese wives of immigrants were accustomed to a bilateral family system, and it seems
safe to assume that they sought to perpetuate the types of family
relationships which they had learned to expect; that is, they
sought to maintain close ties with their own as well as their
husbands' families, and with their daughters' as well as their sons'
families.

Matrilocal residence rarely occurred in China. It could be
brought about only by what amounted to adoption of the husband
by the wife's family. This meant a change of name and ancestors,

and was therefore not a desirable prospect for the Chinese male. Matrilocal residence according to Javanese custom, however, did not involve nearly as great a break from traditional Chinese ideals and prejudices. The family name and ancestor worship in the male line could be maintained. Therefore the Javanese system provided an attractive solution for the Chinese male who, for reasons of convenience or economic co-operation, wanted to live with his wife's kin. It was also a welcome alternative for wives who were eager to escape the traditional domination of their mothers-in-law, and for many Chinese parents who, because of personal attachment or other reasons, wanted a married daughter and her family to reside with them.

These are some of the factors which have made matrilocal residence relatively common in the Chinese community. And, as Murdock has clearly demonstrated, such changes in residence customs can ordinarily be expected to eventuate in changes of lineal groupings.[6] In this case, then, one of the reasons for the emergence of bilateral family relations was the advent of bilocal residence practices. Two other reasons, discussed above, were the rising status of women and the influence of Javanese culture.

Family Size

According to municipal statistics, the average birth rate of the Chinese population of Semarang for the years 1951–1953 was about 40. The death rate during the same years averaged 9.3. The corresponding figures for the Indonesian population of Semarang were about 28 and 22.[7] These figures indicate the relatively low standard of living, the poor health conditions, and the acute lack of medical services among the Indonesians. Such conditions are reflected in abnormally high rates of still birth and infant mor-

[6] George Peter Murdock, *Social Structure* (New York, 1949), ch. viii.

[7] Dr. R. Soeharto, "Kesehatan di Indonesia" (text of a speech delivered to the Fifth Conference of the Ikatan Doktor Indonesia in Semarang, Dec. 20, 1954).

tality—about 3 per cent and 12 per cent, respectively, of all births in Semarang, according to public health authorities.[8] Medical services and health conditions are far better among the Chinese. Nevertheless, 49 per cent of the Chinese questionnaire respondents indicated that one or more of their brothers or sisters were "no longer living"; 10 per cent had three or more deceased siblings. In the figures for family size which follow, only the number of living children are taken into account in the respondents' generation, whereas all siblings of the parents who were known to the respondents were included in the parents' generation. Thus the figures for different generations are only roughly comparable.

In previous chapters, family size has been discussed in connection with socioeconomic and religious differences and differences between Totoks and Peranakans. In the survey results, only the latter comparison showed significant differences in family size. If the questionnaire results are weighted according to the proper proportion of Totoks and Peranakans in the Chinese population, the average number of living children per family in the respondents' generation is 6.2, and in their parents' generation 6.3. The comparable figures for the Indonesian population are 5.7 and 6.0. It may be concluded that in both ethnic groups large families are the norm, and have been for some time.

Nevertheless, there is some indication that changes are taking place. Questionnaire respondents were asked: "If you get married, how many children would you like to have?" The average number desired by the Chinese respondents was 4.4, and by the Indonesians, 5.0. Since knowledge and use of modern contraceptive methods are exceedingly limited in Semarang, it is likely that many of these young people will have larger families than they now consider ideal. In any case, it is evident that most educated young people do not have the traditional ideal of a very large family. And there is reason to believe that, as the number of educated people increases, average family size will decrease.

[8] *Ibid.*

The questionnaire results show a relationship between education and family size, at least for women. Among respondents' fathers who did not attend high school, the average number of children was 5.9; among those fathers who had at least some high school education, the average was 5.2. The difference, however, is not statistically significant. Among respondents' mothers who had no education at all, the average number of children was 6.9; among those mothers with primary school education, the average was 5.0; and among those with at least some high school education, the average was 4.8. The differences between the last two figures and the first are significant at the .01 level. Within each of the three socioeconomic categories used for analytic purposes, differences in education were consistently related to differences in family size. Again the greatest differences were among the women. On the other hand, within educational categories, there was no consistent pattern of relationship between family size and socioeconomic status.

These findings indicate that the most important correlate of family size is the education of the mother. The writer believes that at least four causal factors are involved in this relationship. First, the educated woman is usually one whose family background and individual predisposition encourage her to seek a less traditional role. Second, education itself may give her aspirations incompatible with a large family. Third, education may delay marriage, thus shortening the child-bearing period. Fourth, education raises the status of women vis-à-vis their husbands, and therefore gives them more voice in determining family size. Women may want to limit family size for several reasons: to reduce the burdens of motherhood, to provide more time for recreation or activities outside the home, or to emulate the "modern" women of their own or other societies. The uneducated Chinese woman is likely to be more traditional in her goals and expectations. Even if she desires to limit family size, she is not in as good a position to do so as is the educated woman.

The proportion of girls who are attending primary and secondary schools and even universities is steadily increasing, and educated young people of both sexes want fewer children than their parents had. For these and other reasons, it seems likely that the average family size will decline in the next few decades.

The Treatment and Training of Children

Considerable differences in the treatment and training of children exist between and within different groups in the Chinese community. Even in a group in which differences are small enough to be safely ignored, only intimate and lengthy observation can yield systematic data for a researcher in this field. Therefore it was quite impossible for the writer to obtain detailed and accurate information on this subject. In the discussion which follows, sketchy questionnaire data will be supplemented by impressionistic observations and material from printed sources. These will serve to give a general picture of the treatment and training of children and of the ways in which these are changing.

In both Totok and Peranakan homes, the writer observed that infants are given much attention, affection, and care. They are treated with great indulgence. Disciplinary action is mild and infrequent. Apparently the treatment of infants is little different, if at all, from their treatment in traditional and modern families of mainland China.[9]

Marked changes have taken place in the treatment of children between four years of age or younger and the first few years of adolescence. Traditionally, this period was one of considerable strain for boys because severe discipline was imposed, primarily by the father. For girls it was a period of increasing seclusion in the home. Between World Wars I and II, discipline was relaxed considerably in modern or "transitional" families of China.[10] The same trend has been apparent among the Semarang Chinese, partly because of modernist influences, and partly because of the earlier influence of Indonesian mothers and grandmothers.

Modern or Western ideas of child training have been learned

[9] Levy, *op. cit.*, pp. 69–70, 289–290. [10] *Ibid.*, pp. 75–84, 290–294.

from publications and moving pictures and from observation of the treatment of European children by their parents. It is not uncommon to find Dr. Spock quoted or translated at length in Indonesian Chinese publications. The occasional articles on child training in such periodicals as the *Star Weekly* usually advocate a progressive approach.[11] Yet there is also a fairly widespread concern that "Western" leniency with children may go too far. The following quotation from an editorial in the *Star Weekly* is an indication of the changes taking place, as well as of one reaction to them:

DUTCHIFICATION

Although the Dutch no longer hold power here, the influence of the ideas of white society is still felt among our people, and this influence is not always good.

Eastern people are usually extremely careful with their children who are still small. These children are not allowed to play alone on the streets. Children aged six, seven, or eight are taken to school by nursemaids, or, if there are no nursemaids, by their mothers or grandmothers. Again their parents have to spend time or money for meeting them after school and bringing them home. Fathers and mothers are especially afraid of the danger of water [drowning].

This attitude is in striking contrast to that of the white mothers and fathers, mostly Dutch, who used to reside here. They were more willing to have their small children come home from school alone, to allow them to play in the streets, and to leave them at home alone when they themselves were out. The influence of this attitude has spread among Eastern people, sometimes merely because they like to Dutchify themselves.[12]

In the interview survey, Chinese mothers often stated that they treat their children in a more "modern" or "Western" way than they themselves were treated as children. Usually, however, they

[11] For instance, "Omong-omong tentang Anak-anak jang Berumur antara 6 dan 12 Tahun," in *Star Weekly*, no. 463 (Nov. 13, 1954), pp. 10–11.

[12] *Star Weekly*, no. 464 (Nov. 20, 1954), p. 2.

also declared that they believed only in taking the best from the West, while maintaining the good in Eastern tradition. In general, this means a compromise between the discipline and restrictions imposed upon the children of traditional Chinese families on the one hand and the relative freedom and independence which is allowed in Western middle-class urban families on the other. In one Totok family known to the writer, for instance, corporal punishment and other forms of severe discipline are rarely, if ever, used. Children are not forced to show the subservience and exaggerated respect toward adults which tradition demands. A degree of companionship between parents and children has been encouraged. Nevertheless, all activities of the children are carefully supervised. Even the adolescent children must be home by eight o'clock in the evening. If they want to see moving pictures, they must go to the five-o'clock show. Certain traditional forms of etiquette are required of them, such as passing or offering with both hands instead of one. Thus "modern" ideas are being accepted and put into practice along with many traditional ones.

The Semarang Chinese commonly ascribe to Western influence their increased leniency in treatment of children. The writer, however, is convinced that the attitudes and methods of Indonesian mothers and grandmothers of previous generations have also caused changes in this direction.

The fact that Peranakans, at least, have unknowingly accepted many Indonesian ideas of child training may be illustrated by material from a book by Moerman on the Chinese of Djakarta.[13] To this Dutch teacher, Chinese child training appeared to consist primarily of "Do" and "Don't." From his Chinese students, who were doubtless all Peranakans, he gathered a list of seventeen childhood prohibitions, which they said were common among the Chinese. For instance: "After six o'clock children must not play hide-and-seek; otherwise evil spirits will hide them and they

[13] J. Moerman, *In en om de Chineesche Kamp* (Amsterdam, 1932), pp. 173–177.

will never come back." The writer showed a copy of this list first to a Totok couple and then to an Indonesian friend, without revealing its origin or his purpose in doing so. Among the seventeen prohibitions, the Totok couple recognized only two as being wholly Chinese. Three others were similar to prohibitions with which they were familiar. On the other hand, the Indonesian friend identified thirteen as being common ones in Javanese families. This seems to indicate that the great majority of prohibitions which Peranakan children learn have Indonesian, and not Chinese, origins.

The writer believes that relatively lenient treatment of children became part of Peranakan culture in the same way as these prohibitions—that is, through Javanese mothers and grandmothers of previous generations and through Javanese servants and nursemaids. If this is so, traditional strictness and discipline were undergoing change well before the impact of Western or modern Chinese ideas.

Filial Piety

In Chapter IX the nature of the Chinese principle of *hauw*, or filial piety, was discussed, and its relation to ancestor worship was explained. Theoretically, filial piety was supposed to be a natural and freely accepted attitude, as the following excerpt, written in 1798 and translated into English in 1849, will demonstrate:

I have heard that Ong-tae-hae, when at Semarang, was entertained in the house of the Kap-pit-tan, where his dress and food were elegant and complete, with scores of female attendants around him; and yet he would not be one of those most happy people, because Ong had an old mother at home, whom he longed to see; wherefore he looked upon all as a dream of the southern forest, and whisking his sleeve he returned home, with as little regret as if he had been throwing away an old shoe; considering the coarse vegetables of his native village as sweeter by far than all the delicacies of the south; after which he set to work ploughing with his tongue [school teaching] as before. For it was a thought of filial piety that sprung up in his breast, and the delights of Semarang could not hold him back.[14]

In practice, however, filial piety involved respectful behavior, obedience, and attentiveness, which often had to be imposed by stern discipline. The relationship of son to father, especially, was characterized far more by fear and resentment than by love and admiration.[15] Indeed, the frustrations of severe discipline were such that the positive aspects of filial piety were reduced to a minimum. Perhaps for this reason, one of the best-known leaders of the Chinese "Renaissance Movement," Dr. Hu Shih, has maintained that filial piety scarcely ever existed and that "in those rare cases where it was consciously cultivated the price paid for it was nothing short of intense suppression resulting in mental and physical agony." [16] This view of filial piety may be somewhat exaggerated, but in any case it suggests that traditional families in China very often failed to inculcate the kind of filial piety which tradition idealized.

An attempt will now be made to assess the degree to which filial piety exists among the young Chinese of Semarang—or, more precisely, among Chinese high school students there. The questionnaire included the item: "What feelings do you have toward your father and mother?" Respondents were asked to reply by checking as many items as were applicable in the following list: intimacy, respect, fear, love, dislike, submissiveness, admiration, desire to avoid, companionship. Separate lists were checked for mother and father. Unfortunately, words for these various feelings bear different connotations in Indonesian, Chinese, and English. Therefore the results for the Indonesian language questionnaire

[14] Ong Tai Hae, *The Chinaman Abroad; or, A Desultory Account of the Malayan Archipelago, Particularly of Java* (English trans., Shanghai, 1849), pp. 10–11.

[15] Levy, *op. cit.*, pp. 75–84, 166–175.

[16] Hu Shih, *The Chinese Renaissance* (New York, 1930), p. 110, as quoted in Lang, *op. cit.*, p. 112.

cannot be compared with those for the Chinese form; and reporting the results in the English language may be misleading. Some interesting comparisons can be made, however, and some tentative conclusions suggested.

In place of the Indonesian word for submissiveness, the Chinese word for filial piety was used in the Chinese-language questionnaire. Of the 132 male students who answered the questionnaire in Chinese, 69 per cent claimed that they had feelings of filial piety toward their father. Among the 88 girls, the proportion was 75 per cent. For the Chinese students who answered the Indonesian-language questionnaire, the corresponding results for those checking "submissiveness" toward the father were 47 per cent for boys and 43 per cent for girls. The writer believes that between the two groups of respondents who answered the questionnaire in different languages the actual differences in feelings toward parents were not very great. It seems likely that many of the Chinese-language respondents checked "filial piety," whether candidly or not, merely to conform to a cultural norm. Nevertheless, the large proportion who checked the Indonesian word for "submissiveness," which is little used among the Chinese, suggests that feelings at least akin to filial piety are not rare among the respondents.

Other feelings which are traditionally linked with filial piety were even more frequently checked. Among both boys and girls, about 88 per cent indicated "respect," about 71 per cent indicated "love," and about 49 per cent indicated "admiration" for their fathers. Differences were negligible between Chinese-language and Indonesian-language respondents on these three items. The same three categories were also used in the questionnaires which were administered by Olga Lang to high school students in China in the 1930's.[17] In that survey the corresponding figures were 78

[17] Figures for this survey which are given here and in succeeding paragraphs are taken from Table VII on p. 355 of Dr. Lang's book, *op. cit.*

per cent, 66 per cent, and 30 per cent. These percentages suggest not only that filial feelings are common among the Semarang respondents, but that they are more common in Semarang than in China.

The figures for China are not strictly comparable with those for Semarang because of language differences. Yet it seems safe to say that the Semarang respondents have more positive ties to their parents than had students in China because three other comparisons point in the same direction. Whereas virtually none of the Semarang students indicated a "desire to avoid" their fathers, in China 17 per cent of the male and 7 per cent of the female students checked this category. In Semarang, 24 per cent of the boys and 20 per cent of the girls regard their fathers with "fear." The corresponding figures for China are 64 per cent and 56 per cent. (Needless to say, fear was not supposed to enter into the ideal relationship of filial piety.)

Thus far the figures seem to indicate that there are more feelings akin to filial piety among Semarang students than among students in China about two decades earlier. This cannot, however, be interpreted as a "return" to filial piety. Rather, a new relationship seems to be emerging, that is, one involving less formality and more mutuality. About 33 per cent of the Semarang students checked "companionship" as applying to their relations with their fathers. (There was little difference between boys and girls in this respect, although, as would be expected even in traditional families, the percentage of girls who indicated companionship with their mothers was more than twice as high as that for boys.) In China, on the other hand, only about 6 per cent of both male and female students reported companionship with their fathers. A comparison of other Semarang questionnaire results with data given by Lang [18] makes it evident that Semarang students turn to their parents for advice on personal problems much

[18] *Ibid.,* p. 297.

more frequently than did students in China. Over one-third of the Semarang respondents of both sexes indicated that their relations with their fathers are "intimate."

The relationship between Semarang students and their fathers appears to be very similar to that which Dr. Lang found between students in China and their fathers in those cases where the father had had a modern college education. Her conclusion about the modern group in China could be applied to a much larger proportion of the Chinese in Semarang:

It seems that modern education and modern trends bring the father-son relations closer to the Confucian ideal of genuine love and respect, free of fear and compulsion. A filial modern son of a modern father will not only support him but do it with a happy countenance, just as the old sages wished! [19]

A generation ago many modernist young people, in both China and Indonesia, were disposed to reject filial piety in principle.[20] In Indonesia today, it is often redefined, but seldom rejected. As shown in the questionnaire results, more than two-thirds of the respondents are willing to apply the term "filial piety" to their own feelings toward their parents. *Hauw* is taught directly in some schools and publications, even by the use of the twenty-four classical stories of extreme filial piety.[21]

Acceptance of the principle of filial piety in the Semarang Chinese community, and even among modern young people, can be illustrated by the following incident. The members of a drama club, mostly well-educated young people, were discussing what play they should next present. Someone suggested *Api*, a wartime drama by the Indonesian writer Usmar Ismael. In this play

---

[19] *Ibid.*, p. 301.

[20] See, for instance, the article "Why the religion of Confucius has come to be considered dangerous for the Chinese," in *Sin Po*, IV, no. 161 (May 1, 1926), 902–903.

[21] See the regular children's page in the organ of the Three Religions Society, *Tri Budaja*.

the father, who represents Japan, is the tyrant and villain. One of the leaders of the club pointed out that parts of the dialogue would violate Chinese feelings about *hauw*, especially where the daughter declares that she "hates" her father. Others shared this concern, and it was generally agreed that if this play were chosen, the dialogue should be "modified." This attitude is a far cry from the mood of the militant young intellectuals of the Renaissance Movement in China. In writings such as Mao Tun's novel *Chia* (Family), they bitterly attacked family relations based upon traditional filial piety. *Chia* was rewritten as a play and has been a favorite stage production in China ever since.

In summary, it may be said that in precept and in practice the principle of filial piety is widely accepted in the Semarang Chinese community. However, it has been somewhat redefined, with greater emphasis on love, respect, and mutuality, and less on obedience and submissiveness. As brought out in Chapter IX, the traditional ritual obligations of filial piety, associated as they are with ancestor worship, are rapidly being forgotten.

The Status of Youth

In the foregoing section on filial piety, primarily the feelings of children toward their parents were dealt with. In this section authority and status in parent-child relationships will be discussed. This is, of course, closely related to filial piety.

So far as this writer was able to ascertain, the traditional subordination of young people prevailed in Semarang at least until the time of World War I. Parents regulated the daily lives of their children and made all important decisions for them until they were married, and to a considerable extent even after that. Subsequent to the establishment of modern schools, young people began to demand greater independence. In the 1920's, student and youth organizations were established for the first time. Their principal purpose was to provide sports and recreation. But in their meetings and through their publications the "emancipation" of youth was discussed. The relative freedom of Western young people was before their eyes, and they began to demand the right to have freer boy-girl relationships, to dance, and to select their own marriage partners. They knew that young people were playing a major role in the making of a new China, and they began to see "familism" as the root of many social evils. Nationalism and individualism challenged family loyalty.

All of this amounted to what some Chinese observers have called a "youth movement" in the 1920's and 1930's. This movement was the expression of the conflict between the new and the old generations. The following excerpts, which were written in 1927 by a Chinese columnist in the Indonesian-language periodical *Sin Po*, provide a graphic picture and an interesting interpretation of this conflict:

It is hard to list in detail the differences between our modern generation and the older generation. Dissatisfaction with what already exists and a spirit of revolt are perhaps even more typical of our modern generation than of the new generation in the West. They are weary of all tradition, they hate conventions, and they care not for authority—this has become quite general.

What are the reasons for this frightening change? One of the most important reasons is the entrance of Western morality into the Eastern world. . . . The older generation purposely closed their eyes to the morality and the changes in the West.

It later became apparent this attitude was wrong. It was Japan that first showed that the East must learn from the West. . . .

Since then we have begun to make comparisons. Our morality, customs, virtues, habits, in short, everything is being compared with those of the West. These comparisons are made on the widest possible scale. . . .

[In addition to the political revolution] education, business, organizations, and home life are all experiencing revolution. From clothing to literature, from ceremonies to daily way of life, everything is undergoing revolution. In short, this revolution is running amuck without restraint, because Chinese views concerning ethics and beliefs are also struck by the change-over.

An important problem of the present period is the conflict between the new and the old generation in opinions, ideas, and behavior. . . .

Education has been an important factor in this situation. Our older generation may be said to have had no modern education at all, whereas the younger generation has had almost every opportunity for modern education. . . .

The highest ideals of a businessman father are to make a lot of money and get wealthy, to build a large house to live in with his aging parents, and, if his parents have already died, to build a beautiful grave for them in order to complete his devotion. It is not surprising if such a father, having had no schooling or modern education and busying himself day and night seeking profits, does not know anything about so-called nationalism, patriotism, democracy, emancipated thinking, and so on. But his children get a Western or modern Chinese education. Because of this education, their ideas and thoughts will certainly be very different.

. . . We see not a few mothers and fathers, especially fathers, who are obstinate. They refuse to recognize that there is a wide gulf between them and their children. . . . They send their children to the most modern schools, but at home they firmly maintain the customs and atmosphere of the past. They believe that by doing this they can keep their children "on safe ground," without realizing that every day their children face contradictions which confuse them and heighten their passion for revolt.[22]

This picture may be somewhat exaggerated. For one thing, a large number of young people attended only the first few grades of school, or none at all, and did not participate in any of the youth organizations. And even among educated young people, there were probably many who were not fired by the "spirit of revolt." Nevertheless, it seems clear that a considerable number of young people accepted and defended a way of life which was incompatible with tradition and parental authority.

The modern Chinese youth in Semarang present a somewhat

[22] These excerpts are taken from the regular column "Causerie de Samedi" by "H," in *Sin Po*, V, no. 238 (Oct. 22, 1927), 456–461.

different picture. Although there are youth and student organizations, these are almost entirely concerned with sports, recreation, and fund raising for worthy causes. No "spirit of revolt" or talk of "emancipation" is in evidence. The right of young people to have an important, if not a final, voice in the major decisions of their lives has been accepted by the majority of parents. And parental control over the daily activities of their children has been decreasing steadily.

Young people are not completely satisfied with their status, but serious dissatisfaction is not widespread. Among the questionnaire respondents, about 10 per cent of both boys and girls indicated that they "often" had differences of opinion with their parents. About 31 per cent of the boys and 21 per cent of the girls had "occasional" differences, and 39 per cent of the boys and 46 per cent of the girls had "rare" differences. About 21 per cent in both groups reported no differences of opinion.

Those respondents who differed with their parents were asked to write down the subjects of disagreement. About 28 per cent mentioned differences of outlook, ideals, or way of life. Another 17 per cent mentioned social relationships (especially with the opposite sex), recreation, dancing, or marriage. The figures for other items were as follows: home life and family relationships, 23 per cent; education and schooling, 17 per cent; religion, 9 per cent; politics, citizenship, and international affairs, 6 per cent; future vocation, 6 per cent; and the question of returning to China, 4 per cent.

The figures presented in the foregoing paragraphs do not appear to indicate a revolt of youth against tradition and authority. Indeed, from the questionnaire and interview survey results, as well as from personal impressions, this writer has come to the conclusion that the conflict between generations is only moderate in the Chinese community today. Many of the mothers interviewed in the survey declared that modern youth is "too free" or "going too far." Almost 60 per cent of the questionnaire respondents consider their parents more conservative than they are with regard to marriage and family life. But these differences of opinion very rarely lead to serious or open conflict. As noted earlier, most of the young people have fairly positive attitudes toward their parents and are often willing to submit or defer to them. On the other hand, a large number of the parents who disapprove of their children's behavior make little effort to curb them. Both sides seem willing to compromise. Even grandparents often yield to the times with no more than a regretful shake of the head.

Some of the reasons why youth has achieved a higher status will now be briefly considered—that is, why young people today are allowed considerably more freedom and independence than the young people two generations ago. First, it must be remembered that the young people who were opposing parental authority in the 1920's and 1930's are among the parents of today. No doubt many of them have maintained or only slightly modified their opinions about the rights of youth.

Second, the greater freedom allowed young people today is doubtless in part an extension of the greater leniency with which children are now treated at all ages. Various reasons for this increased leniency have been discussed in a previous section.

Third, young people are now respected for their educational achievements. In Chapter V, it was pointed out that education is of considerable prestige value in the Chinese community. Most young people today have gone considerably farther in their schooling than did their parents. For example, the Chinese questionnaire respondents were all senior high school students. Among their fathers, however, one-eighth had had no schooling at all, and only one-quarter had attended senior high school. Among their mothers, two-fifths had had no schooling, and only about a twentieth had attended senior high school. According to informants and written sources,[23] in cases where young people have

[23] See *ibid.*, pp. 460–461.

obtained considerably more education than their parents, the latter often have an "inferiority complex" and hesitate to assert their authority or impose their will upon their children. This is probably a contributing factor in a significant number of cases.

Economic factors do not appear to have been important in the rising status of youth. Because of their more prolonged education, young people are, if anything, less economically independent than ever. Among the questionnaire respondents, about one-quarter were twenty years of age or older, but only abòut 5 per cent of the boys and 7 per cent of the girls had ever held jobs for which they had received regular pay.

The increasing freedom and independence of youth are no doubt partly due to the demands of the young people themselves. These demands are probably instigated by two interdependent motivations: the desire to be free from frustrating restrictions and the desire to emulate the young people of modern China and the West. The first of these motivations has undoubtedly existed, to some degree, throughout the history of Chinese patriarchy. The second, as demonstrated, has been brought about primarily by modern education.

The Status of Women

Relative to their position in other societies of the world, the status of women in traditional China was very low. When they were children, their brothers were given preferential treatment. When they were adolescents, they were kept secluded in the home. After marriage, they were subordinate to their husbands and dominated by their mothers-in-law. They had no part in public life outside the home.

The extent to which this situation prevailed in the Chinese community of Semarang prior to World War I is difficult to ascertain. The Javanese wives of the Chinese settlers were accustomed to more authority in the home and more independence in economic matters. As they very often played the role of business partner to their husbands, there is no doubt that they enjoyed a higher status than the traditional Chinese wife. Nevertheless, certain features of the Chinese family system remained intact, and many women suffered under them. A prominent Peranakan woman, writing in an Indonesian-language periodical, had this to say of the position of women at the beginning of the twentieth century:

Their way of life actually was more certain and secure, but from her parents' stories [a modern young woman] knows how many tears used to flow.[24]

It is therefore not surprising that, associated with the "youth movement" of the 1920's and 1930's, there was a movement for the "emancipation" of women. The youth associations of that period at first established women's branches and then brought men and women together in single organizations. The position of women in the family and their role in society were much discussed in meetings and in periodicals. The demands of young people, combined with even more important factors which will be discussed at the end of this section, have brought about a rapid rise in the status of women since World War I. The woman writer quoted above summarizes the situation as follows:

Emancipation has very greatly changed the life of women. The field of their activities, which in the past was severely limited, has now become almost as wide as the field of activities of men. The recent world war seems to have speeded up this process of emancipation. In about fifty years the life of women has become as different as day from night.[25]

Perhaps the most noticeable aspect of the "emancipation" of women is their release from the confines of the home. The traditional seclusion of married women and girls in their teens has

[24] Nj. Oei Hien Tjhiang, "Lain Dulu, Lain Sekarang," *Star Weekly*, no. 528 (Feb. 11, 1956), p. 4.

[25] *Ibid.*, p. 4.

virtually disappeared. Girls and women appear on the streets and in all public places without embarrassment. In schools, meetings of organizations, receptions, and social gatherings, formal or informal segregation of the sexes often occurs. But those who feel that women are "out of place" at such events represent a small and diminishing minority.

Women have been released from the home in another way: their household duties are somewhat less time-consuming than those of previous generations, because more prepared foods and ready-made clothing are available in the stores. In addition, most Chinese families have at least one Javanese servant. Among the fifty housewives interviewed, only 12 per cent were without servants; 31 per cent had one servant; 25 per cent had two; and 32 per cent had three or more. About 85 per cent of the student questionnaire respondents had had nursemaids to care for them when they were young. Although these percentages would undoubtedly be lower if derived from a more representative sample, it is clear that a considerable amount of the housework which was done by traditional wives and mothers in the emigrants' families in China is done by servants in Semarang Chinese homes. It should be mentioned, however, that even with the help of servants the average Semarang housewife usually has no more free time than her counterpart in the United States.

In the interview survey, housewives were asked how they spent their "leisure time." About 35 per cent stated that they had no activities aside from housekeeping; 25 per cent reported household arts, such as sewing, embroidery, gardening, and flower arrangement. (As has been noted in a previous chapter on education, many Chinese women spend considerable time taking or giving lessons in these skills.) In the field of home and family recreation, 22 per cent mentioned reading, 6 per cent mentioned music, and another 6 per cent mentioned family outings. As for recreation away from home, 20 per cent mentioned sports, usually either swimming or badminton, and 6 per cent mentioned moving pictures. About 18 per cent participated in clubs and community work, such as church women's associations or the Girl Guide movement. Only one woman mentioned *mahjong*, a Chinese gambling game reported to be common among well-to-do ladies.

The above percentages must be taken only as general indications of the relative popularity of various leisure-time activities among Semarang Chinese women. The small and unrepresentative nature of the sample and the lack of standardization in the way that the question was asked make these figures rather unreliable. Nevertheless, they corroborate the writer's observations and support his conclusion that, in spite of their newly acquired freedom, most Chinese women are still interested primarily in the home. Only a minority regularly participate in activities previously rare among women, such as sports, clubs, and public life.

Although many of the associations described in Chapter VI accept women as members, women have never played an important part in them. Women's branches and temporary women's committees of various organizations have been established from time to time, primarily to help raise funds. Women are very rarely elected to leadership positions in competition with men, and when they are, the positions are more honorary than functional.

The most important women's organization in Semarang is the Fu Nu Hui (Women's Association). It was founded in 1926 and has since grown to an organization of some 700 members, about 300 of whom are married. Its activities are primarily charitable and recreational. Through dramatic performances and other programs, it raises money for various charitable institutions. In addition, it operates a weekly mother-and-baby clinic for those who cannot afford the usual physician's charges. For the benefit of its members, the association has recently established a library. It also arranges picnics and excursions, and has a weekly period reserved for its members at the municipal swimming pool.

Within the Fu Nu Hui there has always been a minority of members who are concerned about the position of women in society and the family. At occasional membership meetings there are lectures and discussions concerning the problems of women. The head of the association, Mrs. Chung Kim Yan, is an advocate of mutuality and companionship in the home and equality for women in society. In addition to leading the Fu Nu Hui, she plays an active part in Chinese community affairs and public life in Semarang.

In this consideration of the changing position of women, the Protestant women's organization "Debora" is of special interest because, so far as the writer was able to ascertain, it has held the only publicly announced lectures on birth control which have been given in Semarang. According to Chinese doctors, only a very small number of Chinese in Semarang have knowledge of or interest in contraception sufficient to practice it or even to seek medical advice about it.

In the field of education, too, there is considerable evidence of change. The first school for girls in Semarang, according to its founder, Mrs. Goei Sin Nio, was established about the turn of the century. It had eighteen officers, all women, and some forty pupils. The language of instruction was Malay, and in addition to reading, writing, and arithmetic, various household arts were taught. After a few years, the school merged with the Tiong Hoa Hwe Koan School, which thus initiated its first classes for girls.

In the few traditional Chinese schools which existed in Semarang before 1900, all the pupils were boys. During the early years of the "modern" schools, the proportion of girls was very small. They were put in separate classes, and their curriculum included household arts. Except in Catholic schools, classes are coeducational today. In the elementary grades, the curriculum is the same for boys and girls, and their numbers are about equal. Schooling is rather expensive, however, and girls are often withdrawn at an earlier age than that of their brothers. Among the questionnaire respondents (who are fairly representative of all Chinese senior high school students in Semarang), there are only one-half as many girls as boys. Many of the boys aspire to a higher education, but for most of the girls this is out of the question. There are perhaps no more than two dozen university graduates among the Chinese women of Semarang, although the number who have been professionally trained as teachers, nurses, and midwives is considerably larger. In general, it may be said that although educational opportunities for girls are not equal to those for boys these opportunities are steadily increasing.

In the field of occupations and economic activities, women are also playing increasingly important roles. It is now common for young unmarried women to take jobs as salesgirls, clerks, typists, and stenographers. Some high school teachers and the majority of elementary school teachers are women. In addition, married women often take an active part in their husbands' enterprises or supplement the family income in various ways. Among the fifty housewives interviewed in the survey, 58 per cent were engaged in some such activity. Twenty of these women were helping in the enterprise managed by their husbands. Seven were managing their own business enterprises—a flower shop, a beauty shop, a kindergarten, for example. There were also one teacher and one midwife. And for twelve of these women, dressmaking was an additional source of income. Among mothers of the questionnaire respondents, almost 30 per cent were reported engaged in some kind of enterprise outside the home. (Presumably this did not include dressmaking, which is almost always done in the home, but did include work in family enterprises attached to the home.)

Unfortunately, the writer did not obtain any systematic information about the position of women in the family. The following tentative generalizations are based on fragmentary observations in perhaps twenty families and on a limited amount of data given by informants. It appears that the average husband is no longer a virtual dictator in the family. Without doubt, however, he is the "head" of the family, at least as far as outsiders are concerned. While he is at home, his wife dutifully attends to his needs. When guests are being entertained, she often stays in the background—serving refreshments and taking little part in the conversation. "Emancipated" though she may be, she accepts the role of housewife and to all appearances enjoys it. On the other hand, the wife often takes an important part in family decisions, such as the education of the children. She usually has almost complete responsibility for the management of the home. She expects, and usually gets, considerate treatment from her husband. Many husbands show a substantial degree of respect for the opinions and wishes of their wives. It is evident that the traditional dominance of the male has been somewhat modified by modernist patterns of mutuality and equalitarianism.

Even greater changes are apparent in the relationship between daughters-in-law and mothers-in-law. In the traditional stem or joint family, this relationship was an extremely frustrating and onerous one for the daughter-in-law. According to one student of the Chinese family, "the mother-in-law's treatment of her subject daughter-in-law was likely to be unfeeling and domineering and was quite frequently harsh, vindictive, and unjust. Her power over her daughter-in-law was well-nigh absolute." [26] In the early immigrant families from which Peranakan culture emerged, both mother-in-law and daughter-in-law were often Javanese. And many young couples did not live with the husband's family. For these reasons, the relationship between mother-in-law and daughter-in-law generally did not acquire the severity which was characteristic of Chinese tradition. Nevertheless, many Peranakan women of recent times have conformed to the traditional Chinese expectations in this respect. For example, a Peranakan informant gave the following account of his grandfather's joint family, into which three of his uncles brought their wives. (The grandfather is now dead.)

[26] Levy, *op. cit.*, pp. 108–110.

The relationship between Djoen's wife and my grandmother is not very good. . . . No, they don't quarrel. She wouldn't dare to quarrel with my grandmother. She would be kicked out of the house. But she minds her own business. She helps as she is required to. She helps out of duty, out of mere duty. And she doesn't do more than is asked of her. But Boen's wife does a lot more. My grandmother doesn't treat her as a servant at all. But she, from her side, tries to do everything to please her mother-in-law. Oen's wife is a regular help to my grandmother too.

The daughters-in-law all recognize grandmother's authority. In waiting on table, they serve grandmother before their husbands, because their way of thinking is this: "This is the mother of my husband. She is more important." And the husbands readily recognize it. At the table, for instance, if the daughter-in-law came first to the husband, he would say, "Go to my mother first."

In case of disagreements between my grandmother and Djoen's wife, it is difficult to say which side Djoen would take. He doesn't love his wife. It was a family-arranged marriage. But Oen—I'm inclined to think that secretly he would choose the side of his wife and would make it clear to her that he sympathizes with her. But this has to be covered up. It must appear that he is siding with his mother.

Systematic data is not available on the prevalence of traditional relationships between mother-in-law and daughter-in-law in Semarang today. But informants made it clear that the traditional pattern is now widely rejected. The young man whose joint family is described above said of his own future spouse: "She will be my wife, not the servant of my mother." Another informant, a Peranakan professional, told the writer: "We moved into our own house when we were first married. We Chinese don't like to live with our relatives, because troubles always arise. My wife wanted to be queen in her own house." This informant's mother and mother-in-law are both living with his family today, but his wife is still "queen." This is an indication of the fact that in many, perhaps most, stem families today it is the parents-in-law who are outsiders or guests; authority has shifted to the primary breadwinner and his wife. As noted in an earlier section, traditional obligations to the older generation are now considered more or less intolerable, and this is one reason for the preferred pattern of neolocal (separate) residence. Economic independence has permitted the younger generation to care for parents in their old age without submitting to their authority.

The rising status of women in society and in the family in recent decades may be ascribed to a number of interdependent factors. Increasing educational achievement has given women new social prestige and has opened new fields of employment to them. Increasing economic independence has likewise raised their prestige and authority, both in society and in the family. Technological progress and sufficient affluence to pay for servants have released women from part of their household duties.

These various factors, combined with emulation of modern China and the West, have resulted in greater freedom and wider fields of activity for women. Thus women have been "emancipated"—not from the role of housewife and mother, but from many of the burdens and frustrations which were associated with woman's traditional position in that role.

Courtship and Marriage

In traditional China there was no such thing as courtship. Marriages were arranged by parents, often through professional matchmakers. Fifty years ago the same was true among the Semarang Chinese, and even today there are several old-lady matchmakers, called *mah djomblang,* who are occasionally called upon to find suitable spouses for the children of middle-class or wealthy Semarang families.

Among the fathers of the questionnaire respondents, only 26 per cent of those over fifty years of age had even been acquainted with their wives before marriage; 55 per cent of those under forty-five years of age had been acquainted before marriage. This difference is significant at the .01 level. Of the ten fathers over sixty (who were probably married about the time of World War I or earlier), only one selected his own spouse; and even among those under forty-five, not more than one-quarter decided for themselves whom they were to marry. Probably only a minority of the family-arranged marriages were handled through matchmakers, however.

In the present generation, about 9 per cent of the boys and 12 per cent of the girls indicated that they would like their parents to select their future marriage partners. On the other hand, about 34 per cent of the boys and 29 per cent of the girls reported that their parents wanted to make the selection. In the interview survey, mothers were asked which kind of marriage they considered better—family-arranged marriages or marriages initiated by the young couples themselves. Only 8 per cent definitely favored parental choice, and another 23 per cent were uncertain. About 27 per cent believed that young people should choose their own partners, and another 42 per cent agreed, but added that parental consent should be obtained. Among these mothers, about 27 per cent were married to husbands chosen by their parents.

From these various figures, it is evident that preference for family-arranged marriages is rapidly disappearing. In its place, the ideal of personal choice widely prevails among young people and even among their parents. Associated with this ideal is a different outlook on marriage itself. The questionnaire respondents were asked to select from a list of ten the three most important things to be considered in choosing a marriage partner. About 97 per cent of the boys and 90 per cent of the girls checked "mutual love." This represents a reversal of the traditional expectation: according to the sages, love was supposed to grow out of marriage, and not vice versa. "Common ideals" were considered important by as many respondents as checked "parental consent," and "education" was more frequently chosen. The writer concludes that to most young people today the ideal basis for marriage is love and mutuality.

It appears, however, that changes in ideals have far outdistanced changes in practice. Courtship patterns consistent with personal choice based upon love and mutuality have not been widely adopted. Insistence on premarital chastity remains strong, and Chinese parents today are almost as fearful as they were a generation ago that freer courtship practices will lead to sexual promiscuity. Therefore parents exercise more control in the boy-girl relationships of their children than in any other field. The Semarang community is considered more conservative in this respect than the Chinese community in Djakarta. One young man told the writer that he prefers Djakarta, because in Semarang it is impossible to get to know young women. He complained that dancing was virtually out of the question in Semarang, except at rare private parties, and that he could not even take a girl to the moving pictures. Another young man said: "If you take a girl to the moving pictures, you are considered 90 per cent married to her!"

Male and female high school students in Semarang engage in many activities together. Once they are out of high school, association is more difficult. There are a few clubs in which young men and young women take part—for example, a mixed swimming club, a dancing club, and some young people's church groups. But even in these, the proportion of women is small, and many of the women are married. Western patterns of "dating" are disapproved by the community and usually forbidden by parents. Young men and women meet one another in clubs, at parties, or on picnics. But on such occasions the unit of social intercourse is always the group, not separate couples. The writer was told that almost the only way for a young man to get to know a girl well was to visit her at her home; and he would then be considered to have "intentions." Greater intimacy and privacy are allowed after engagement. But as young informants pointed out, engagement practically amounts to marriage in a system where family and community pressures make engagements extremely difficult to break.

The writer intends no negative judgment of this system. If comparisons were to be made in moral terms, it might well be considered preferable to Western practices in many respects. The intention is merely to point out that there appears to be a lack of integration—what might be called "cultural confusion"—in the area of courtship and marriage-arrangement ideals and practices. On the one hand, the community (including many of the young people themselves) enforces a system of boy-girl relationships which prevents intimacy and understanding between young couples. On the other hand, there is a widespread belief that marriage should result from free choice based upon love and mutuality. It is not surprising, then, that there is no consistent pattern of courtship and marriage arrangement. The following information from a young Peranakan intellectual will serve to illustrate this point:

I have two brothers. The way our three marriages were arranged was quite different. My older brother was married some years ago. His bride was chosen by the family, and he had a traditional wedding.

On the other hand, I met my wife at the university. We participated in various activities together. Occasionally we went out together, but only in the daytime. (Here in Semarang you can't go out at night with a girl unless you are engaged.) Finally, we decided to get married, and each of us told our families and got their consent. Of course, her family had to investigate me and my family. Chinese families are always very careful about prospective spouses! Then my mother went to her family to make the formal request, and our marriage was arranged.

My younger brother's case was quite different. When he turned twenty-five, my mother said to him: "It's time you should be thinking of getting married. Would you like me to find you a bride?" My brother is rather shy and hadn't come to know any girls very well, so he agreed. My mother inquired around until she found a suitable girl whose family was willing. My brother then went to visit the girl at home. They met in the front room and were left alone there by the girl's parents, who withdrew upstairs. After about an hour, the girl's mother came back and inquired whether my mother was well and so on. This meant that my brother had stayed too long and that he should leave! He visited the girl in her home like this once a week for several weeks. Finally, he was invited for a meal. Then the engagement was agreed upon, and the marriage was arranged.

These examples are not unusual. They illustrate the fact that there is as yet no new standard pattern of marriage arrangement in the Chinese community. A multitude of types of marriage arrangement exist, from elopement to family-arranged marriages between strangers. On the basis of the survey results, personal observations, and data from informants, however, the following generalizations can be made. The typical contemporary marriage is initiated by the young people themselves, or at least by the young man. It usually arises out of a period of friendly acquaintance rather than of intimacy or love-making. Parents are consulted, and their consent is obtained. After a more or less formal proposal by one set of parents to the other, the engagement is announced and celebrated. Then follows a period of increasing intimacy. Unless very serious incompatibilities arise, the engagement ends in marriage.

In other words, marriage initiated by one or both partners and agreed to by the parents on both sides is the most common form of marriage arrangement today. Marriage arranged by the parents, but with the consent of the young couple, is also common. Parental arrangement without consultation with the prospective mates has become exceedingly rare. Similarly, marriage without parental consent almost never occurs.

As to some of the reasons for the gradual disappearance of family-arranged marriages, the Chinese themselves usually ascribe the fact to modern education. Both the interview data and the questionnaire results support this view. For example, among the fathers of questionnaire respondents, only about 3 per cent of those with a primary school education or less were reported to have chosen their own brides; but about 41 per cent of those with at least some high school education were reported to have done so.

The number of respondents who answered the two questions involved in this comparison was exceedingly small, and the percentages have a wide margin of error. Nevertheless, the difference is significant at the .01 level.

Education has had a triple effect on marriage arrangement among the Semarang Chinese. In the first place, it has given them knowledge of the courtship patterns of the West and of opposition to the traditional family system by their contemporaries in China. As brought out in previous chapters, both modern China and the West have been widely emulated because of their prestige. In the second place, most of the Chinese schools in Semarang have long been coeducational. It has been common for boys and girls to form attachments in school which they want to extend into marriage. In the third place, as an earlier section makes clear, education has raised the status of young people. Thus they have demanded and have been able to win more control over their own affairs, including the selection of a life partner.

No factors other than education were found to correlate significantly with marriage arrangement. For instance, differences by socioeconomic status and religion were very small, and could be accounted for by educational differences within these groups. It may be concluded that the factors associated with education are the primary social variables which account for the rising preference for personal choice in marriage.

Divorce

According to Chinese tradition, divorce was permissible on a number of grounds, including mutual consent. Yet it rarely occurred, because it was considered a family tragedy and was strongly disapproved in public opinion.[27] A Semarang informant stated that a divorce is remembered in a family for three or four generations and that divorces are regarded with shame because they are considered to have "blackened the name of the family." The Chinese

27 Lang, op. cit., pp. 40–41.

strongly disapprove of the frequency with which divorces occur among Indonesians. Nevertheless, informants reported that divorce is becoming somewhat more frequent among the Semarang Chinese. Although municipal divorce records are very incomplete, they appear to confirm this report.

Almost half of the women interviewed in the survey expressed strong disapproval of divorce; others disapproved, but mentioned circumstances under which they considered it justifiable. By a few it was accepted with qualifications, but without adverse comment. The written answers to a questionnaire item on divorce indicate that more of the young respondents take a tolerant attitude toward it than do the housewives who were interviewed. These data, compared to informants' reports of the traditional attitude, suggest the conclusion that public opposition to divorce is declining.

More important than changes in the frequency of divorce and in public attitudes toward it have been changes in its nature. Traditionally, it was a virtually exclusive prerogative of men. This tradition was originally given official sanction by the Dutch government. From 1717, the written consent of one of the appointed Chinese officers was required in every case of marriage or divorce.[28] The Chinese officers were expected to use this power to enforce traditional customs. After 1919, Dutch family law was applied to the Indies-born Chinese. This did not affect marriage customs appreciably. But it did affect divorce. Under Dutch law, either husband or wife could sue for divorce by laying a charge either of adultery or of prolonged desertion. Thus women gained a right which they had not previously enjoyed, and men were restricted in the grounds for which they might obtain divorce.

Among the fifteen cases of divorce between Chinese which were taken to the Semarang court in 1954, only three were initiated by the husband. Of the twelve cases in which charges were laid by

[28] Dr. J. Th. Vermeulen, "Remarks about the Dutch East India Company's Administration of Justice for the Chinese Community in the 17th and 18th Centuries," *Jade*, XII, no. 2 (1948), 27–37.

the wife, some probably involved collusion. Few were contested. Nevertheless, there is no doubt that in a number of cases the wives were obtaining divorces which, under the customary law applied by the Chinese officers, would not have been available to them. It is of interest to note that among the fifteen divorce cases ten involved couples with no children and five of these ten had been married for four years or longer. Thus childlessness may have been a contributing factor in the deterioration of the marital relationship.

In the previous section, it was found that marriage is increasingly regarded as a matter between two persons rather than between two families. By implication the same is true of divorce. The writer believes that this viewpoint has been a major factor in modifying public attitudes against it. And the weakening of family and community opposition to divorce is undoubtedly an important reason for its increasing frequency. (It is not likely that a divorce is easier or cheaper to obtain today than it was under the administration of Chinese officers. Nor is it likely that there are more unhappy marriages.) The fact that now women, rather than men, usually initiate divorce proceedings may be ascribed to two factors: the change in the law, which made this possible, and the rising status of women, which gave new aspirations to women.

Concubinage

According to Chinese law and tradition, a man could marry only one principal wife, but he could take any number of secondary wives or concubines. Although both wife and concubine lived in the husband's household, there was a great difference between them. The wife came from a family approximately equal in social standing to that of the husband; the concubine was almost always from a poor family. Whereas the wife's family usually refused the monetary gifts offered at the time of marriage, the concubine's family received either a large cash payment or continuous financial support. Usually no marriage ceremony accompanied the taking of a concubine, and she could be repudiated or sold at any time. The wife shared the rank and station of her husband and appeared in public with him; the concubine retained her low status and never accompanied him publicly. The wife managed the household; the concubine was subordinate to her. The wife was considered the legal mother of all her husband's children, including those of the concubine.[29]

In early times and throughout the nineteenth century, concubinage was a socially accepted practice among the Chinese in the Indies. Wealthy men were expected to take concubines, and usually did. Most of the Chinese officers took several. One of the outstanding Chinese officers of Semarang, Major Oei Tiong Ham, had four or five concubines. Each of his twenty-six children inherited his name and part of his wealth. But well before his death in 1924, the Chinese community was already beginning to disapprove of concubinage.[30] He took his last concubine about 1915. According to one informant, she was a "modern, well-educated girl," and many of her friends strongly opposed the match; she herself agreed only because it would help her father out of financial difficulties.

Since that time, public disapproval of concubinage has become very widespread. Among the women interviewed in the survey, only three saw no objection to the practice, and two others thought it justified under certain conditions—as when a man's wife is childless. But forty others were definitely opposed to the practice. In written answers to a questionnaire item, 77 per cent of the student respondents categorically disapproved of concubinage even when the women involved have no objections themselves; another 10

[29] P. H. Fromberg, *Verspreide Geschriften* (Leiden, 1926), pp. 269–270. This source offers extended discussions of the position of Chinese concubines in China and the Dutch East Indies in the early years of the twentieth century. See, especially, pp. 353–357.

[30] Even as early as 1903, Fromberg noted that the Chinese concubine in Indonesia at that time "seems to exist more secretly and not publicly" (*ibid.*, p. 356).

per cent gave qualified replies; and only 13 per cent gave their approval under the above conditions. This represents a great change from the public acceptance of concubinage which existed only fifty years earlier.

In spite of the fact that concubinage is generally disapproved today and that it is strongly condemned in the press and in public speeches, a certain number of Chinese men have continued the practice. In one of the divorce cases mentioned in the previous section, the wife brought suit because she did not wish to share her home with her husband's concubines. The writer, during his stay in Semarang, heard of about a dozen other cases of concubinage. For example, the wife and the concubine of a retail store owner were living in the same household; it was reported that the two women got along very well, went to the moving pictures and to vacation resorts together, and even made common cause against the husband. The two "wives" of another businessman were living in the same house, but were said never to speak to one another.

The cases just cited seem to fit the traditional pattern of concubinage. But in most cases today, a concubine is kept in a separate household, usually in a different part of the city. She differs from a mistress in that the relationship is not clandestine: she and her children are well known to her husband's wife and to the community. Nevertheless, the man who has a concubine no longer speaks of her openly; and conversation about concubines is equivalent to gossip.

Concubines may be Chinese or Javanese. The owner of a small restaurant in Semarang took one of his Javanese waitresses as a concubine. When he died recently, she inherited the restaurant. Javanese concubines are almost always maintained in a separate household.

Informants said that most of the men who take concubines are fairly well-to-do merchants or businessmen who have little education. But the writer heard of several exceptions—a carpenter, a clerk, and a Dutch-educated professional.

Concubinage is very much less common, even in its new form, than it used to be. This is no doubt mainly due to rising public opposition. The changed attitudes toward concubinage, in turn, probably result primarily from acceptance of modernist Chinese and Western standards in this respect and from the rising status of women. Concubinage is considered an offense to the dignity of women, both of wives and of concubines, and fewer women will accept it today than formerly. One Peranakan woman told the writer: "There is still a good deal of concubinage among well-to-do Chinese here in Semarang. It is up to us women to oppose it. It is a sign of inequality—that we women are treated like toys: men can play with one, and when weary of it, get another, and another."

Social Relations with Kin

Clans and lineages were basic units in the social structure of traditional China. Clans do not exist in Semarang, and lineages are of greatly reduced importance. Nevertheless, relations with kin are of considerable significance in the lives of the Semarang Chinese. The average person knows the personal names and the relationship to himself of a large number of relatives. Toward all of these he feels degrees of interest and obligation considerably greater than toward other strangers or toward acquaintances. Even among Peranakans who cannot speak Chinese, many of the very large number of traditional Hokkian relationship terms are used in addressing or referring to kin. It is still customary for relatives, even distant relatives, to visit one another at New Year's time. Children and young people are expected to pay their respects to all older relatives during this holiday. This may mean visiting as many as a dozen or two dozen homes. In those families which still maintain ancestral altars, all descendants of the ancestors represented there are expected to gather for worship at least at New Year's time. Families may travel hundreds of miles in order to get together with their relatives for this traditional festival.

Other evidences of the importance of kinship in the Chinese

community could be cited. For present purposes, however, it is more important to note ways in which relations with kin are changing.

Obligations to kinsmen outside the conjugal family are not felt so strongly as they were formerly. Increasing dependence upon contractual relations in business activities has been accompanied by decreasing willingness to seek assistance from, or offer assistance to, kinsmen. Growing preference for the conjugal family has been associated with a weakening of social and economic interdependence even among close kin. Ancestor worship is gradually disappearing, and with it the periodic gathering of relatives around the family altar. The circle of relatives who must be visited at New Year's time is becoming more and more narrowly circumscribed.

According to Chinese tradition, all persons of any one surname were considered relatives and were supposed to treat one another accordingly. A man could not marry a woman of the same surname, even when no actual relationship could be traced. In Indonesia, the Chinese officers generally enforced this rule until 1919, when marriages were removed from their jurisdiction.[31] Semarang's first registered marriage between persons of the same surname did not occur until 1930. There were six such marriages in 1940, thirteen in 1954. Informants agreed that the great majority of Semarang Chinese no longer consider persons of the same surname to be relatives, unless the relationship can be traced.

There are many reasons for the declining importance of kinship in the Chinese community. Business and professional opportunities have scattered Semarang families to different towns and cities throughout Java. With a great increase in the number of salaried and professional positions open to young people, conjugal families have become more independent. In traditional China, the land belonging to family and clan created a strong tie between relatives. In the trading economy of Semarang, there has been no such immovable tie. It is likely that knowledge of the family system of the West and news of the modernist Chinese attack on the traditional

[31] Vermeulen, *op. cit.*

system in China have also been contributing causes. In view of these various factors, as well as the friction and frustration which are known to have existed in traditional joint-family relations, it is not surprising that Semarang Chinese have concentrated more and more of their loyalty and interest within the conjugal family.

Summary

Although about one-half of the Semarang Chinese families are still of the joint or stem types, the conjugal type is preferred by an increasingly great majority. The traditional patrilineal family system has been largely replaced by a bilateral system, in which the wife's relatives are as important as the husband's.

The training and treatment of children has become increasingly lenient, and the prevailing concept of filial piety puts much more emphasis on love and mutuality than on obedience and subservience. The status of youth has risen steadily. Women have been emancipated from the seclusion and complete submission of their traditional role, but they still usually center their interests and activities within the household.

Although marriage arrangement was traditionally a parental responsibility, it is now a matter for consultation between parents and young people, usually on the initiative of the latter. Divorce is still rare, but it is not as strongly disapproved as formerly. Whereas divorce was the traditional prerogative of men, the majority of recent cases in Semarang have been initiated by women. Though concubinage still occasionally occurs, it is now widely condemned in the Chinese community. Mutual obligations and social relations among kin are much less important than they used to be.

Thus it may be concluded that in their family system, as in other aspects of their social relations and their culture, the Semarang Chinese have developed distinct patterns which represent unique and changing combinations of elements from traditional China, modern China, Indonesia, and the West.

EPILOGUE

An Approach to Theories
of Sociocultural Change

In this chapter certain theoretical orientations and propositions which grew out of the study of the Chinese community in Semarang will be presented. These will be illustrated by material from the study, but there will be no attempt to make a comprehensive theoretical analysis of social and cultural change in all aspects of the life of the community.[1] The general theory to be presented here draws upon the work of many sociologists and anthropologists. Its first formulation, which was based upon extensive reading in the field of social and cultural change, was used in planning the research project. The theory was developed further in the course of the field work, especially in connection with the preparation of the questionnaire. Additional modification and elaboration resulted from subsequent analysis of the data and further reading in the literature.

[1] Detailed analyses of the most important changes are made in the "theoretical discussions" at the end of each chapter in Donald E. Willmott, "Sociocultural Change among the Chinese of Semarang, Indonesia" (doctoral dissertation, Cornell University, 1958).

Evaluation of Theories of Sociocultural Change

In order to evaluate theories and hypotheses about sociocultural change, it is first necessary to draw up general criteria by which to appraise them. This must be done in terms of the long-range goals of social science and the intermediate goals which appear to be necessary steps toward them.

The goal of social science has often been stated as understanding, prediction, and control of human social behavior. Since actual control of social processes is more properly a task for politicians and social engineers, the scientist will be well satisfied if he can make predictions such that the results of alternative programs of control can be foreseen. Thus "control" seems unnecessary to the definition, except insofar as it implies that the predictions must be reliable. Many social scientists would also eliminate the term "prediction"; to them, "understanding" alone is the final goal. In the opinion of the writer, however, the greatest degree of understanding is that which makes prediction possible. Prediction therefore becomes the test of the adequacy of understanding. Thus the ability to make reliable predictions about social phenomena may be considered the ultimate goal of social science.

Ideally, a theory of sociocultural change would consist of a limited number of general propositions which were determinate enough so that specific hypotheses deduced from them could be used to predict the outcome of change processes. Such hypotheses should be capable of combination, in order to account for cases in which a number of significant variables are expected to have divergent effects. The correct prediction of the outcome of combined variables, however, would require a measure of quantification not foreseeable in the immediate future of social science.

In the opinion of the writer, sociologists might well adopt an intermediate goal of developing a series of hypotheses, each of which would make prediction possible in situations that represent relatively pure cases of the hypothesized relationships. Predictions about average social situations, which are likely to involve a complexity of variables, would then have to be made on the basis of an impressionistic combining of several hypotheses, and consideration of a number of intuitive hunches and unspecified conditions as well.

This is to say that although social science may never attain the precision of the physical sciences it should aspire at least to the level of predictability which has been achieved in medical science. The doctor can make a fairly precise assessment of the physical condition of the patient, in terms of body temperature, blood and pulse counts, body chemistry, types and extent of infection, and so on. He knows the probable effects of a large number of such factors taken singly or in standard combinations. He also knows the therapeutic effects and some of the secondary effects of a large number of drugs. But when faced by an actual patient, he cannot combine all of the relevant information into exact predictions. The prescription that he gives is not obtained by means of an automatic formula. It is the result of an impressionistic weighing of a number of medical laws and intuitive hunches in the doctor's mind.

This type of understanding and prediction may serve as an intermediate, yet distant, goal for social science. The writer believes that development toward this goal will be forwarded by careful work on all levels of analysis, from the most concrete and descriptive to the most abstract and theoretical. It is too early for social scientists to rule out each other's approaches as fruitless.

As examples of analysis on a very concrete level, Chapin's *Cultural Change* and Ogburn's *Social Change* may be cited. The emphasis in these works is on the concrete processes by which technological changes have affected modern Western society. Many of what Merton has called "empirical generalizations" and "*post factum* interpretations" are presented. But these constitute the raw material out of which theory may be constructed, not theory itself. The major point of theoretical significance in these works is the concept of "cultural lag." Although this concept is useful in that it alerts the observer to the wider consequences of change processes, it has not proved useful in the formulation of propositions which make possible substantive prediction of change.

At the most generalized level, theories of sociocultural change deal with whole social systems, and specify under what conditions these systems change from one type to another. The Marxian interpretation of history is a case in point. Julian Steward, in his book *Theory of Culture Change: The Methodology of Multilinear Evolution,* has advanced the initial formulations of another theory of this kind. He maintains that societies can be classified into a limited number of types (primarily according to their modes of adaptation to the environment and their levels of sociocultural integration) and that the causal factors which bring about each type can be specified in a series of hypotheses. For instance, he suggests four causal factors by which one may predict the development of any relatively primitive society into a type which he designates as the "patrilineal band." [2] In another chapter, he shows the "developmental regularities" of societies dependent upon irrigation agriculture and suggests the factors which cause such societies to change from one rather general stage to the next.[3] This approach seems promising for the reconstruction of the development of preliterate societies and for the interpretation of the history of premodern societies. But it appears to be of little utility in the analysis of change in contemporary societies. Steward himself makes no application of the theory in the one chapter of his book which deals with a contemporary situation; the final chapter on the effects of industrialization in various subcultures of Puerto Rican society is wholly descriptive.

Another theory of sociocultural change which has been formulated at a very high level of abstraction is that found in Sorokin's

[2] Julian H. Steward, *Theory of Culture Change: The Methodology of Multilinear Evolution* (Urbana, Ill., 1955), p. 135.

[3] *Ibid.,* pp. 178–209.

Social and Cultural Dynamics. In this case, all societies are classified into three major categories—the ideational, the idealistic, and the sensate—and the processes of development from one type to another are outlined. Aside from the question of whether or not this theory is well founded, it appears that most of its propositions are still too general to enable useful predictions to be made.

Presumably in criticism of this type of theorizing, Talcott Parsons has stated that

a general theory of the processes of change of social systems is not possible in the present state of knowledge. The reason is very simply that such a theory would imply complete knowledge of the laws of process of the system and this knowledge we do not possess. The theory of change in the structure of social systems must, therefore, be a theory of particular sub-processes of change *within* such systems, not of the over-all process of change *of* the systems as systems.[4] [Italics are in the original.]

This writer does not share Parsons' pessimism about general theories of change of "systems as systems." Surely we have enough knowledge so that intensive historical and comparative study of many societies could produce at least the beginnings of reliable theory about major changes from agricultural to industrial societies, from colonial to independent, or from feudal or capitalist to socialist. The fact that this kind of study is so rarely undertaken by contemporary sociologists may be a reflection more of their personal and collective interests and predispositions than of any inherent obstacles to the task.

Nevertheless, the problems with which most sociologists (including this writer) are concerned require theory about "sub-processes of change" such as Parsons advocates. For example, with regard to such matters as the assimilation of minority groups, the effects of migration on the family, the diffusion of new techniques, or the possibilities of legislated change, predictions cannot be based

[4] Talcott Parsons, *The Social System* (Glencoe, Ill., 1951), p. 486.

upon general theories of the change of whole systems. Similarly, the writer found that changes in the culture and social relations of the Semarang Chinese had to be interpreted in terms of theories of "sub-processes."

One type of "theory of particular sub-processes of change" would be a series of systematic hypotheses about change within analytic subsystems of a society. In his book *Social Structure,* Murdock develops a promising set of propositions to account for changes in kinship systems.[5] Another approach is to elaborate hypotheses about one type of change process. Miller and Dollard have developed such a series of hypotheses about the process of diffusion.[6] On the basis of a similar psychological approach, Gillin has proposed four hypotheses to account for acculturation.[7] These various contributions constitute what Merton calls "theories of the middle range"—

theories intermediate to the minor working hypotheses evolved in abundance during the day-to-day routines of research, and the all-inclusive speculations comprising a master conceptual scheme from which it is hoped to derive a large number of empirically observed uniformities of social behavior.[8]

Middle-range theories of sociocultural change are not comprehensive or "all-inclusive" because they deal only with relatively simple or short-run change processes or with particular aspects of social systems. This writer believes that it should now be possible to initiate work on a more general theory which would consolidate and systematize these various middle-range contributions without attempting to deal with high-range generalities about changes in

[5] George Peter Murdock, *Social Structure* (New York, 1949), pp. 184–259.

[6] N. E. Miller and John Dollard, *Social Learning and Imitation* (New Haven, 1941), pp. 253–273.

[7] John Gillin, "Parallel Cultures and the Inhibitions to Acculturation in a Guatemalan Community," *Social Forces,* Oct., 1945, p. 9.

[8] Robert K. Merton, *Social Theory and Social Structure* (rev. ed.; Glencoe, Ill., 1957), pp. 5–6.

whole systems. In some respects, H. G. Barnett's book *Innovation: The Basis of Culture Change* prefigures this type of theory. The model which he uses for the analysis of change is a simple one: every change is regarded as a process extending from the appearance of an innovation to its final acceptance as part of a sociocultural system. This model subsumes the various types of change which have previously been elaborated, such as diffusion, acculturation, assimilation, and social adjustment.

Barnett's approach is also systematic and comprehensive. He isolates, describes, and categorizes a multitude of variables which may be involved in culture change. Thus far, however, this work is primarily taxonomic. Barnett does not attempt to elaborate a substantive theory of culture change; that is, he does not propose a comprehensive series of propositions which can be tested and used for predictive purposes. Many of the variables which he names and outlines will be of use to theory builders, but unfortunately he has too often left to others the task of illuminating their interconnections with existing concepts and theories in sociology and anthropology.

From this examination of various social and cultural change theories, the writer concludes that an attempt to systematize existing middle-range theories may be the most promising next step in theory development. In the section which follows, various types of change hypotheses are evaluated, in order to determine what types are most suitable for the theory to be proposed.

Evaluation of Sociocultural Change Hypotheses

Without trying to construct a comprehensive typology of hypotheses, the writer will here arbitrarily label, describe, and evaluate some of the types which have appeared in the literature on sociocultural change.

1. The *determinate change hypothesis* specifies the nature of changes which may be expected to occur under stated conditions. For example, Zimmerman proposes the hypothesis that, when

church and state become weak or incapable of functioning, the family system will change toward the "trustee" type, which is characterized by strong authoritarian controls, high solidarity, and multiplicity of functions.[9] This type of hypothesis is the most valuable for an over-all theory of change, because it is specific enough so that it can be tested and, if substantiated, can be used for determinate prediction.

2. The *indeterminate change hypothesis* specifies that there will (or will not) be change under certain stated conditions, but it does not specify the nature of the changes which will (or will not) emerge. Consider the following examples:

Strain, tension, contradiction, or discrepancy between component elements of a social and cultural structure . . . exert pressure for change. When social mechanisms for controlling them are operating effectively, these strains are kept within such bounds as to limit change of the social structure.[10]

When research opportunities and consumer choices are kept fully free, and when makers of cultural choices are provided with available information as to the probable effects of alternative choices upon their own valued ends, the fulfillment of those ends, as measured by the most reliable measurable indexes, will progress at accelerating rates of acceleration.[11]

Even when, for many members of the society, the gains from the new culture element outweigh its disadvantages, it will still be abandoned if it proves a threat to the advantage or privilege of the members of one of the dominant categories.[12]

Hypotheses such as these enable social scientists to predict which aspects of a system will change and to identify some of the initiating and inhibiting factors in the change process. Their utility is

[9] Carle C. Zimmerman, *Family and Civilization* (New York, 1947), pp. 719–721.

[10] Merton, *op. cit.*, p. 122.

[11] Hornell Hart, "Social Theory and Social Change," in Llewelyn Gross, ed., *Symposium on Sociological Theory* (Evanston, Ill., 1959), p. 202.

[12] Ralph Linton, ed., *Acculturation in Seven American Indian Tribes* (New York, 1940), p. 475.

limited by the fact that they give little indication of what new structures will emerge. It is usually the case, however, that determinate hypotheses can be deduced or derived from them, though partly on the basis of empirical observations. The following is one possible determinate derivation of the third hypotheses quoted above:

> Even when the extended-family system is a source of friction and strain, neolocal residence will not become the accepted norm in a patrilineal society in which fathers benefit from the dependency and proximity of married sons.

Similarly, Hornell Hart has suggested a number of specific derivatives of the second hypothesis quoted above. He demonstrates the applicability of these hypotheses to past trends and argues that they may also be used for predictive purposes, provided that the conditions which invalidate predictions based upon trends are taken into account.[13]

The writer concludes that although indeterminate change hypotheses are of limited utility for predictive purposes, they may serve the useful theoretical function of unifying, at a high level of generalization, a large number of derivative determinate hypotheses.

3. The *indeterminate innovation hypothesis* states conditions under which innovations are likely to occur. It is different from the indeterminate change hypothesis in that it does not attempt to state conditions sufficient for predicting the group acceptance of the expected innovations. For example, Barnett declares that, where there is a tradition of learning, curiosity, and initiative or where exchange of ideas is encouraged, innovations are more likely to occur; where there is secrecy among subgroups or little communication of ideas, innovations will be fewer.[14] This type of hypothesis may suggest in which cultures, or which aspects of a given

[13] Hart, *op. cit.*, pp. 202–216.
[14] H. G. Barnett, *Innovation: The Basis of Culture Change* (New York, 1953), pp. 41–42.

culture, innovations may be expected. But for determinate prediction, it must be combined with hypotheses specifying what
forms of innovation will occur and under what conditions they
will be accepted. Its utility is therefore relatively low. It will be
kept in mind by the social scientist, but probably will not appear
in his substantive theory.

4. The *historical hypothesis* is a statement of the observed or
recorded conditions which are assumed to have determined specific
changes that have occurred. In using the term "historical hypothesis," the writer does not intend to include general propositions induced from a considerable number of similar historical situations. These would be "determinate (or indeterminate) change
hypotheses." They would be difficult to test, but, once established,
would be useful for prediction. By a "historical hypothesis" is
meant only the interpretation of a particular change process, which
is necessarily hypothetical. For example, in describing acculturation in Cayuá culture, J. B. Watson suggests that the diminishing economic role of women led to a weakening of the custom
of bride service through temporary matrilocal residence, which
in turn contributed to the establishment of neolocal residence as
a regular part of the culture.[15]

Some authors present their historical hypotheses as if they were
established fact. Others present them as "theories." In sociological
terminology they are neither. Historical hypotheses are descrip-
tions of sequences of events. The assumed causal connections are,
at best, highly plausible. They are often subject to alternative interpretations. These hypotheses are on the lowest level of generalization (description of the concrete case) and as such cannot be
incorporated into theories. Nevertheless, at the present stage of
the development of social science, they are of considerable importance, because they furnish the raw material and inspiration from

[15] James B. Watson, "Cayuá Culture Change: A Study in Acculturation and
Methodology," *American Anthropologist,* Memoir no. 73, vol. LIV, no. 2,
pt. II (1952), p. 110.

which general hypotheses are fashioned. They are still the most common type of change hypothesis to be found in sociological and anthropological literature, although their hypothetical nature is not always recognized. The present study of the Semarang Chinese community contains a large number of "historical hypotheses."

5. The *functional hypothesis* specifies an interdependence between two or more variables such that they can be expected always to appear together or to vary proportionately. For instance, a discussion of the American family system by Talcott Parsons [16] suggests the following functional hypothesis:

Where marriage rules require that a person be incorporated into an existing group of his spouse's kin, such as a clan, the kin will have an important influence in marriage choice; free choice of spouse is to be expected where marriage does not bring either spouse into the other's kin group. [The present writer must take responsibility for this wording of Parsons' thought.]

The importance of this type of hypothesis for the prediction of change has been pointed out by Levy.[17] If the relation between interdependent variables is known, the effects on one of changing the other may be predicted. Thus functional hypotheses can often be converted into determinate change hypotheses. For example, the above hypothesis might be converted as follows:

Given a society in which traditional marriage rules require that a person be incorporated into an existing group of his spouse's kin—if these rules break down, there will be a change from family-arranged marriages to free choice of spouse.

As a further example, the functional relationship between the conjugal-family system and industrial society may be considered. Wilbert E. Moore has made an especially penetrating analysis of

16 Talcott Parsons, "The Kinship System of the Contemporary United States," *American Anthropologist*, XLV (1943), 30.
17 Marion J. Levy, *The Structure of Society* (Princeton, N.J., 1952), p. 44.

their mutual interdependence.[18] This same relationship has been embodied in a determinate change hypothesis by Levy:

When the patterns of economic production in a society change in the direction of highly industrialized patterns (i.e., high multiplications of human effort by means of tools and heavy reliance on inanimate sources of power), the family patterns will change in the direction of a multilineal conjugal type (i.e., of the sort in the modern United States) unless, of course, family patterns of that type already existed.[19] [Parentheses are Levy's.]

Conversions from functional to determinate change hypotheses can be safely made only when it is apparent that the interdependent variables are dependent upon one another to a greater extent than upon other elements of the system. Thus in the case of Levy's hypothesis above, if (by a stretch of the imagination) the family system were more closely related to religious factors than to the socioeconomic system in a given society, a change in the latter might not affect the family system to any significant degree.

Functional hypotheses will be found useful also in assessing resistance to hypothesized changes and in predicting the structural effects of the accomplished incorporation or substitution of a new element in a system. Thus functional hypotheses, which are rarely stated in terms of change, may be of considerable utility in a theory of change.

Although Merton has made a distinction between functional hypotheses which specify an interdependence in terms of survival or adjustment and those which merely specify a mathematical correlation,[20] the writer believes that the above commentary applies to both types. Where a mathematical correlation between variables has been demonstrated, it can be assumed that change in one

[18] Wilbert E. Moore, "The Aged in Industrial Societies," in *The Aged and Society* (Industrial Relations Research Association, Publication no. 5; Champaign, Ill., 1950), p. 36.

[19] Levy, *op. cit.,* p. 44.

[20] Merton, *op. cit.,* p. 21.

variable will result in change in the other. Where a relationship has been established in terms of functional prerequisites for survival or adjustment, the implications for change are more complicated. These will be discussed in a later section.

Consideration of the various kinds of hypotheses brings the writer to the conclusion that determinate change hypotheses are the most useful for predictive purposes, whereas indeterminate change hypotheses may be of use in organizing these into a theoretical system. Indeterminate innovation hypotheses are of minor importance for sociocultural change theory, but historical hypotheses may be generalized and functional hypotheses may be converted into determinate change hypotheses.

Proposals for a Theory of Sociocultural Change

On the basis of the foregoing evaluation of theories and hypotheses, the writer came to the following conclusions about the kind of a sociocultural change theory which might now be attempted.

1. The theory should deal with the process of sociocultural change in a form general enough to apply to all types of change, such as assimilation, acculturation, diffusion, and social adjustment. A possible model for change analysis that satisfies this requirement is one which includes the following terms: structure (and environment, if relevant), innovation, acceptance. Assimilation and acculturation are types of change which involve group acceptance of innovations deriving from alien societies and cultures (elements of the environment). Similarly, diffusion, or the "borrowing" of cultural or social elements from outside groups, may be seen as innovation acceptance arising out of contacts with the environment. Social adjustment is the acceptance of innovations necessitated by the cultural, social, or sociopsychological structure of the group. The concept of "innovation" includes both borrowed elements which are new in a system and elements independently invented within a system. In either case, the novel

element does not become part of the system until it has been accepted by the group or society.

2. If the theory is to have predictive value, it must include determinate change hypotheses—that is, hypotheses which specify the types of innovation that will be accepted under certain conditions.

3. A cumulative list of numerous hypotheses of various types and levels of generality does not constitute a theory. A useful theory is one that takes the form of a limited number of parallel hypotheses at a fairly high level of generalization, under which can be subsumed all relevant hypotheses of lower levels of generalization. In view of the fact that the number of determinate hypotheses necessary for prediction in many fields is very large, it is clear that the major hypotheses of the theory (if their number is to be small) must be indeterminate. But if so, they must also be such that determinate hypotheses can be derived from them. Such derivative hypotheses are an essential part of a theory.

4. The theory must be such as to facilitate the incorporation of existing hypotheses into it, either as major or as derivative hypotheses. That is, it must be capable of serving as a basis for the consolidation or "codification" of available empirical generalizations and hypotheses, as suggested by Merton.[21]

5. The theory should not attempt to predict the secondary effects of innovation acceptance. These effects are usually numerous —in the opinion of the writer, too numerous to be specified in the hypotheses of a middle-range theory. To construct a theory which included a comprehensive series of propositions specifying multiple elements of social and cultural structures, both before and after given changes, would involve a very large number of exceedingly complex hypotheses. The criteria of feasibility and manageability seem to demand that the hypotheses of the theory go no farther than to specify that an innovation will be accepted or rejected. Prediction of the effects of rejection would appear to

21 *Ibid.*, pp. 9–10, 12–13, 101.

demand a separate theory. Effects of innovation acceptance may be dealt with by applying different hypotheses of the theory, this time to the new structure which consists of old structure plus accepted innovation; this new structure may be such that the theory will indicate that certain new innovations are also likely to be accepted.

6. In spite of the foregoing conclusion, the theory should be comprehensive. That is, it should have the potentiality of including hypotheses which are applicable to any particular subprocess of change in any part of a social or cultural system.

7. The variables of the hypotheses at all levels should be made as determinate as possible; that is, they should be defined specifically enough for empirical utility.

Clearly these various criteria for a useful theory of sociocultural change would be very difficult to fulfill completely. This writer first approached the problem by listing various types of sociocultural change as a basis for a limited number of general hypotheses. The typology was based upon the different "salient variables" which seem to exert pressure for change. This list was consolidated into the following five major types.

1. *Purposive change* results from the deliberate adoption of innovations for the purpose of attaining culturally defined goals or values.

2. *Emergent change* "emerges" from dissatisfaction and unfulfilled needs among the members of a society.

3. *Necessitated change* arises out of incompatibilities between elements of the structure of a social system or between elements of the system on the one hand and the environment on the other. (Such incompatibilities, in turn, arise out of other changes in the system or the environment.)

4. *Imposed change* takes place when innovations are forced upon a group by persons with power over the group.

5. *Emulative change* occurs when a group adopts innovations because of the high prestige of the innovators or when a group

adopts elements of an alien culture because of the high prestige of the culture-bearers.

Corresponding to each of these five types of change, an indeterminate innovation-acceptance hypothesis was formulated. These specify that an innovation will be accepted in a group when the appropriate salient variable comes into play. It was immediately apparent, however, that these hypotheses had to be modified by at least general statements of the "if and when" conditions under which salient variables may be expected to effect change. At this level of generalization, it seemed sufficient to group such conditions into two categories: "change readiness factors" and "stability factors." These will be discussed in detail in later sections. They are intended to include only those elements of a system or its environment which are immediately relevant to the specific change process in question.

It is of course recognized that any actual change process may involve more than one of the types of change outlined above, especially among the different subgroups of a society undergoing change. That is, there may be more than one salient variable "pressing" for the acceptance of a particular innovation. In such cases, hypotheses based upon these salient variables may be used in combination, thus increasing the likelihood of determinate prediction.

At the most general level, then, the proposed theory consists of the following five hypotheses, each of which must be modified by the proviso that precedes them all:

Given appropriate change readiness factors and subject to the effects of stability factors:

1. *An innovation will be accepted in a group if it constitutes a more efficient means of achieving culturally defined goals or values than do existing means alone.* (Purposive change)

2. *An innovation will be accepted in a group if it minimizes the dissatisfactions or fulfills the individual needs of group mem-*

bers more adequately than do existing structural elements. (Emergent change)

3. *An innovation will be accepted in a group if it is necessitated by incompatibilities arising out of irreversible changes in the environment or in the social or cultural structure of the group.* (Necessitated change)

4. *An innovation will be accepted in a group if it is imposed by persons with power over the group.* (Imposed change)

5. *An innovation will be accepted in a group if it is introduced by persons with high prestige in the group.* (Emulative change)

This is a statement of the theory at the most abstract level. In this form, it is highly indeterminate—that is, it has little predictive value. The writer has proceeded on the hope (as yet far from a conviction) that the elaboration of the initial formulation may produce the beginnings of a theory which shows promise of fulfilling the criteria outlined at the beginning of the section.

The elaboration must take two directions: (1) specification of change readiness factors and stability factors, and formulation of hypotheses indicating their importance and relevance to various change processes, and (2) cumulation of derivative hypotheses which are determinate in that they specify the *types* of innovation for which acceptance is predicted. In the following sections major concepts will be defined, various structural factors will be discussed, and some of the derivative hypotheses which emerged from the study of the Semarang Chinese community will be presented.[22] The crucial task of compiling a comprehensive list of the determinate hypotheses which appear in the literature on sociocultural change, and of attempting to incorporate these into the present theory, cannot be undertaken at this time.

[22] Over twenty such hypotheses were suggested by the data of the Semarang study. These are reported and discussed in the theoretical sections at the end of each chapter in Willmott, *op. cit.*

STRUCTURE: TYPE OF GROUP

"Structure" is an abstract description of a system which specifies the pattern of regular elements and their relationships as observed in that system over a period of time short enough so that the passage of time is not a significant variable.

The initial point of reference for all change analysis is a statement of regularities existing prior to the change process, that is, the description of structural uniformities in relevant areas. It has been well argued that change analysis is not complete until the resultant structure, including the new elements and interrelationships, is also described.[23] However, this would involve far too great complications in a middle-range theory of sociocultural change. Therefore the proposed hypotheses will specify only those pre-existing structural features which are of most direct relevance to the hypothesized change. These will include any characterization of the group which is indispensable to the hypothesis, as well as the most important stability and change readiness factors.

Each one of the general hypotheses begins with the words "An innovation will be accepted in a group if . . ." It is assumed that many of the more determinate derivative hypotheses will be applicable only to certain types of groups. For instance, certain hypotheses might apply only to groups with a patrilineal kinship system, with a *Gemeinschaft* culture, or with a hunting and food-gathering economy. Steward has developed fairly determinate hypotheses about changes in irrigation-agriculture societies.[24] Many of the more determinate hypotheses of the theory will undoubtedly be limited in this way. Others may be applicable to any group, from a married couple to a total society.

STRUCTURE: STABILITY FACTORS

Stability factors are elements in a system which tend to prevent change and perpetuate the structure of the system. In the case of

23 Levy, *op. cit.*, pp. 44–45.
24 Steward, *op. cit.*, pp. 178–209.

each of the general change hypotheses, the expected acceptance of an innovation is said to be "subject to the effects of stability factors." The effects may be of two kinds: either complete rejection of the innovation or modification of its form or meaning.[25] Whether the innovation will be rejected, accepted with modifications, or accepted with virtually no change depends upon the relative strength and number of stability factors as against change readiness factors and salient variables.

A large part of the literature on sociocultural change deals with stability factors.[26] Some of these factors may be considered to be constant for any given system—for example, climate, the "inertia" of habit, the embodiment of tradition in the language, and so on. Such factors will be given consideration by the social analyst; but in the opinion of the writer, they need not be incorporated into the system of hypotheses of a theory of change. The limits which they set upon potential change are usually either so wide as to be of little significance or so obvious as to be taken for granted.

Similarly, the factors of isolation from other societies and lack of knowledge of alternative patterns may be dropped from a systematic list of stability factors. They do minimize diffusion; but in the presence of salient variables pressing for change, they have no deterring effect. For reasons to be discussed in a later section, the theory being presented here deals only with the acceptance or rejection of innovations already presented to a group.

The remaining stability factors will be consolidated into seven general categories. The utility of each of these will be discussed separately.

1. *Social control.* In this category are included all the means which groups use to assure conformity to group expectations and

[25] Linton, *op. cit.*, pp. 476–478; Melville J. Herskovits, *Man and His Works* (New York, 1949), p. 556; Pitirim A. Sorokin, *Social and Cultural Dynamics*, IV (New York, 1941), 253.

[26] A detailed list of such factors, along with references to the sources where they are proposed and discussed, is given in Willmott, *op. cit.*, pp. 39–41.

norms, as well as the power or influence utilized by dominant subgroups or outsiders to prevent changes in the group. These controls include not only sanctions and punishments, from mild
ridicule to exile or death, but also rewards and social or cultural
mechanisms, such as certain religious beliefs, which help to recon-
cile potential deviants to the *status quo*. Sociocultural change can
never be predicted without taking into account the potential social
controls which may be used to prevent it. Thus social control is
a variable of very great importance, which can rarely, if ever, be
omitted from consideration when applying a determinate change
hypothesis. Its degree of determinacy is fairly high: on the one
hand, the types of phenomena which it denotes can be fairly
precisely specified; on the other hand, where a prediction is to be
made for a specific case, the nature and extent of these various
types of social control can be observed or ascertained from the
way the group or its leaders deal with deviants.

2. *In-group solidarity and out-group hostility.* This factor includes such group characteristics as race prejudice, caste exclusiveness, nationalism, class consciousness, and group pride. It is
relevant only when the innovation originates outside the group
or subgroup for which change is to be predicted. Thus it is a
variable of considerable importance to any type of change hypothesis applied to assimilation or acculturation situations, and
to all imposed change hypotheses. Although the concept of group
solidarity remains somewhat indeterminate, enough work has
been done on various kinds of out-group hostility to give this
variable a fairly high measure of determinacy.

3. *Conservative values.* Where conservatism, traditionalism, or
hostility and suspicion toward novelty are part of the culture, an
innovation may be rejected or modified which would otherwise
be accepted. If this factor is strong in the area for which change
is to be predicted, it becomes a variable of some importance. It
appears to the writer, however, that conservative values alone are
rarely a crucial factor when salient variables are pressing for

change. The determinacy of this factor seems adequate: it can be given fairly precise definition, and in concrete situations it is ascertainable through observation and questioning.

4. *Conservative personality traits.* Included here are such traits or tendencies as a strong superego, inflexibility, fear or anxiety about the new, dependence upon authority, and rigid internalization of culture patterns. Whereas the previous factor refers to explicit, recognized, and socially sanctioned values, this factor consists only of implicit, indirectly taught, and usually unrecognized psychological tendencies. Such personality traits are not relevant to sociocultural change unless regularized socialization procedures or other aspects of the social structure cause them to appear to a high degree in the personalities of most of the members of the particular group in question or of a dominant subgroup. This factor would be most important where potential change is closely related to personality—for example, where new role definitions, such as reduced parental authority, are being proposed. In such cases, personality factors may have to be given some weight in considering the probabilities of change. Even so, the writer believes that the specification of personality traits will only rarely be essential in the application of determinate change hypotheses. There is the further limitation that methods by which one can establish the widespread existence of such personality traits in a group are still far from adequate. Thus much additional work must be done before this variable can be considered determinate.

5. *Vested interests.* The desire to maintain and protect personal power, influence, prestige, property, or wealth often lies behind the efforts of dominant groups to prevent change. Where an innovation is not in accord with the interests of dominant persons or groups, this factor becomes important to the prediction of change. But it is important only to the extent that those with vested interests can exercise social control. Therefore it is a variable which must be used in combination with the variable of

social control. Combined with that factor, it is often of considerable importance in the change process. Its determinacy would seem to be adequate.

6. *Group difficulty in perceiving, understanding, or learning the nature or use of a new element.* This factor depends partly upon the previous experience or training of members of the group and partly upon the nature of the innovation. It is likely to be exceedingly difficult to determine or specify in advance, and for this reason probably will remain an indeterminate and largely unaccounted-for variable. Its significance is confined, for the most part, to situations involving the acceptance or rejection of complicated technological innovations.

7. *Functional integration.* This concept derives from the theory of functionalism. A system is said to be functionally integrated when there exist a high degree of interdependence, compatibility, and harmony among its various elements, and a minimum of conflict, tension, and strain. As Merton points out, traditional functionalists fallaciously assumed that all sociocultural systems were highly integrated in this sense, whereas a more careful analysis indicates that functional integration is a variable "changing for the same society from time to time and differing among various societies." [27] Merton suggests the significance of functional integration for sociocultural change in these words: "The interdependence of the elements of a social structure limits the effective possibilities of change or functional alternatives." [28] The more functional interconnection each element has with other elements, the less likely it will be that any new (alternative) element can take the place and fulfill the functions of one of the elements of the system.[29]

An example of this is Kardiner's contention that consistency (that is, integration) between the prescribed value and goal systems learned by members of a culture and the social roles they

[27] Merton, *op. cit.,* p. 27.   [28] *Ibid.,* p. 52.   [29] *Ibid.,* p. 81.

must play is a necessary condition for stability.[30] Thus if a given role is closely related to a number of values of a cultural system, and serves to facilitate achievement of prescribed goals, it can be replaced by an alternative role only with great difficulty.

The writer concludes that functional integration may be a stability factor of considerable importance. As an aspect of a total system, it is a variable which is extremely difficult to observe or assess. But this indeterminacy is less marked when only the structure immediately involved in a subprocess of change is considered. The factor of "compatibility of an innovation with the existing system" is often discussed in this connection. It is merely another way of looking at the functional integration of those parts of a system directly implicated in a specific case of potential change. Functional integration in this limited sense may be assessed on an impressionistic basis, but its determinacy varies considerably from concrete case to concrete case and can rarely be accurately assessed in advance. Nevertheless, it is an important factor in most change processes and therefore must be accounted for.

STRUCTURE: CHANGE READINESS FACTORS

Involved in a process of change there may be not only salient variables which exert pressure for change and stability factors which exert opposite pressures, but also certain other variables which increase the probability of change. These other factors range from indispensable to merely permissive conditions for change. Some operate as catalysts, others as "boosters." All of them may be called "change readiness factors." They are elements of the existing sociocultural structure which in themselves have little or no power to create change; but they provide a context for the emergence of salient change factors, or add to the strength of such factors.

[30] Abram Kardiner and associates, *The Psychological Frontiers of Society* (New York, 1945), p. 423.

Considerable attention has been given to change readiness factors in the literature on sociocultural change.[31] The number and diversity of such factors is very great. They range from environmental factors, such as natural catastrophe, invasion, and trade, to social and cultural variables, such as progressive or scientific ideology, competition, cultural diversity, and internal crisis. Study of these various factors suggests that although they provide favorable conditions for change they are rarely crucial enough to require their specification as variables in determinate change hypotheses.

There is, however, one change readiness factor which must be present in the structure of a system if change is to take place: it consists of the extensive and efficient channels of communication which are indispensable to the acceptance of an innovation in a group. This factor must therefore be considered an implicit variable in *all* the hypotheses of the proposed sociocultural change theory. Other change readiness factors, including many which have not been mentioned above, may also be taken into account in the application of change hypotheses in order to increase the determinacy of prediction.

INNOVATION

Innovation, or the appearance of a new element in a sociocultural system, is an important step in every change process. Barnett, whose book *Innovation* is the most comprehensive treatment of this concept, defines innovation as

any thought, behavior, or thing that is new because it is qualitatively different from existing forms.[32]

This definition raises a difficulty which is recognized but not satisfactorily solved by Barnett. As he points out, according to his definition *every* event is an innovation, because no event is ever

[31] A detailed list of such factors, along with references to the sources where they are proposed and discussed, is given in Willmott, *op. cit.*, pp. 47–48.

[32] Barnett, *op. cit.*, p. 7.

identical with any other event. He maintains, however, that all innovations can be ranged along a continuum of relative difference from other events, and that the innovations of interest to the social scientist are those on the greater-difference end of the continuum.[33]

Herskovits uses a definition of innovation which eliminates this difficulty, but raises others:

A cultural innovation is one which enough members of a society accept to make of it a recognized element in the range of traditions and modes of behavior to be found among the group.[34]

This definition has two shortcomings. First, it defines a phenomenon in terms of its results rather than its own qualities. Thus the label can be assigned to objective phenomena only in retrospect. Second, it rules out an important range of phenomena which are often discussed under the label "innovation"—that is, new elements which are introduced into a sociocultural system, but are ultimately rejected by the group.

To the present writer, it seems desirable to define innovation in such a way as to eliminate the minor variations and individual idiosyncrasies of human behavior which are irrelevant to sociological analysis. It appears that this can be done only by referring to the descriptive categories and the level of generalization used in any particular analysis. The following definition is suggested:

An innovation is an element in a sociocultural system which is new in that it must be described in terms of a category or com bination of categories that has not been applied, at a given level of generalization, to any previous regular element in the same system.

In his book *Innovation,* Barnett has classified and described in great detail various motivations which may lead to innovation.

[33] *Ibid.*
[34] Herskovits, *op. cit.,* p. 559.

These range from such "credit wants" as the desire to be distinct from the ordinary rank and file, to such "central subliminal wants" as the need for meaning, orientation, and structuralization of perceptions and conceptions.[35] In addition, Barnett offers a detailed analysis of the mental process involved in innovative behavior, including "recombination of configurations," five kinds of "prototypes," and many other factors. The purpose of all this is presumably to make possible the understanding and prediction of innovative behavior.

Barnett's work is based upon insightful introspective experience, impressive knowledge of the psychological principles of the *Gestalt* school (and none other), illustrative and anecdotal material from anthropological studies, common sense, and a propensity for cataloguing. Nevertheless, he has not convinced this writer of either the possibility or the desirability of including a psychological theory of innovation in a theory of sociocultural change.

In the first place, for most practical purposes, innovation can be taken for granted in analyses of sociocultural change. Most propositions about change refer to either of two types of situations: (1) changes necessitated by circumstances or (2) changes arising out of the borrowing, rather than the inventing, of new elements. In both cases, the psychological motivations of the first innovator may be overlooked.

In the second place, again for most practical purposes, the prediction of individual innovative behavior is becoming less and less crucial to the understanding and prediction of change. The variability of human behavior, the amount of deviancy in all cultures, the prolific inventiveness of modern civilization, and especially the increasing extent of communication and culture contact throughout the world provide most groups with an almost unlimited stock of potential innovations as models for acceptance. More and more, the prediction of change will involve foreseeing

[35] Barnett, *op. cit.*, pp. 101–180.

what innovations a group will be willing to adopt, rather than what individual inventions will be made within the group.

This suggests a third, more theoretical consideration. The psychological factors which may be used to predict that certain inventions will be made in a group are also factors which will determine the acceptance of such innovations. That is, these factors determine the whole process of change and not merely the first step, innovation. Suppose the specification, of certain conditions of a group could make possible the prediction that some member of the group would make a certain kind of innovation. Whatever these conditions were, they would act on other members of the group as well, and cause them to make the same innovation independently or to imitate the first innovator. Thus the conditions for invention are also conditions for acceptance, at least by as many other members of the group as are affected by the stated conditions.

A psychological theory of innovation, as distinct from psychological hypotheses about group acceptance, would have to go beyond psychological characteristics of all or most group members to psychological characteristics of particular individuals. This would be quite unmanageable in practice. To predict whether a certain innovation will be invented would involve the question: is there *any* member of the group who has the requisite psychological characteristics? The answer to this would require detailed personality data on a large number of people, including all those who might be suspected of being potential innovators in the field in question.

For these various reasons, it appears feasible and economical to develop a theory of sociocultural change which takes initial innovation for granted and seeks to specify only the conditions for acceptance of innovations already available. The major problems, then, are those concerning the process of acceptance.

GROUP ACCEPTANCE

Group acceptance of an innovation may vary in type or in degree. In the first place, on the basis of distinctions proposed by Merton,[36] it is noted that innovations may become either permitted, preferred, or prescribed alternatives to previous elements. For instance, neolocal residence may be accepted as a permissible alternative to patrilocal residence; it may come to be a preferred but not always practiced alternative; or it may be substituted for patrilocal residence in all cases. Of course, an innovation may be such that it must be accepted by the whole group or not at all— for example, alterations in community activities such as public ceremonies. But except for such cases, it is usually very difficult to predict whether an innovation will be adopted as a permitted, a preferred, or a prescribed alternative. When applying a change hypotheses, one may find that a thoughtful assessment of the relative strengths of salient variables, stability factors, and change readiness factors will indicate which type of acceptance should be predicted. When this is not feasible, minimum acceptance (that is, group acceptance as a permissible alternative) will be considered a sufficient goal for prediction.

In the second place, many innovations are appropriate only for certain subgroups within a community—for instance, an age, sex, or occupational group. Group acceptance of such innovations involves adoption in practice by some and merely assent or passive recognition by others. Consider the example of a change toward neolocal residence. This innovation can be put into practice only by married couples, but unless they are willing to cause considerable conflict, its acceptance requires the assent of their elders.

In the third place, an innovation may be accepted by the total membership of a group or by various parts or proportions of it. For present purposes, the term "group acceptance" will be taken to mean acceptance by at least a simple majority of the members, including most of those in dominant positions.

[36] Merton, *op. cit.*, p. 133.

In spite of the way in which this last aspect of group acceptance has been stated, the writer does not regard sociocultural change merely as the personal acceptance of an innovation by a certain number of individuals. He believes that the distinction between group acceptance and individual acceptance is just as useful and important as the distinction between group decision and individual decision. Indeed, the analogy is extremely close. The study of group decision making draws on theories of individual decision making; but each involves variables and processes which are not taken into account in the other. Similarly, either the individual or the group may be taken as the primary object of attention in the study of sociocultural change.

When the individual is the unit of analysis, the theory will emphasize such processes as selective perception, cognitive reorganization, resistance, attitude change, and so on. The five general hypotheses of the theory presented in this chapter could be converted into individual change hypotheses. However, this would require the use of a different (though partly overlapping) set of stability factors and change readiness factors. Variables which are usually disregarded in group analysis, such as individual differences in perception, motivation, personality, and perhaps even heredity would have to be taken into account. Attention would be centered on the process of change within individuals. Such an approach to sociocultural change would be both valid and valuable. But it is not the one intended here.

In the group approach, the process to be analyzed is not primarily within individuals, but between them. Group acceptance is seen as a process of group interaction which involves not only individual changes, but also such factors as communication of information and opinions in private conversation, overt practice and demonstration of the innovation, group discussion, and public recognition. The interaction process is conditioned by various group factors, such as social control or in-group solidarity. Psychological factors are relevant only when they are characteristic of most of the members of the group or at least of the dominant members. Social or cultural change is considered to have taken place only when an innovation is openly practiced and recognized in the group; the private acceptance of the innovation by a majority of individuals is only part of the phenomenon.

The theory presented in this chapter was developed with the assumption that the group approach would best serve the writer's purposes. Unlike Durkheim, however, the writer found that individual or psychological variables were useful at times. He was led to the conclusion that it is no more advisable for the sociologist to avoid social psychology than for the physiologist to avoid biochemistry.

The foregoing discussion may be summarized by stating that, in the theory presented here, group acceptance involves the following conditions: (1) an innovation must be accepted at least as a permissible alternative to previous social or cultural elements; (2) this acceptance may consist of anything from active practice to passive assent; (3) at least a majority of the members of a group, including most of the dominant members, must accept the innovation in one of these ways; (4) acceptance of the innovation, whether by practice or assent, must be public.

A more detailed discussion of the various processes of innovation acceptance is now necessary. To make the definition of variables sufficiently determinate will be a primary concern.

PURPOSIVE CHANGE

An innovation will be accepted in a group if it constitutes a more efficient means of achieving culturally defined goals or values than do existing means alone.

This type of change occurs when members of a group deliberately adopt an innovation with the expectation that it will be useful, advantageous, or desirable in terms of culturally defined goals or values. Since it is voluntarily and deliberately accepted, the innovation must be one that is "compatible" with those parts of the existing sociocultural structure which are most closely

related to it. After initial acceptance, it may later be rejected because of unanticipated, undesirable consequences in more remote
areas of the sociocultural system. In the middle-range theory, however, initial acceptance followed by rejection cannot be analyzed
or predicted on the basis of a single hypothesis. Instead, the initial
acceptance must be dealt with by one hypothesis, and the later
rejection by another. It is not that ultimate rejection can never be
foreseen. But ultimate rejection is to be explained in terms of
new salient variables, such as "strain" or dissatisfaction, rather
than in terms of stability factors existing prior to the application
of the initial acceptance hypothesis. In such cases, rejection is to
be considered as a new innovation, though a negative one, arising
out of the structure which resulted from the initial acceptance
of the positive innovation.

This hypothesis, then, assumes the manifest compatibility of an
innovation with group goals and values in a limited area. If the
innovation is incompatible with other aspects of the sociocultural
system in ways which the group itself may be expected to perceive,
the stability factor called "functional integration" must be considered. If the innovation is incompatible with other aspects of
the sociocultural system in ways which only the trained and experienced observer can foresee, an initial acceptance hypothesis
may be supplemented with a second hypothesis concerning
ultimate rejection.

The purposive change hypothesis has, of course, been proposed
in various forms by many writers. Such factors as the following
have been used to account for change: expectation of advantages
to be gained from adopting an innovation, the "utility" of an
innovation as perceived by the prospective accepters, and, for certain members of a society, the impossibility of attaining culturally
defined goals by legitimate means.[37]

Probably the most common examples of purposive change are

[37] For references to sources in which these and a number of other such
factors are discussed, see Willmott, *op. cit.*, pp. 57–58.

to be found in the area of technological development. In the study of the Chinese community in Semarang, however, purposive change was evident in other areas of the culture as well. For instance, Javanese charms and petitionary prayer at Javanese holy places were deliberately added to the traditional Chinese ways of gaining supernatural aid. Development of the educational system was also largely purposive. The Chinese school boards introduced educational policies and curriculum changes in accordance with current community values. The turn from Confucianist to nationalist teachings, for example, reflected changing ideology in the community; and the introduction of commercial courses was a deliberate adjustment to the utilitarian, economic, and vocational values of Chinese overseas society.

EMERGENT CHANGE

An innovation will be accepted in a group if it minimizes dissatisfaction or fulfills the individual needs of group members more adequately than do existing structural elements.

This hypothesis refers to changes which "emerge" out of individual motivations (usually dissatisfactions) which are not legitimized by the culture of a group. Whereas purposive change involves innovation only in means to culturally defined ends, emergent change often involves innovation in the ends themselves —that is, in norms, goals, and values. In purposive change, the motives are socially and culturally sanctioned; in emergent change, they are not. In emergent change, the existing culture is seen as undesirable or intolerable; in purposive change it is merely inadequate.

Ultimately it may appear possible and desirable to frame this hypothesis in terms of cultural and social inadequacies rather than psychological motivations of individuals. These inadequacies have been conceptualized under such labels as "strain," "inconsistency," "net balance of dysfunctions," and "unfulfilled functional prerequisites." Merton, who is actively concerned with making concepts researchable, recognizes that these are still highly indeterminate.[38]

The question whether or not modern science is "incompatible" with supernaturalistic religion might be taken as an example. To some groups, it certainly has been. In the Enlightenment period of the eighteenth century, the "strain" between science and religion apparently was great, for many intellectuals renounced the one to embrace the other. Even earlier, in the Renaissance period, the strain must also have been great, for the church felt so threatened by science that attempts were made to torture or terrorize people into giving it up. But such has not always been the case. Many great scientists have been pious believers, and in modern times one finds scientific research and teaching carried on in many religious schools and universities.

This illustrates the difficulty of determining whether strain exists between two structural elements or not. Some elements can be pronounced incompatible on *a priori* grounds. Neolocal residence, for instance, would be incompatible with a patriarchal, extended-family system. In the first place, it would be physically impossible for a father to exercise continual authority and supervision over sons who are not living nearby. In the second place, the very existence of an extended family depends upon daily social and economic co-operation within a single household. Nevertheless, in many cases where strain is actually found, it could not be predicted on logical grounds alone. And in other cases where strain seems logically indicated, it does not appear. Anthropologists have again and again documented the fact that people can accustom themselves to seemingly incompatible culture traits.

In many cases, this problem may be dealt with by introducing psychological factors into the definition of strain. Parsons has defined it as a "disturbance" in the expectation system which is

[38] Merton, *op. cit.*, pp. 51–54.

an essential part of the integration of individual need dispositions and culture patterns.[39] How to identify such disturbances, however, is not clearly specified, and the definition remains a somewhat indeterminate one. It might be more determinate to define strain as a relationship between two or more elements in a social or cultural system which produces irreconcilable motivations or expectations in the participants in the system (as indicated by anxiety, mental conflict, or dissatisfaction). With such a definition in hand, one could look for indications of anxiety or conflict in the behavior or verbal responses of a people, and where these were found to be related to discrepancies between sociocultural elements, strain would be identified.

The following quotation from Linton indicates the utility of identifying strain (or, in this case, "incompatibility") by its psychological aspects:

New elements may be given up even when they are more effective than the old ones for reasons which we may lump under the rather vague term incompatibility with the preëxisting culture patterns. It is safe to say that no group, when it accepts a novelty, is able to foresee the full extent of the consequences. . . . As time passes, the effects of the new thing on the life of the group begin to be apparent. These effects may be abstractly phrased in terms of culture derangement, but concretely they produce discomfort and bewilderment for the society's members. It becomes a question of whether the advantages to be derived from the novelty outweigh the trouble it causes. The group may conclude that they do not, and go back to the old ways.[40]

It appears that, at least for the time being, the empirical application of the functionalist concepts under discussion must be primarily determined either by vague individual judgment or by

[39] Talcott Parsons, *The Social System* (Glencoe, Ill., 1951), p. 491.

[40] From *Acculturation in Seven American Indian Tribes,* edited by Ralph Linton, pp. 474–475. Copyright, 1940, D. Appleton–Century Co., Inc. By permission of Appleton-Century-Crofts, Inc.

psychological definition. The latter seems preferable, in that it facilitates more determinate empirical application. Nevertheless, much more work must be done before such concepts as "incompatibility," "net balance of dysfunctions," or "unfulfilled functional prerequisites" can be used in an empirically relevant theory.

Instead of struggling with the problem of developing determinate definitions for these sociological concepts, the writer has chosen at this point to employ psychological variables directly. This has proved helpful also in that it permits the "emergent change" hypothesis to include a range of phenomena which do not appear to be adequately covered by concepts of cultural incompatibility and which are only obscurely related to the concept of unfulfilled functional prerequisites.

Every society puts certain limitations on the freedom and independence of the individual. These restrictions usually generate a certain amount of dissatisfaction. Yet they may be accepted for generations, or even centuries, especially if they are supported by the dominant groups in the society. Close contact with other societies, however, is almost certain to reveal that restrictions in certain areas can be considerably less onerous, and this is likely to intensify and make more widespread the dissatisfaction with existing restrictions. Thus emergent change, or change instigated by dissatisfactions or unfulfilled needs, is almost certain to occur in cases of close cultural contact. In Semarang, for example, when Chinese young people became aware of the relative freedom of their peers in both Western and modern Chinese society, they proceeded to demand greater independence for themselves. As was shown in Chapter X, young people now have new freedom and status in the community.

Other instances of emergent change have resulted from the particular dissatisfactions with Dutch rule which were discussed in Chapter II. As was shown there, these grievances played a large part in the reorientation of the Chinese community toward China. They also resulted in changes of leadership in the community and in the establishment of new organizations.

Consideration of these changes again suggests the economy of using the concepts "dissatisfaction" and "unfulfilled needs" as salient variables, rather than sociological terms which as yet are not adequately related to the phenomena under discussion here.

NECESSITATED CHANGE

An innovation will be accepted in a group if it is necessitated by incompatibilities arising out of irreversible changes in the environment or in the sociocultural structure of the group.

This hypothesis refers to changes which are objectively necessary. In the previous section it was stated that certain incompatibilities set up "strains" which are manifested in dissatisfactions and individually felt need for change. From this type of incompatibility, which results in "emergent change," are distinguished objective incompatibilities, which result in "necessitated change." Emergent changes may be no less necessary, but the necessity is psychological. In what is here called "necessitated change," necessity is mechanical; that is, the incompatibility does not merely create strains—it is plainly unworkable.

Actually, incompatibilities may be ranged along a continuum of increasingly obvious unworkability. The writer believes, however, that it is useful to distinguish between the polar types and, further, that the distribution of relevant empirical situations is sufficiently bimodal to make classification fairly determinate. There are certain incompatibilities which no group could possibly maintain. For instance, the exhaustion of a natural resource is incompatible with an economy based upon it, and change of the economy will follow immediately. Most of the "objective" incompatibilities, however, are not so inescapably obvious. In an earlier section, the incompatibility of a rule of neolocal residence with a patriarchal, extended-family system was discussed. A group trying to maintain both sides of this incompatibility can be envisioned, but it is not possible to imagine them succeeding for very long. Change in one custom or the other seems objectively necessary.

It was suggested earlier that many functional hypotheses can be converted into determinate change hypotheses. When this is done, the result is a "necessitated change hypothesis." If a functional relationship between two variables can be demonstrated, it may be assumed that a change in one will "necessitate" a change in the other. The change toward a conjugal-family pattern in an industrializing society does not occur because the incompatibility of the original family system with the requirements of industry creates dissatisfactions which lead to change. On the contrary, dissatisfactions arising out of this incompatibility may be directed against the development of industry rather than against the old family system. In any case, industrialization necessarily involves certain factors, such as mobility and universalistic job competition, which require changes in the family system regardless of the motivations of the individuals involved.

The writer concludes that changes arising from incompatibilities are of two types: (1) those in which psychological variables are irrelevant for predictive purposes and (2) those in which dissatisfaction is a salient change variable. Those of the latter type are grouped together with other changes in which motivational variables (such as unfulfilled needs) are salient, and they are called "emergent changes." Those of the former type are "necessitated changes."

Most of the determinate change hypotheses which have been proposed by other writers involve "necessitated change." Steward's hypotheses about the factors which create different types of societies [41] and most of Murdock's propositions about changes in kinship systems [42] are of this type.

In the analysis of the Chinese community in Semarang, many instances of necessitated change were found. Intermarriage with

[41] Steward, *op. cit., passim.*   [42] Murdock, *op. cit.,* pp. 184–259.

Javanese women, for example, inevitably led to the adoption of a new language and many new customs in the home. Rather exclusive concentration in commercial occupations resulted in other changes, such as the lack of a scholarly tradition and the very high evaluation of commercial success. In Chapter VII, it was apparent that certain changes in the structure of the community necessitated more concentrated leadership at particular times and very dispersed leadership at others.

IMPOSED CHANGE

An innovation will be accepted in a group if it is imposed by persons with power over the group.

This type of change is so obvious that it has received little theoretical attention by writers on sociocultural change. Nevertheless, if the amount of legislated change in Western societies and of decreed change in colonial and totalitarian areas is considered, it is clear that a very significant proportion of all change. in the modern world is partly or wholly imposed. Therefore this kind of change must not be omitted from the proposed theory.

Although this hypothesis is "obvious" in its most general form, it involves the theoretical and practical problem of how much power is required to impose an innovation on a group. The hypothesis cannot be used to make predictions in particular cases unless the degrees of coercion and of expected resistance can in some way be weighed against each other. It seems unlikely that this can ever be done precisely, but consideration of appropriate stability factors and change readiness factors may be expected to increase the probability of correct prediction when applying the hypothesis.

Persons having power to effect sociocultural change in a group may be either powerful outsiders or dominant members of the group itself. Imposed changes by both group members and outsiders have been discussed briefly by several previous writers.[43]

43 For references, see Willmott, *op. cit.*, p. 63.

Many of the imposed changes observed among the Chinese of Semarang derive from the governmental regulation, police power, and economic strength of the Dutch and, more recently, of the Indonesians as well. Dutch commercial law and, after 1919, most of Dutch family law were applied to the Chinese. This meant that they had to accept new business practices in many of their economic dealings, and other new practices in such matters as divorce, polygyny, and inheritance.

In these examples, changes were imposed by outsiders. Changes were also noted which stemmed from the power of certain groups within the Chinese community. Young people won a greater voice in marriage arrangement, presumably through newly acquired "power" deriving from educational achievement and vocational independence. Similarly, women won higher status largely because of their economic importance; and this new "power" was partly responsible for male acceptance of bilateral family relations and even, frequently, matrilocal residence.

EMULATIVE CHANGE

An innovation will be accepted in a group if it is introduced by persons with high prestige in the group.

This hypothesis refers to changes in which a group adopts a new element because of the prestige of those who introduce it. Barnett, Herskovits, Linton, Lowie, and others have discussed this type of change.[44] It is directly implied, also, in Merton's discussion of nonmembership reference groups. Merton speaks of "identification" with "reference groups" and "reference individuals," and of "emulation" of some or all of their roles and values.[45] When such identification objects (persons with prestige) display novel attitudes or behavior, their emulation by a group results in social or cultural change.

The utility of the hypothesis as it is stated above depends upon the determinacy of the variable "prestige," and this concept will

[44] *Ibid.* [45] Merton, *op. cit.*, p. 303.

now be examined in the light of psychological theories. In studies by Miller and Dollard [46] and Queener,[47] prestige was linked to imitation. The prestige of person A in the eyes of person B was considered a function of the frequency with which B's copying of A's responses had previously led to reward. The more often B is rewarded for responses copied from A, the higher the "prestige" of A will become for B. In the process, B learns a generalized tendency to copy A; that is, he comes to depend upon A to suggest appropriate responses in a wide variety of situations. This type of generalized imitation, which Miller and Dollard call "matched-dependent imitation," may be distinguished from simple "copying." In the latter B deliberately imitates A when he sees that A's responses are appropriate to his own ends.

If these concepts are applied to the proposed theory, it is evident that the simple copying of an innovation is an instance of "purposive change." In this case, the copying results from the observation that someone else's behavior is appropriate to one's purposes. But when innovation acceptance results primarily from a generalized, habitual tendency to copy, without more specific ends in view, it is an instance of "emulative change."

In matched-dependent imitation, the prestige involved is the prestige of the expert, the person who can demonstrate the most efficient ways of achieving goals. But this is not the only basis for a generalized tendency to copy. Linton, for instance, points out that behind all questions of concrete rewards that may be gained from borrowing (copying or imitation) "there lies the deeper question of whether borrowers want to be like the donors or not." [48] The prestige of the "donors" in this conception is the prestige of a reference group or a reference individual. The psychological mechanism involved is identification.

[46] Miller and Dollard, *op. cit., passim.*

[47] Llewellyn Queener, "The Development of International Attitudes: II, Attitude Cues and Prestige," *Journal of Social Psychology,* XXIX (1949), 237–252.

[48] Linton, *op. cit.,* p. 497.

Identification has only recently received systematic attention from psychologists. Sears [49] and Mowrer,[50] especially, have distinguished it from imitation and have explored its nature and genesis. Their work has been concerned primarily with identification between individuals. In their view, identification arises out of three aspects of a relationship: (1) dependence of the identifier; (2) nurturance (rewards) offered by the identification object; (3) standards of behavior and attitude demanded or expected by the identification object.

The result of the first and second of these conditions is a strong affective tie between the two persons. Nurturance assures that the affect will be partly or primarily positive, but dependence may introduce negative affect as well. Without the third condition, however, the affective tie does not lead to identification. The "spoiled" child is an example of this: although he is extremely dependent and is constantly rewarded, he does not internalize the attitudes or behavior patterns of his parents because no standards are consistently imposed. When demands are made, and made consistently, the child who has a positive relationship with his parents feels internally rewarded when he conforms to them. Theoretically, this is because the gratifying feelings associated with the parents are elicited by any response which is characteristic of the parents or highly valued by them. It is the self-rewarding nature of identification which explains why many instances of copying occur and persist when there are no overt rewards and even when there are considerable punishments involved.

With this theoretical background, "prestige" can now be defined as the distinctive attribute of a person or group when he or it is the object of identification or matched-dependent imitation by another person or group. Unfortunately, such psychological processes cannot be observed directly. Therefore it is necessary to

[49] Robert R. Sears, "Memorandum on Identification" (unpublished paper, Harvard Univ., 1951).

[50] Hobart O. Mowrer, *Learning Theory and Personality Dynamics* (New York, 1950), *passim*.

infer their presence or absence from antecedent conditions or behavioral responses, as suggested by the theory. On this basis, the prestige of A in the eyes of B may be assumed when all or most of the following conditions are found:

1. B frequently copies A, that is, adopts attitudes or behavior patterns characteristic of A.

2. B copies things from A for which there are no external rewards, no obvious advantages.

3. B is dependent upon A; A is more powerful or dominant or is indispensable to B's welfare or status.

4. A's techniques for achieving various goals are more efficient than B's.

5. A is a source of regular rewards and gratifications for B.

6. B is emotionally attached to A.

7. B expresses high respect or esteem for A.

8. B shows concern for acceptance by A.

9. A sets certain standards of behavior and attitude for B.

The combination of several of the above indicators of identification or matched-dependent imitation should serve as a reasonably reliable "operational definition" for prestige. These indicators are derived from interpersonal psychological theory, but the writer believes that they can be extended to apply to groups without serious difficulty. In a review of the literature on identification, the writer found no suggestion that the psychological processes of identification with groups are essentially different from those of identification with individuals. Indeed, at least two authorities state the contrary:

Space will not be taken to elaborate upon the problems of identification with a group. But such group identification seems to involve practically the same principles as identification with a single individual.[51]

[51] Edward C. Tolman, "Learning and the Psychodynamic Mechanisms," in Talcott Parsons and Edward A. Shils, eds., *Toward a General Theory of Action* (New York, 1951), p. 310.

The psychological mechanism underlying group identification is presumably no different from that underlying an individual's identification with his family, his children, his possessions, the fruit of his work.[52]

In a detailed analysis of the relations between the Semarang Chinese and three other groups (the West, as represented chiefly by the Dutch; China, and especially its modernists; and the Indonesian people), the writer found that the indicators listed above gave high determinacy to the concept "prestige." [53] The analysis showed that modern China and the West, but not Indonesia, have acquired high prestige in the Chinese community—that is, prestige involving sufficient psychological identification to encourage emulation of many social and cultural traits. There was evidence for the prestige of the Chinese modernists in all nine categories of prestige indicators.

With regard to the Dutch, the evidence for prestige was found to be weak in two of the nine categories. Expressed respect for the West was found to be much more limited than for modern China, and the discrepancy was even greater in the case of emotional attachment. In addition, the Chinese entertained many grievances, and therefore considerable hostility, toward the Dutch. However, these circumstances are not incompatible with psychological identification. As was mentioned earlier in this section, in order to have identification occur it is not necessary that negative feelings be absent, but merely that positive attachments, including dependence, be present. For example, children who have very ambivalent feelings toward their parents may be strongly identified with them. The prestige of the Dutch may be compared to that of authoritarian parents, whereas the prestige of modern China has been more like that of an idealized hero.

With regard to the Indonesian people and their culture, the

[52] David Krech and Richard S. Crutchfield, *Theory and Problems of Social Psychology* (New York, 1951), p. 413.

[53] For the details of this analysis, see Willmott, *op. cit.*, pp. 116–120.

situation seems to be changing from one in which they enjoyed little, if any, prestige in Chinese eyes to one in which they may be in a position to attain prestige. Before World War II, almost the only attitude among the Chinese which approached respect for Indonesian culture was their fairly widespread appreciation of Indonesian music, dancing, and literature. Recently, however, the Chinese have become dependent upon the Indonesian government. If that government is able to create some positive ties with the Chinese, by offering significant concessions and benefits, it will no doubt acquire a measure of prestige among the Chinese. If it consistently discriminates against even those Chinese who are citizens, there will be no basis for identification. In terms of the analogy used above, the authoritarian parent who shows no affection and offers no rewards or gratifications is usually rejected by the child and therefore has no prestige in the child's eyes.

Changes in the clothing preferences of Chinese men well illustrate the influence of prestige in cultural change. As one would expect from the above analysis, Chinese men are rarely seen wearing items of apparel which are distinctively Indonesian. On the other hand, relatively expensive and uncomfortable articles of Western dress, such as neckties, suit coats, and leather shoes, are very common. Among those who most strongly identify with modern China, the military-type uniform made popular by Sun Yat-sen is also popular.

It is to be expected that emulative change will be most common in those areas of taste and preference which are most visible and least implicated in complex patterns of traditional relationships. But emulation has been found to be a salient variable in more significant changes as well. For instance, the prestige of modernist China and the West has been an important factor in many of the changes observed in the family system: the opposition to concubinage, the aspirations of women and young people for greater independence, the new ideal of personal choice in marriage, and the preference for the conjugal-family type. Emulative change has also been apparent in the field of religion. Given the emergence of motivation to seek new religious orientations, those for whom Western culture has high prestige tend to view Christianity with favor, and those who identify with Chinese culture tend to favor neotraditionalism.

The Elaboration of Derivative Hypotheses

It has been suggested that the general theory presented here is of little value unless a substantial number of determinate change hypotheses can be incorporated into it as derivatives of its five major propositions. The most important task in this connection—and the crucial test of the utility of the present formulation of the theory—would be to gather a considerable number of change hypotheses from sociological and anthropological writings and to see whether they could be reformulated to fit systematically into the theory. In this section, however, a much more modest task of codification will be undertaken—the way in which determinate change hypotheses can be derived from empirical data and current sociological concepts will be illustrated. For this purpose, use will be made of the material on economic life presented in Chapter III and the "pattern variables" proposed by Parsons and Shils.[54]

In the competitive, rational economic system of the Chinese community, affective neutrality and achievement are in the dominant normative pattern; affectivity and ascription are at a minimum. No marked trend with regard to these variables has been discerned. Similarly, in economic relationships (except those within the extended family), self-orientation has remained dominant over collectivity-orientation. With regard to this variable, however, certain changes have been noticed. Self-orientation in the community of newly arrived immigrants, as seen in individualistic competition and a restriction of moral obligations, was at a maximum. In the more settled Peranakan group, considerations of family reputation in the community and of ethnic group relations

54 Parsons and Shils, *op. cit.*, pp. 80–84.

with the Dutch and Indonesian groups tended to increase the amount of collectivity-orientation in the normative pattern of economic activities.

The increase of self-orientation in the immigrant communities, as compared to the homeland communities, may be attributed to the relative lack of social controls. Given this lack, personal motives for economic well-being were unchecked, and the expectation of self-oriented action became widely accepted. This phase of the change is an instance of emergent change, since the salient variable was unfulfilled individual desire. The breakdown of social control, however, was a prior phase. Strong social controls were incompatible with the mobility and heterogeneity of the immigrant community in the "plural society" of Indonesia. Thus the first phase of the change toward increased self-orientation may be seen as necessitated change. From these considerations, three general hypotheses are derived. These, and others to be presented below, will serve as derivative hypotheses in the theory of socio-cultural change.

3A. *A decline in social controls will be accepted in a group in which mobility has increased.*

3B. *A decline in social controls will be accepted in a group in which heterogeneity has increased.*

2A. *Increased self-orientation will be accepted in a group in which social controls have declined.*

In presenting derivative hypotheses, numbers are assigned to indicate which of the five major hypotheses they are instances of, and capital letters to give them separate designation. Thus the "3B" before the second hypothesis above indicates that it is an instance of the third major hypothesis of the proposed theory (necessitated change) and that it is to be distinguished from "3A," another instance of the same major hypothesis. A lower-case letter is added to the designation of a hypothesis which is a specific instance of a derivative hypothesis. For example, the following hypothesis, suggested by the data, is one of many less general formulations which may be derived from "2A" above:

2Aa. *Increased individualistic competition and a restriction of moral obligations in economic activities will be accepted in a group in which social controls have declined.*

With regard to the particularism-universalism dimension of social interaction, it is evident that the economic activities of the Chinese in Semarang have been dominated by particularism. This is seen in nepotism, in the typical familism of business organization, in the raising of credit through friends, in the use of arbitration rather than court litigation, and in the reluctance to enter into co-operative ventures with strangers. On the other hand, it was found that universalistic business practices have been increasing—for example, the introduction of personnel policies based upon merit, the organization of public corporations, the formation of new trade associations, and the use of and adherence to contracts.

As to the variable diffuseness-specificity, a similar situation exists. Role expectations in traditional Chinese economic relationships were almost exclusively diffuse. The effectiveness of the go-between depended upon his having a diffuse relationship with both parties in an undertaking. The *langganan* (regular client) relationship typically developed from specificity (a simple economic transaction) to diffuseness (mutual obligations, mutual concern, and sometimes friendship). The co-operative loan club, with its feasting and sociability, typifies the emphasis on diffuseness. The "creepy" feeling which many Chinese businessmen have toward government officials, notaries, public accountants, and the like no doubt derives from the fact that they are accustomed to more diffuse (and particularistic) relationships.

But specificity is increasing in the normative patterns of economic activity among the Semarang Chinese. Relationships with European trading companies, with banks, with Indonesian business "partners," with government officials, and with other members of trade associations are usually primarily specific. The number of such relationships has been increasing in frequency and importance in recent years.

Universalistic and specific economic relationships are generally more efficient than particularistic and diffuse ones in areas where business success involves large-scale organization or dependence upon a relatively large number of persons or organizations outside a particular enterprise. This is evident from the fact that small importers can compete with large importers only by banding together in co-operative ventures and by increasing their impersonal, specialized contacts with government officials, foreign businessmen, and other relative strangers. The changes here under discussion are, then, partly purposive: the salient variable is the motive to achieve the culturally defined values of efficiency and economic gain.

On the other hand, many of these changes are, in part, necessitated changes. Large-scale organization and widening interdependence in any area of activity reach a point at which certain particularistic and diffuse normative patterns become unworkable. In a large business enterprise, for instance, the employer cannot possibly develop diffuse relationships with all his employees. Again, the myriad contacts and transactions of an insurance company, representing its dependence upon a large number of scattered individuals and groups, cannot possibly be particularistic relationships. Thus large-scale organization and widening interdependence will bring about both purposive change (based upon considerations of efficiency and gain) and necessitated change (based upon the elimination of incompatibilities) toward more universalistic and specific patterns. From these considerations, the following general hypotheses are derived.

1A and 3C. *A greater degree of universalism and specificity in normative patterns will gain group acceptance in sociocultural areas in which large-scale organization develops.*

1B and 3D. *A greater degree of universalism and specificity in normative patterns will gain group acceptance in sociocultural areas in which interdependence among a large number of people has developed.*

In Chapter III, a trend from "trust relations" to "contractual relations" in the economic activities of the Chinese in Semarang was described. These concepts are now re-examined in the light of the foregoing discussion. Whereas the "pattern variables" of Parsons and Shils are theoretically present in all social relationships, the variables of trust and contractual relations occur only in cases of deliberate, goal-oriented co-operation. A trust relation may be viewed as a diffuse, particularistic relationship in which deliberate co-operation is based upon the informal sanctions of the primary group and the individual conscience. A contractual relation is a specific, universalistic relationship in which co-operation is based upon the formal sanctions of economic power or government law and authority. Both the data presented in Chapter III and theoretical consistency with the above hypotheses suggest the following second-level derivative hypotheses:

1A and 3Ca. *Greater dependence upon contractual relations and less dependence upon trust relations will gain group acceptance in sociocultural areas in which large-scale organization develops.*

1B and 3Da. *Greater dependence upon contractual relations and less dependence upon trust relations will gain group acceptance in sociocultural areas in which interdependence among a large number of people has developed.*

The reciprocal statements of these two hypotheses, with the direction of change reversed, would no doubt be equally valid, although such phenomena were not observed in Semarang. One can easily imagine plausible examples, however. Consider the branch stores which Chinese merchants establish in small rural villages. Those who operate these stores must forget the city ways of business. They must develop trust relations with the whole community.

Even these second-level derivative hypotheses are formulated at a fairly high level of generality. They could apply as well to political relations as to economic. In the economic field, a number of lower-level hypotheses could be elaborated, but these would approach the level of interpretation which has been used in reporting the data. In any case, they would be too specific, and therefore too numerous, to merit a place in the theoretical system. One example will suffice:

1A and 3Caa. *Personnel policies based more on personal merit and less on nepotism will be accepted in business concerns which become large-scale enterprises.*

Thus far the derivation of hypotheses through the examination of empirical data in the light of a general theory has produced nothing new. Indeed, it may be said that the hypotheses are merely restatements of generalizations already common in sociological writings. This accords with the writer's aim of elaborating a theory which can incorporate existing hypotheses. A hypothesis will now be ventured which is somewhat outside the main current of sociological thinking to date. It is also alien to the general orientation of the writer, but it was suggested by observation and appears worthy of further attention. It was derived from the data on different child-rearing practices and concomitant attitudes toward work which were described at the end of Chapter III.

2B. *Normative patterns of activity characterized by less striving and lower levels of aspiration will be accepted in a group in which child-rearing practices have become more permissive over a period of one or more generations.*

The writer considers that this hypothesis involves emergent change because the more easygoing normative patterns are hypothesized to derive from motivations in the new generation which are not culturally sanctioned. If the hypothesis can be substantiated by more reliable observation or experiment, it will be of considerable sociological interest: child-rearing practices will have been shown to have a potential effect not only on "projective systems," as proposed by Kardiner and Linton, but on other important sociocultural areas, such as the economy, as well.

Before closing this chapter, it will be well to remind the reader that all proposed hypotheses are subject to the proviso "given appropriate change readiness factors and subject to the effects of stability factors." The preceding hypothesis, for instance, could be used for prediction only in conjunction with an evaluation of the probable effects of such stability factors as the social control of the older generation, vested interests in high standards of achievement, or a functional integration which requires striving among adults. On the other hand, the hypothesized change process might be supported by such change readiness factors as social disorganization and family disorganization, a customary emphasis on individual independence and freedom, or a rapidly rising standard of living.

Summary and Prospects

The writer has elaborated five major hypotheses of a theory of sociocultural change and has enumerated various general stability factors and change readiness factors which must be combined with these for predictive purposes. An endeavor has also been made to clarify the major concepts of the theory, such as "innovation," "group acceptance," "incompatibility," and "prestige," in order that these can be applied in concrete situations with some degree of determinacy. Finally, the way has been shown in which derivative determinate change hypotheses may be formulated on the basis of empirical data and existing theory.

As it stands, the theory has many limitations. It does not deal with the changes of whole sociocultural systems. Nor does it deal directly with secondary effects of innovation acceptance and rejection. Because it was developed in the course of research and has been conceived in terms of its empirical relevance, it lacks logical refinement—in the mixing of psychological and sociological variables, for example. Finally, it remains to be seen whether a sufficiently large number of useful hypotheses can be incorporated into the theory to justify its present formulation. As stated earlier, the writer has not presented new hypotheses—only an integrated system. If this system turns out to be unsuited to the elaboration of derivative hypotheses and the further incorporation of existing hypotheses, it will have little utility.

As yet the theory does not include a wide range of hypotheses suitable for predictive purposes, but it does provide a relatively comprehensive specification of the general factors which are likely to be important in any change situation. The stability and change readiness factors, as well as the five salient variables, can be used as a "checklist" of factors to be looked for and taken into account when changes in real situations are to be assessed. They may also be used in *post factum* interpretation of sociocultural change in particular cases. Determinate change hypotheses may be examined even more rigorously in the light of their correspondence with the realities of actual change processes. This means that the theory is "testable": by confrontation with empirical data, it can be expanded and refined, or rejected.

Obviously, much more work is required. The strength of various stability and change readiness factors and their relevance for various types of change situations must be further investigated and assessed. Determinate change hypotheses must be elaborated. Not only the few such hypotheses which have been presented here, but many others which may be incorporated into the theory, must be refined, modified, or rejected as the result of sociological observation or experiment. It is in the belief that these tasks can best be carried out with the co-operation and criticism of colleagues that the writer ventures to display in print a theory in such a rudimentary form.

The Questionnaire Survey

The questionnaire survey was undertaken in order to obtain systematic information on a variety of subjects about which informants would not have reliable knowledge, such as the distribution of family sizes in different groups, the attitudes of youth, and the social and cultural correlates of adherence to various religions.

Ideas for items to include on the questionnaire came from various sources: from extensive reading in the field of family sociology; from discussions with Olga Lang, author of *Chinese Family and Society;* from the interview schedule used by Dr. Lang in the surveys she undertook in China; from discussions and interviews with Chinese informants in Semarang; and from general and specific hypotheses which the writer developed as a basis for his investigations. The initial list of potential questions, which included well over one hundred items, was discussed, translated into Indonesian, and revised by four Indonesian and Chinese friends, one of them a language teacher.

On this basis, a preliminary questionnaire was prepared and administered to about forty Indonesian secondary school students in a social-work course. As a result of analysis of this "pretest," about twenty-five items were revised, and an equal number were dropped altogether. This was done in consultation with several informants, including both teachers and students. The final form was translated into Chinese by a Totok woman and checked by her husband and a Totok school principal. Both Indonesian and Chinese versions were then mimeographed in quantity.[1]

Unfortunately, the number of items dropped from the preliminary questionnaire was not sufficient to make the final form short enough for the average student to complete in the standard class period of about one hour. In most schools it was impossible to arrange for longer periods, so the number of items had to be further reduced. This was done by dividing the students of each school into several groups which answered different, though overlapping, series of questions.

School principals were approached personally, after the project was approved by the provincial educational authorities. All principals were co-operative, and some were especially helpful. Questionnaire administration was scheduled and carried out in four government normal schools, one regular government high school, one Islamic high school, three Christian schools, and all five Chinese high schools of the city.

In each school the questionnaire was administered to at least two classes. In Chinese, Indonesian, or both these languages, the writer explained to each class the purposes of the survey and the method of filling out the questionnaire. He supervised the class throughout the period and answered the students' many questions. In some classes the teacher or principal gave unsolicited (and sometimes unfortunate) assistance in supervision.

The composition of the sample was as follows: among the Chinese students, 436 boys and 215 girls; among the Indonesian students, 500 boys and 150 girls. This makes a total of 1,301 respondents, half of them Chinese and half Indonesian. In both ethnic groups, the median age of the boys was nineteen, and that of the

[1] An English translation of the questionnaire may be found in Donald E. Willmott, "Sociocultural Change among the Chinese of Semarang, Indonesia" (doctoral dissertation, Cornell University, 1958), pp. 479–485.

girls eighteen. The respondents were in their tenth, eleventh, or twelfth year of schooling, except for a quarter of the Indonesians, who were in their ninth. In both ethnic groups the largest proportion of students were eleventh-graders. Among the 651 Chinese respondents, 422 completed the Indonesian language questionnaire and 229 completed the Chinese form. The author estimates that the Chinese respondents constitute a sample of between one-third and one-half of all Chinese students in the last three grades of high school in Semarang. The proportion of Indonesians is very much smaller.

The answers from each completed questionnaire were coded according to a standard procedure and transferred to a one-page code sheet. Four assistants helped in the work of coding. This task was completed before the writer's departure from Indonesia. Later, in Calgary, Alberta, IBM cards were prepared from the code sheets. On the basis of several hundred sorting runs on a standard IBM sorter, tabulations of the results of the survey were made. Every operation was checked at least once.

A number of shortcomings of the survey should be considered. Although complete anonymity was intended, in most classrooms students were seated almost shoulder to shoulder. In spite of instructions and requests to the contrary, many students looked at the replies of their classmates, and some even copied them directly. Occasionally teachers or principals misled the students with faulty instructions or peered at their replies as they wrote.

In spite of the pretest, several of the questionnaire items proved to be too difficult or too ambiguous for some of the respondents. The Chinese and Indonesian versions of the questionnaire could not be exactly equivalent, and in several cases the difference in meaning was so great that comparison or combination of the results from the two groups was clearly unjustifiable.

The writer had hoped to use the questionnaire data to test some hypotheses interrelating child-rearing practices, identifications, and sociocultural change. The questionnaire results were not adequate, however, for the elaborate statistical analysis which would have been necessary. This was due to errors and misunderstandings in questionnaire completion and to an insufficient number of cases for controlled comparisons of subgroups. Because the questionnaire was too long, as mentioned above, many respondents had been instructed to omit certain items, and others to omit different items.

It would appear that for most purposes the questionnaire respondents constitute a reasonably valid sample of Chinese and Indonesian students in the upper grades of Semarang schools. With regard to matters which show a marked difference from school to school, however, the representativeness of the total sample is marred by the fact that considerably different proportions of the upper-grade students completed the questionnaire in the different schools. Furthermore, it would have been advantageous to reach conclusions about Semarang Chinese or Indonesian youth in general. But it is clear that in most matters high school students cannot be taken as representative of all young people. The high school group no doubt differs from the nonattenders in such crucial matters as socioeconomic status, vocational orientation, social attitudes, and personal and national identifications. Thus the generalizations sometimes had to be limited to the school-attending group. At other times questionnaire data has been used to suggest conclusions about all Chinese young people. In such cases, however, the conclusions must be taken with a large measure of caution and skepticism.

APPENDIX II

Municipal Statistics

Two kinds of municipal statistics are widely used in this report: city population reports and civil registration records. Population figures are compiled by the municipal government on the basis of monthly reports from the 114 *lurah* (ward headmen). Close examination of these statistics reveals that they include many errors and inaccuracies. For example, different tables which are supposed to include some of the same information often disagree. Certain population subtotals remain unchanged for months at a time, and this probably indicates that some of the *lurah* failed to report. Between May and June, 1953, the adult Chinese population of one large district dropped by about 30 per cent, whereas among the Chinese children of the same district the number of boys decreased only slightly and the number of girls increased considerably.

Such inaccuracies are not surprising in view of the fact that the *lurah* are nonsalaried, semiliterate, and overworked officials. They are expected to make monthly enumerations not only of people, but of trees, livestock, and even dogs, cats, and rabbits. For pigs and cows, as for humans, they must give monthly figures for in- and out-migration, births, and deaths (with separate categories for natural death and slaughter). In addition, the *lurah* must compile monthly reports of the prices of a long list of commodities. Obviously, some of this reporting must be sheer guesswork. Population figures are likely to be more accurate than the other figures, because each *lurah* knows every family in his ward and is usually informed of every birth and death. Thus, if he has the time, the motivation, and the arithmetical ability to do it, he can make a fairly accurate population enumeration from his own desk. Apparently few *lurah* have all the necessary prerequisites, however, and the resulting population figures are mere approximations.

During the writer's stay in Semarang, all aliens were required to register with the immigration department and with the police. Newspapers reported that about 17,000 alien Chinese registered in the municipality of Semarang. Because of a certain amount of confusion about citizenship regulations, the exact status of many Chinese had not been finally established. Nevertheless, alien registration statistics may be taken as a fairly complete enumeration of those who considered themselves aliens. By contrast, the *lurah* reports put the number of alien Chinese in Semarang at about 14,000. It seems likely that the 18 per cent difference between these two figures is much greater than the error in the general population totals given by the *lurah*. These officials undoubtedly know which families in their wards are Chinese, but they have no clear idea as to which Chinese are alien. The writer believes that the error in the municipal population figures given by the *lurah* is rarely more than 10 per cent and usually in the vicinity of 5 per cent.

In the matter of civil registration statistics, the Office of Civil Registration itself provides no figures for births, deaths, or marriages. Therefore it was necessary for the writer to compile his own statistics by counting duplicate marriage certificates and tabulating information from them. Over six thousand certificates were counted and categorized according to ethnic groups of bride and bridegroom. More detailed information was tabulated from over one thousand of them, such as marriage age, birthplace, surname of both parties, and occupation of bridegroom and bridegroom's father.

Certain shortcomings of the records should be pointed out. In the first place, a number of volumes were missing, and others were so badly soiled as to be useless. Even in the period when the writer was working in the Civil Registration Office, the records for 1952 and 1953 were lost in a fire which destroyed most of the provincial government building. More important is the fact that ever since registration was first required in 1919 many Chinese have neglected to register their marriages. Furthermore, it is apparent that the proportion of unregistered marriages has varied over the years. For instance, the registered marriage rate in 1930 was about 4.8 per thousand, whereas in 1954 it was 7.2. However, of the 431 registered marriages of Chinese in 1954, 96 involved couples who already had children. This is probably almost entirely due to the fact that marriage certificates had been added to the list of documents which Chinese were required to display in various official dealings. When these long-standing marriages are subtracted from the 1954 figures, the rate for that year drops to 5.6. In 1954 the crude marriage rate in Western countries varied from 9.2 in the United States to an exceptional low of 5.4 in Ireland. In Japan and Taiwan it was 7.9 and 8.9 respectively. In Canada, where the age distribution of the population and the average ages of marriage are similar to those of the Semarang Chinese, the marriage rate was 8.5. In view of these figures, it seems probable that the actual crude marriage rate of the Semarang Chinese is between 7.5 and 9.0. Therefore it is likely that the proportion of Chinese marriages in Semarang which are not registered is between 25 per cent and 38 per cent, or about one-third. Since the registration rate in different sectors of the Chinese community undoubtedly varies considerably, the registered marriages cannot be considered a representative sample of all Chinese marriages in Semarang.

There is no difficulty in identifying Chinese in the marriage records. In the first place, there is a separate register for the marriages of Chinese men. Very few marriages involving Chinese are in other registers. Chinese men who have been "legally assimilated" are included in the register for Europeans, and the Chinese wives of Europeans and of Christian Indonesians are registered with their husbands. In both cases, however, the Chinese are easy to identify by their names.

Some of the names of Christian Indonesians and most of the names of Eurasians are difficult, if not impossible, to distinguish from Dutch names. Thus, in the case of mixed marriages, it was not always possible to identify the ethnic group of the wives of Chinese men.

No registration has been required for the marriages of Moslem men. Therefore there is no record of the marriages of non-Christian Indonesian men to Chinese women or of the Chinese men who have nominally or actually adopted the Mohammedan faith in order to marry Indonesian women. However, the number of marriages in these two categories is not likely to have been very large.

These various facts about the population statistics and marriage records of the municipality of Semarang have been taken into account in the interpretations given in this book. But the reader will now better understand the tentativeness and caution with which conclusions have been expressed.

APPENDIX III

The Interview Survey

The interviewing in this survey was carried out by a young Peranakan woman who was employed on a part-time basis. She was given training in interviewing by the writer. In her approach to the work she proved capable and intelligent.

The interview schedule contained only topical headings. The interviewer was instructed to obtain the information required under each heading in a conversational way and in any convenient order. The topics covered included family composition, socio-economic status, religious life, recreation, education, family activities, marriage arrangement, and opinions on such matters as polygamy, divorce, and joint-family relations.

Originally it was hoped that a representative sample of Chinese housewives could be interviewed. Initial attempts to obtain interviews met with considerable suspicion, however, and the more aggressive sampling methods which have been used in Western societies had to be given up. It was decided, therefore, to send introductory letters to potential interviewees, along with return postal cards to be mailed back by those who did not want to be interviewed. The difficulty was to obtain the names. A list of the membership of a Chinese women's club was supplemented by names supplied by acquaintances of the writer and by the interviewer herself. It was the intention of the writer to see that the various significant groupings in the Chinese community were represented in this sample in approximately correct proportions. But there proved to be time for only about fifty interviews before the writer's departure from Semarang, and the goal of a fairly large, representative sample had to be given up.

The sample actually obtained contains an overrepresentation of Peranakans, of Christians, of the comparatively well to do, and of the better-educated groups. Thus it cannot be used to make valid generalizations for the whole community. In addition, generalizations would not be reliable because of the small number of cases. Therefore the interview survey material has been used with considerable caution, and primarily for illustrative purposes.

APPENDIX IV

Statistical Procedures

Wherever a comparison between two groups is based upon statistical information derived from samples, an apparent difference may be spurious; that is, samples drawn from two groups may differ when the actual groups do not. However, it is possible, by the use of standard formulas, to calculate the probability that each observed difference could be due to chance variables alone. Only when this probability is very low is the difference considered real, or "significant." If it is quite possible that the observed difference is due to the element of chance involved in selecting the samples, no confidence may be placed in it.

The "levels of significance" referred to in the text are measures of the probability that an observed difference between samples represents a real difference between the groups sampled. Two such levels have been used: the .01 level and the .05 level. A difference which is significant at the .01 level would occur only once in one hundred selections of samples from two populations which were actually the same. An observed difference with such a small probability of chance error is generally taken to be worthy of considerable confidence. At the .05 level, however, the element of chance in the drawing of samples could result in five spurious differences in every one hundred sample selections. A difference which is significant at this level is therefore considered interesting and relevant, but not conclusive.

In the analysis of survey results, every arithmetical or statistical calculation has been checked at least once, and many have been checked twice.

INDEX

Acculturation, 308, 315, 322
  Chinese, 15, 22-23
  see also Dutch, influences, *and*
    Indonesian, influences
Agnosticism, 187, 195, 219
Ancestor worship, 199-205, 210-212,
  218, 236-237, 300-301
  ancestor tablets, 199-200, 206
  ancestral altars, 188, 197-198, 200,
    206, 227-228
  belief in, 196, 201-203, 205
  beliefs of, 199, 202-203
  ceremonies, 198-199, 203
  Confucius and, 195
  decline of, 205
  moral obligations of, 187, 200, 204
  relation to family system, 204-205
  relation to religion, 196
  Totok-Peranakan differences, 107
Arbitration of disputes, 64, 148-149,
  151
Assimilation, 307, 315
  Chinese, 15, 62, 89
  see also Ethnic group relations *and*
    Intermarriage
Astrology, 124, 221-222

Banks, 21, 24, 40, 56
  see also Loans and credit
BAPERKI (Badan Permusjawaratan
  Indonesia), 133-134, 156, 161-
  162, 165
Barnett, H. G., 309, 311, 326-328, 341
Bastin, John, 6
Bilateral family, 265
Bilocal residence, 265-266

Boen Hian Tong, 130, 145, 157, 162
Books, *see* Publications
British in Indonesia, *see* Government, British
Buddhism, 195, 251, 253
  Goddess of Mercy, Kwan Iem, 206,
    213-214
  mixture with other religions, 182,
    185, 197, 251
  monk, 252-253
  Totok-Peranakan differences, 108
Business (and trade):
  Chinese-Dutch relations, 5, 58-60,
    66, 71-72
  Chinese-Indonesian relations, 56-
    58, 62-63, 66, 70-71
  fields of, 3-5, 24, 40-47, 101-103
  organization, 47-58, 70
  orientations, 67-79
  regulations, 60, 62-63, 69
  relations among the Chinese, 60-
    62, 66, 69-72, 98, 108-109
  see also Corporations, Moneylend-
    ing, Monopoly concessions,
    and Trade associations

Catholics, Roman:
  activities, 230-231
  attitudes to ancestor worship, 237
  attitudes to dancing, 238
  belief in "magical" prayer, 226
  intermarriage among, 184, 235
  numbers of, 230
  political orientation of, 142, 238-
    239
  proportions in schools, 245-246